MW01485720

A GLOBAL LIFE INSPIRED BY FAMILY
AND A FORTUNE TELLER

Pray
Standing

Pray Standing: A global life inspired by family and a fortune teller

By Frank Ling

Copyright 2013 by Frank Ling

Published in 2013 by
Frank Hegyi Publications
1240 Kilborn Place, Unit 5
Ottawa, Ontario
Canada K1H 1B4

Canadian Cataloguing in Publication Date: 2013
Main entry under title:
Pray Standing: A global life inspired by family and a fortune teller

ISBN # 978-0-9812495-5-1

Editor: Rosalind Tosh
Design: One Girl Media + Design

For my wife and family, the answer to my prayer.

Introduction

In the early evening of October 23, 2009, I was admitted to the Emergency Room of the Ottawa General Hospital suffering with chest congestion, nausea, fever and mental confusion. It was five days after my return from a ten-day trip to Beijing. The medical team determined that I was in septic shock and transferred me to the Intensive Care Unit.

Within minutes, my wife and daughter were at my bedside and word had been sent summoning our son and his family from Toronto. Unbeknownst to me, a priest was standing by, waiting for the arrival of my whole family including my four grandchildren. The expectation was that I might not make it through the night.

But I did. And after five days in the ICU and a further nine days in hospital, I was well enough to be discharged and was soon restored to good health. Those weeks of unexpected 'down time' made me reflect on my life and it struck me forcefully that what had just happened was the third life-threatening situation I had survived in the span of seven decades lived on three continents.

One of those incidents stands out with particular clarity. It was 1944. Allied bombing raids on Japanese-occupied Hong Kong had become an almost daily occurrence and we lived our lives as normally as we could in spite of them. The warning sirens began their spine-tingling wail one day as my mother and I were walking to church and we quickly ran beneath a tree, the only thing near us that offered any hope of shelter. My six-year-old pounding heart desperately sought reassurance: "Mother, can you pray standing?" My mother grasped my hand and unhesitatingly nodded her head. The calm certainty of that unvoiced response was to become the guiding focus of my life: with trust, all is indeed well, no matter what.

My hospital stint persuaded me it was time to share my experiences of war and peace, danger and opportunity, tears and laughter with my family. I decided to retrace the journey that brought me from beneath that tree to where I am today, seven decades later – and perhaps in doing so to discover where I might take my thrice-spared life from here. And so, let my journey begin.

Pray standing.

FRANK LING
Ottawa, Canada
May, 2013

Acknowledgements

Hunched over the keyboard, willing my two-finger typing to keep up with the avalanche of memories flashing one after another through my mind – seven decades worth – I wondered at times if this book would ever get written. Then my good friend Jackie Holzman, Ottawa's former mayor who knows just about everyone in the city, introduced me to author and publisher Frank Hegyi, who agreed to assist this neophyte, and when Frank suffered a medical emergency not long afterwards, Jackie put me in touch with Rosalind Tosh who then stepped in to fill the void. This book may not have made it beyond the metaphorical drawing board without Rosalind's clear deciphering of my multi-layered stories and frequent diversions into sub-plots, her supportive background research and her creative input. Then Frank Hegyi, well on his way to full recovery, kindly resumed the role of publisher and worked with Rosalind and graphic designer Cynthia French (of One Girl Media + Design) to physically produce the final product. A truly first-class team.

For helping fill in the gaps around events in my childhood in Hong Kong, I owe a huge debt of gratitude to three people who shared much of that time with me: my paternal cousin Phoon Wai-wor (now a physician living in Philadelphia), my maternal cousin Deborah Chung (now a scientist in Buffalo, NY), and my old friend Ng Ping Keun (now a retired engineer living in Toronto).

For helping refresh my memory of events at the Canadian Museum of Nature, I am deeply appreciative of former museum vice-president and chief operating officer Colin Eades and former board secretary Irene Byrne.

For providing important supporting information regarding many of my community involvements especially my work with the Ottawa Police, I am most grateful to Robert Yip, a long-time friend and my sounding board in the Chinese community of Ottawa.

Finally, for their unfailing encouragement that kept me sane and cheerful as I worked on the manuscript over the course of three years, including on the beaches of Southeast Asia when we were supposed to be on vacation, I am deeply and forever indebted to my wife Loretta, my children Theo and Kim, my daughter-in-law Charlene and each one of my grandchildren. Family history in the making.

Table of Contents

9

Architect and Chinese-Canadian (1972-1987)

10

Bridge Builder (1987-2012)

Endgame

Roots and Wings – Baby and the Chinese Origins

Japanese Invasion and Occupation 1

(1941-1945)

THE CLOUD BEFORE THE STORM

My lessons in survival began when I was four years old. It was the autumn of 1941 and Hong Kong was about to be invaded by Japan.

Hong Kong Island where I was born, along with Kowloon Peninsula to the north across Victoria Harbour and the vast countryside on the adjacent southern tip of mainland China called the New Territories, had been a British Crown Colony for a century, but that was about to change. Japanese troops arrived on our doorstep in October 1938 with the occupation of the Chinese city of Canton (present-day Guangzhou), and for the next three years it was just a matter of time.

That summer of 1941, Hong Kong's defences consisted of just four regiments of artillery, four battalions of infantry, a naval reserve, and the Hong Kong Volunteer Defence Corps headed by British businessmen and civil servants. Air and naval defences were all but non-existent. In mid-November, a mere three weeks before the invasion began, two battalions of reinforcements arrived from Canada, however the soldiers of the Winnipeg Grenadiers and the Royal Rifles of Canada had no battlefield experience and lacked essential equipment, the ship transporting their heavy equipment having been diverted to the Philippines.

As part of the reinforcement effort, Britain reached an understanding with China's Nationalist government under Chiang Kai-shek to coordinate their respective military operations in the event of a Japanese attack on the crown colony: Once hostilities started, the Chinese army would attack the Japanese forces from the rear to relieve the pressure on the vastly outnumbered Hong Kong garrison. Britain also explored the possibility of cooperating with Chinese Communist guerrillas operating in the vicinity of Hong Kong. Neither scenario, however, was to materialize.

Local Chinese manpower in Hong Kong was not utilized to any great extent, with a mere twenty-two hundred out of a possible one-and-a-half million being enrolled into the volunteer defence corps and a similarly marginal number serving as air raid wardens and auxiliary firefighters. The attempted raising of a regular Hong Kong Chinese Regiment occurred too late in the game and its recruits were nowhere near trained when the Japanese made their move.

Four of my mother's five brothers – all those old enough to fight – joined the volunteer corps and were assigned as gunners to various defence posts on the island. When they came to say goodbye, proudly showing off their military uniforms, steel helmets and alien-looking gas masks, I thought it all a marvellous adventure.

Though the British government knew that it was impossible for Hong Kong to hold out for long against the Japanese, no such lack of confidence was ever publicly admitted, with the result that the majority of Hong Kong's population, my own family included, failed to grasp the seriousness of the situation. Complacency prevailed. Conditioned by centuries of imperial privilege and systemic racism, many of the expatriate British totally underestimated the ability of the invaders on the doorstep, even believing that Japanese troops were incapable of night movement and their pilots incapable of night navigation. Among the

Chinese community, most still believed in the might of the British Empire and were content to count on its protection.

I was always conscious of the fact that mine was not a typical household. Unlike that of most of my relatives and friends, my immediate family consisted of more than just my parents, my brother and myself. I was the youngest, four years behind *Taaî Ló* (Cantonese casual address for "Elder brother").

My father was the only son in a family of five children. He was a quiet man who never seemed to greatly enjoy playing with us children, so it was puzzling to me when I would see him acting the "little brother" to his two older sisters, submitting to their authority with little resistance. He was House Manager at the King's Theatre, overseeing the day-to-day operation of the large cinema and live production venue on Queen's Road, Central, a popular downtown Hong Kong commercial area. My brother and I were told that our father had hated school and had not attended university, and we were sternly admonished not to follow in those footsteps.

My mother was a devoted and endlessly patient parent and a dedicated English language teacher at the highly regarded *Ying Wa* ("Anglo-Chinese") Girls' School. She too had not gone to university, though for a different reason: as the eldest of six children, her income had been needed to help her widowed mother support her family.

My father's eldest sister, *Taaî Koo-Má* ("Eldest paternal aunt"), had taken on the role of family matriarch and in respect for her important position my brother and I simply addressed her as *Koo-Má* ("Aunt"), without the need to include the prefix *Taaî* ("Eldest"). Aunt was married to a prominent physician who had both the heart and the means to be the head of our family. My brother and I addressed him as *Koo-Cheüg* ("Paternal aunt's husband" or "Uncle"). Uncle had a successful practice with four other doctors in the King's Theatre Building and one of my father's two younger sisters, Sź Koo-tsé ("Fourth Aunt"), was his clinic nurse.

It was probably Aunt's idea that *À Yē* ("Grandfather") and *À Mā* ("Grandmother") should also live with us. That way, my father would be recognized as the *haaù shun* ("filial") son, even though he could not afford to support them without her help. The arrangement made good sense to all of us as Uncle and Aunt had no children of their own and they could help to raise my brother and me as the future hope of our family. This was the Chinese way.

We all lived under the wing of Uncle and Aunt in a three-bedroom flat on the third floor of a low-rise building at Ning Yeung Terrace on Bonham Road in the comfortable neighbourhood of Mid-levels. Indeed, this was where my brother and I had been born, both of us delivered by Aunt, who was a midwife, under the supervision of Uncle, a specialist in obstetrics and gynaecology.

Living across the hallway from our flat was the family of my father's second eldest sister, my *Î Koo-Má* ("Second paternal aunt"), who was married to a doctor from Singapore, my *Î Koo-Cheùg* ("Second paternal uncle). My brother and I played often with their three children, who also had been delivered by Aunt, as had the many children of our landlord, Mr. Ng Wah, whose large family occupied the ground floor and one of the two second-floor flats.

Ning Yeung Terrace was the backdrop for so many of my first memories of relatives and friends, warm memories of togetherness and security. Then in early 1941, not knowing what was just around the corner, our family moved to a more comfortable – certainly a more spacious – home. Uncle had purchased a two-storey garden house in Pokfulam, a prestigious suburban district in the western portion of Hong Kong Island.

Our new home was in a quiet neighbourhood with breath-taking views. From our balconies and garden, we looked out across acres of green and yellow pastureland, home to the cattle of the historic Hong Kong Dairy Farm, sloping down towards the western inlet of Victoria Harbour and distant offshore islands. The gate of our rear garden gave access to a pathway leading up the hill to the Queen Mary Hospital, the largest government health facility in Hong Kong. Little did we know that it would very soon become an important treatment centre for the Red Cross. We were also not far from Mount Davis, which had been a key artillery depot for British forces since 1911, with three nine point two inch guns still in evidence thirty years later, along with barracks and bunkers.

Fourth Aunt, Uncle's clinic nurse, now also lived with us and we had a household staff of seven – a chauffeur, a gardener, a head maid, an under maid (we called the maids "Amah", a colonial term inherited from the British), a young girl who attended to Aunt, a chef, and a pastry chef named Ching who also looked after Uncle's English pantry. Ching was by far my favourite, not least because he happily indulged my inability to resist fresh-from-the-oven cookies.

My memories of the few idyllic months before the Japanese takeover are vivid and bittersweet. I remember my cousins and brother laughing in delight from the top of an amusement park Ferris wheel while I watched enviously from below, not understanding that I was too young to join in their adventure. I remember falling asleep to the blissful sound of my mother's voice as she sang my favourite nursery tunes. I remember being taken by Aunt to a tea party where there were lots of games and even a roller-skating contest for us children – I was thrilled when my brother won a box of English toffees – and to an early Christmas party where, to my amazement, we were handed presents by none other than Santa Claus himself.

I also remember Uncle pointing out camouflaged military bunkers and caves on the hillsides as we drove to the beach at Repulse Bay: we children were simply told that they were places for storing rations. And I recall all the windows of our house being taped over with diagonal crosses made out of strips of newspaper, and the wooden shutters and drapes being tightly closed as soon as darkness began to fall. When I noticed oil lamps and candles appearing on tables, I simply thought the grownups were preparing for a party.

I started Junior Kindergarten at *Pui Ying* ("Cultivating Talents") Primary School in the autumn of 1941. My teacher was Miss Tam Cheuk-lan, a beautiful lady with a smiling face, and I loved her with all my four-year-old heart. She gave us hot Ovaltine and sweet English biscuits before the end of class each morning and I never wanted to miss out on these delights. Then came the morning of Monday, December 8.

Our mother accompanied my brother and me to school as usual, but when we arrived at my classroom, nothing was as usual. It was a grim-faced Miss Tam who greeted us. "You must go home right away," she entreated urgently. "The Japanese are coming."

That was the last time I ever saw her.

THE BATTLE OF HONG KONG

The attack on Hong Kong had begun shortly after eight o'clock on that clear, sunny, Monday morning, with the bombing of Kai Tak Airport on the Kowloon Peninsula just across Victoria Harbour from the island. Within five minutes, Japan had gained complete air supremacy. Two of the defence force's three torpedo bombers and both its amphibian biplanes were destroyed, and so too were most of the civil aircraft including any that could have been used by the Hong Kong Volunteer Defence Corp. The few naval vessels in the area were ordered to relocate to Singapore. From then on, the Allied forces in the area and the volunteer corps would have to fight on the ground.

It was revealed much later that the Japanese had superb intelligence about Hong Kong's defences, gained by agents working locally as waiters, barmen, hairdressers, masseurs and prostitutes servicing British officials and military officers. Thus, even before the invasion began, they were assured a smooth ride through the defence positions into the heart of the colony. Poised to attack Hong Kong was the 23rd Corps of the Japanese Army under Lieutenant General Sakai Takashi, who also had overall command of the air and naval units supporting the assault. The actual invasion force was the battle-hardened 38th Division led by Lieutenant General Sano Tadayoshi and reinforced by two brigades and six battalions of artillery, tanks and other logistical units. They were augmented by sixty-three bombers, thirteen fighters and ten other aircraft, as well as a light cruiser, three destroyers, four torpedo boats, three gunboats, two ancillary ships and five naval aircraft.

With such armed might and at fifty-two thousand personnel strong – almost three times greater than the number of defenders – it was no surprise that the New Territories region of Hong Kong was lost in less than three days. On the evening of December 11, the Allies began their evacuation from Kowloon Peninsula across Victoria Harbour to Hong Kong Island under aerial bombardment and artillery barrage.

The defence of our island was about to begin.

After we were sent home from school on December 8, bomb blasts and heavy artillery shock waves kept us on edge around the clock. The whole family began sleeping on mattresses on the ground floor of the house and our household staff was gradually, a few at a time, released by Aunt, most of them finding escape routes back to their ancestral villages in southern China. With the Mount Davis artillery depot a likely military target, Pokfulam was no longer a safe place. It was time to seek safer shelter and we headed back to Ning Yeung Terrace.

The Japanese made a demand for surrender on December 13. It was rejected. Two days later, the systematic bombardment and shelling of Hong Kong Island began.

All of us children and some of the adults living in the upper-floor flats at Ning Yeung Terrace moved to the landlord's ground floor unit for safety. During daylight hours, we sat along the corridor in the protection of the building's inner walls, and at night we slept there on shared mattresses laid out on the floor. I remember being given a cotton handkerchief with the instruction to jam it between my teeth to help absorb the shockwaves caused by the frequent bomb explosions. To torment us further, there was also a homegrown threat. Local Chinese gangsters were ransacking stores and homes, creating fear and havoc under the guise of being 'victory fighters.' The front door of our building had to be kept securely locked and reinforced with heavy wooden bars.

I also remember the sheer fun and excitement that the close sharing of accommodation brought to us children. We happily played cards and many other games for hours on end and I can still picture the girls and some of the boys passing the time with attempts at mastering the skill of knitting.

Japan's second demand for surrender came on December 17. It too was rejected, and an even more intense phase of what would become known as the Battle of Hong Kong began. As a consequence, during the night of December 18, the defences of Hong Kong Island were breached by six Japanese battalions who succeeded in crossing Victoria Harbour at its eastern end, with at least twenty of the defending gunners who surrendered to them being massacred. My mother heard nothing about the fate of her four brothers.

On the morning of December 19, the strategic headquarters of the West Brigade – the home force defending the southwest and western portion of the island – was annihilated and its commanding officer killed. The Japanese also made surprise landings along secluded parts of the coast and succeeded in making their way towards downtown. Again there was a massacre of prisoners, including medical corps personnel.

Now the island was split in two, with the defending force still holding on to the west in spite of the loss of their commanding officer, and to Stanley Peninsula in the south. When the invading forces captured the island's reservoirs, however, it was the beginning of the end. On the morning of December 25, Japanese soldiers entered the British field hospital in the southern town of Stanley, brutally killing more than sixty patients and medical staff, and by the afternoon it was clear that further resistance was futile.

That evening, British officials headed by Hong Kong Governor Sir Mark Aitchison Young surrendered at the Japanese headquarters on the third floor of the Peninsula Hotel in Kowloon. It was the first time a British Crown Colony had capitulated to an invading force. The garrison had held for seventeen days.

Christmas Day 1941 is remembered in Hong Kong as Black Christmas.

CONQUERORS AND SURVIVORS

In the first few days after Hong Kong's capture, treatment of the local population was extremely harsh and large numbers of suspected dissidents were executed. Military prisoners of war were incarcerated in camps on the island, on Kowloon Peninsula and in Japan. Civilian prisoners of war, including Governor Young, were confined in the Stanley Internment Camp on the south side of the island.

For the next three years and eight months, Hong Kong would be subject to martial law administered from the Japanese command post in the Peninsula Hotel in Kowloon. The military government enacted stringent regulations and established executive bureaus with power over every aspect of life for all Hong Kong residents.

It became unlawful to own Hong Kong dollars, which were replaced by the Japanese Military Yen, a currency without reserves issued by the Imperial Japanese Army administration. Two Japanese banks, the Yokohama Specie Bank and the Bank of Taiwan, replaced the Hong Kong and Shanghai Bank (present day HSBC Bank) and the Mercantile Bank, and were responsible for issuing banknotes.

The ten local Chinese newspapers were reduced to five and placed under heavy censorship. Radio was used for Japanese propaganda and movie theatres including the King's Theatre screened only Japanese films. A Japanese curriculum was compulsory at those schools allowed to remain open, with English forbidden everywhere. My brother and I, however, were taught at home – in Chinese by our grandfather and in the outlawed English by our mother.

Hyperinflation and food rationing became the norm. There was a great shortage of essential commodities such as rice, oil, flour, salt and sugar. I remember being horrified by stories about starving people fighting over dog, cat or rat meat – and utterly terrified by whispered rumours of children being kidnapped for the same end.

Each household was limited to six-point-four taels (about one-quarter of a kilogram or half a pound) of white rice a day, enough to make no more than ten bowls a day in total when normal consumption would average two bowls per person per meal. In our twelve-person household – my family plus three servants – ten bowls a day did not go far. We conserved the precious white rice for dinnertime, eating inferior red rice purchased on the black market at other meals – it tasted awful, but hunger is indeed a good sauce. We sold the brass fixtures from our home – the Japanese war machine gobbled up the metal – in exchange for extra white rice and Uncle was occasionally paid in the coveted grain for his medical services. In addition, my mother sometimes received a small bag in return for giving English tuition, an illegal and extremely risky enterprise on her part.

Given the logistics involved in feeding a population of more than one and a half million after its economy has been destroyed, the Japanese worked assiduously to reduce Hong Kong's population. Some half a million were to die over the course of the next four years, and another half-million were 'repatriated' to the famine- and disease-ridden areas of the mainland from which many had come just a few years earlier, fleeing the conflict of the Second Sino-Japanese War. This enforced deportation was fortuitous for some as it facilitated the escape of former members of the Hong Kong Volunteer Defence Corps – my mother's four brothers among them.

My *Sź K'aŭ-foô* ("Fourth maternal uncle") Wah-chiu had been stationed at the Lei Yue Mun Fort, a strategic defence outpost guarding the eastern inlet to Victoria Harbour. When the Japanese took the fort on December 14, he was captured along with his surviving service comrades. A few days later, he was in the parade of captives being marched to a prison camp on the Kowloon Peninsula and when they were passing through a narrow street lined with many onlookers he managed to slip into the crowd. As he made his way through this sea of people, sensing that someone was tailing him, he raced up a flight of stairs only to be cornered at the top by the gun-wielding pursuer. It was then that he discovered his pursuer was in fact only after his money and after handing over the little he had, he was allowed to go free. Eventually, he made his way back to Hong Kong Island to be reunited with *Sź K'aŭ-mŏ* ("Fourth maternal uncle's wife") Wan-fun and both of them later managed to escape to mainland China, with him dressed as a labourer and her disguised as a boy.

My *Lûk K'aŭ-foô* ("Sixth maternal uncle") Wah-leung had also been assigned to Lei Yue Mun Fort and his specific duty was to handle grenade launching. When their position was under heavy shelling by the advancing Japanese, he was injured – a facial nerve was broken, causing facial paralysis – and he was rendered unconscious. He was a shortsighted person whose glasses had been shattered by earlier shell shockwaves, but when he regained consciousness he found an unbroken pair lying beside him. It seemed like a miracle. Much later, it was learned that they belonged to my *Paàt K'aŭ-foô* ("Eighth maternal uncle") Wah-cheung, who had placed his own glasses beside his injured older brother before obeying the order for his unit to retreat from the fort.

Uncle Wah-leung, along with his 'miracle' glasses, was taken to Queen Mary Hospital, though little medical treatment was available during those besieged days. After the Allies surrendered on December 25, however, he walked out of the hospital and made his way down the hill to hide in Uncle's vacant Pokfulam house. His daughter tells a story that her father recounted about that time, yet another 'miracle' he experienced: One day, feeling rather low, he tried to bolster his spirits by singing hymns when suddenly a Japanese military officer appeared at the house, but instead of arresting Uncle Wah-leung, the officer asked if he could join him in the singing. Afterwards, he left his card, and that card, inscribed with a note from the officer, enabled Uncle Wah-leung to leave Hong Kong for mainland China in safety.

We later learned that my mother's other two brothers were also able to make their way to China.

For those of us in the family remaining in Hong Kong, the immediate challenge was to deal with two essential aspects of survival: finding an adequate food supply and more stable accommodation. Uncle started dealing with the accommodation problem by seeking help from the founding partner of his medical clinic, Dr. Ma Luk-sun, whose wife, one of Aunt's close friends, was Japanese. Her influence was to come in handy.

British faculty members at the University of Hong Kong – those who had not managed to escape to China – had been arrested and sent to the internment camp at Stanley. Most of their residences had been taken over by the Japanese, but a few were still empty. Through Mrs. Ma's negotiation with the Japanese military, Uncle was permitted to exchange our Pokfulam house for a pair of semi-detached houses on the university campus, not too far from the overcrowded Ning Yeung Terrace.

We were permitted to combine the semi-detached units by opening up a party wall, making the home more than large enough for our big family: Uncle and Aunt, my grandparents and parents, Fourth Aunt, my brother and me. A kitchen and quarters for our few remaining domestic helpers were at the back of the house. Our accommodation problem was solved, even if it included the uncomfortable reality of living next to the homes of various Japanese military officials.

Interestingly, one of the two units we lived in had been the residence of Dr. Gordon King, Professor of Obstetrics and Gynaecology at the university. Shortly after the Hong Kong surrender, Professor King took as many of the medical students as he could and fled to China, leaving behind his home and its library of medical books and journals. Uncle, working in the same specialized field of medicine, turned out to be the natural custodian of that library, the collections of which were duly returned to Professor King after the war.

To supplement our food rations, we began raising chickens and ducks and planted corn, tomatoes and beans in the front yard. My brother and I were responsible for the delicate task of collecting any eggs laid by the poultry and for fertilizing the vegetable garden, noses firmly pinched as we spread our household's daily waste. Goat's milk was available now and then from street hawkers and there were occasional nuggets of extravagance when a grateful patient would present Uncle with a precious gift of Taikoo sugar cubes or English biscuits.

Others were not as fortunate. Almost every day, I saw Chinese women cutting grass or collecting tree branches to use as cooking fuel. One early afternoon, I saw a bayonet-wielding soldier drag one such woman, screaming and helpless, into the house of a Japanese military neighbour. I did not see her coming out again.

The young servants of another neighbouring household invited me to play in their quarters one afternoon. Their Japanese master came home just as I was about to leave and indicated by hand gestures that I was to go into his dining room, a command I was much too scared to ignore. Once there, he pulled out a sword and began to chase me around the large dining table, laughing uproariously at his invented game. To my six-year-old self, it was completely terrifying. I cried out for help until finally he tired of this entertainment and let me go, but my ordeal was not quite over – a German Shepherd dog came bounding after me as I raced down the front steps and I was certain that this time there would be no reprieve. Fortunately, the master materialized at the top of the steps yelling in Japanese, whereupon the dog retreated and I was finally free to run home, my heart almost bursting out of my chest. Needless to say, I never again visited that house or the house of any other Japanese neighbour.

However, I also remember a pleasant Japanese soldier coming to our home from time to time to visit with my grandparents, communicating with them by writing *Kanji* (Japanese term for Han or Chinese characters). He would tell them that he was feeling homesick and missed his parents.

One evening, my father failed to come home from work. We got word from his colleagues at the King's Theatre that he had been arrested by the Kempeitai, the notorious Japanese military police who also performed secret police functions. We had no idea of the reason for the arrest or of his whereabouts. For four agonizing days, our family was in shock as we had heard many stories about the Kempeitai's reign of terror employing excruciating methods of torture inflicted in sinister places of execution.

At the end of the four days, to our great joy and relief, my father came home. He had been arrested for accompanying a friend to a house that the Japanese suspected was the home of spies, and so he was assumed to be a probable accomplice. At the dreadful moment when he was taken into a chamber for interrogation, an officer entered the room, recognized him, and spoke in his defence. That officer had interacted with my father frequently at the King's Theatre, which was often expropriated for Japanese army entertainment activities. There is no doubt his serendipitous and timely arrival saved my father's life.

My father was badly shaken by this experience, so much so that he became fearful of remaining in Hong Kong. He made up his mind to escape to China along with my mother, my brother and me, and instructed my mother to begin making all of us warm winter clothing and broad cotton belts with pockets for holding rations and money. Had this plan gone through, my life path would have taken a completely different direction, but instead Aunt was able to talk her little brother out of the decision, persuading him that he would in fact be taking his family into a life of certain danger and starvation. Persuaded further by my grandparents, he finally gave up on the idea.

I experienced a particularly personal lesson in survival one afternoon while playing a favourite game with my brother and cousins in our sloping backyard that sat atop a high retaining wall. 'Soldiers and Bandits' entailed a lot of running, chasing and brandishing of weapons – golf clubs and field-hockey sticks that had been left behind by the previous residents of our house. I, being the youngest, had to work hard at not getting caught. I remember panicking, slipping, and the vivid slow-motion seconds of falling from the top of the retaining wall to the ground some three metres (ten feet) below.

My next recollection is of lying in bed, with the worried faces of Uncle, Aunt and Fourth Aunt staring down at me. My mother was holding my hand. When I was told all that had happened, I even then recognized its rather extraordinary place in my personal history.

I had lost consciousness when I hit the ground, bleeding from the right side of my skull. My brother and cousins ran inside to get help. Uncle and Fourth Aunt were at the clinic and it would take too long for them to get home, so my grandfather came to the rescue. He had in his medicine cabinet a herbal mixture called *Dieda Shang* ("Fallen hit powder"), a composition of conium, saffron, cinnamon and other herbs that doctors of Chinese medicine apply to stop bleeding and to treat traumatic injury, and when my grandfather applied the composition to my head wound, the bleeding did indeed stop. Next, he ordered my brother to urinate into a cup, urine being a substitute for ammonia, known for restoring consciousness – my grandfather insisted that it had to be the urine of a virgin boy – and he forced the liquid down my throat. It worked. But undoubtedly it had to be my most distasteful survival experience, in every sense of that word.

BORROWED TIME, ALLIED BOMBING AND VICTORY DAY

Two years into the Japanese occupation, the people of Hong Kong had become somewhat used to living under martial law and to exploring its limits, resulting in increased activities in the community. Sunday church services and social gatherings were now tolerated. Tutorial classes were offered by organizations such as the YWCA. Children were encouraged to learn Japanese – even I, at such a young age, was able to memorize most of the Japanese alphabet and many useful words. Some restaurants and stores reopened, although their names were often changed to Japanese renditions of the originals, and I particularly remember a few mouth-watering displays of red bean and green tea desserts – such a luxurious rarity in those days – though I never had a chance to sample any.

The only forms of public transportation available were electric trams that ran between the western and eastern ends of the urban core, and a few cross-harbour ferries. Everywhere else, if they did not want to walk or cycle, people used sedan chairs, rickshaws or trolleys propelled by men. Aunt would take my grandmother out from time to time seated on a sedan chair carried by two bearers and then she was transferred to a single-passenger rickshaw. I loved being small enough to sometimes share the rides with her.

My grandfather seldom went out but friends frequently visited him at our home. He was a keen follower of Confucius and, being an atheist, would sometimes make derisive remarks about Jesus to which I would retaliate with jokes about Confucius. This invariably led to a scolding from Aunt. In contrast to my rebellious nature, my brother was a well-mannered child who, it seemed to me, was favoured by my grandfather and by Aunt as the appropriate heir to the family's good name.

Uncle continued to be the principal provider for our family. He was permitted to continue his clinic practice with Fourth Aunt as his nurse, and from time to time the Japanese would summon him for medical duties. One night he was fetched by an official car for an emergency house call and was shocked to discover that the vehicle he was riding in was his own car that had been confiscated by the Japanese and now repainted in white with a red cross.

He was a caring substitute for my father, who was seldom home. I remember being almost asleep one Christmas Eve when I sensed someone placing a gift beside me, a rare thing in those destitute years. Beneath the paper I detected what seemed to be a pair of knitting needles, filling me with disappointment, however next morning's unwrapping revealed a welcome pair of chopsticks, a thoughtful gift from Uncle, who often reminded us during those difficult years to be thankful that our family unit remained intact, alive and healthy.

Family gatherings at dinnertime were always interesting, no matter how sparse the food. That's when I got to listen to the grownups gossip and relay the news about the war, a war that was ever present even when only in the form of power cuts and curfews.

By the summer of 1943, the British counter-offensive in Burma was making steady progress, assisted by the Chinese. As well, American troops were gaining ground in the Pacific theatre, engaged in an operation to liberate south China including the Canton-Hong Kong region. The 1st American Volunteer Group, consisting mostly of former U.S. Army, Navy and Marine Corps pilots and ground crew, had become a key component of the Allies' Hong Kong offensive. Nicknamed the Flying Tigers, this group was made up of three fighter squadrons with about twenty aircraft apiece, each painted with an iconic shark face and the twelve-point sun of the Chinese Air Force.

The Flying Tigers were commanded by General Claire Lee Chennault, who preached a radically different approach to air combat based on his study of Japanese tactics and equipment, his observation of the tactics used by Soviet pilots in China, and his judgement of the strengths and weaknesses of his own pilots and aircraft. Some Chinese cadets were trained and joined the group.

The Allies' air raids on Hong Kong began in early 1944. They usually took place during the day, the ascending pitch of the warning siren quickly followed by the thunderous noise of explosions, often causing shockwaves as though the bombs had landed very close at hand. Out of fascinated curiosity, I sometimes tried to get a glimpse of the action through a window, oblivious to the possibility of flying shrapnel. My brother, however, was old enough to be aware of the danger and would accompany our grandfather under the staircase to take shelter as soon as the siren began its eerie wail – the concern for my brother's safety was a spontaneous one on the part of my grandfather, who must have felt he had a responsibility to protect the eldest grandson of the family. The remainder of the family would quickly follow and none of us relaxed until we heard the descending pitch of the second siren, signifying that the bombing was over for the time being.

Hong Kong had not been very noticeably damaged during the invasion of 1941, as the bombing of Kai Tak Airport had lasted for only one day and the subsequent shelling was targeted mainly at defence outposts. The Allied air raids, however, would largely destroy Hong Kong's infrastructure, targeting any location that might have strategic value to the Japanese. In addition to five-hundred pound bombs, incendiary bombs were also dropped. They destroyed by starting fires once they reached their target, burning at a very high temperature. Because of their relatively light weight, however, incendiary bombs would sometimes miss their intended targets on a windy day, destroying 'innocent' homes and businesses instead, so the pilots had to fly low in order to increase accuracy. During one of the occasions when I was stealing a forbidden peek outside, I caught a glimpse of several of these low-flying planes and vividly remember the painted twelve-point sun on the underside of their wings. It was an exciting moment for me.

These low-flying aircraft became easy targets for the Japanese artillery. Captured pilots were usually executed and I remember seeing

Allied flying suits, headgear, boots and parachutes displayed in shop windows as evidence of Japan's military superiority.

My most dramatic recollection of the Allied air raids was the bombing of a fuel storage depot on Kowloon Peninsula across Victoria Harbour and quite visible from our house on the university campus. The first thing that caught my eye was sunlight glinting off several aircraft in the distant sky and then I noticed objects falling from each fuselage. When the fuel tanks below were hit, immediate and dramatic explosions erupted. Very quickly, the whole depot became a raging inferno. It burned for an entire week and was so bright there was no need for us to light the candles in our home at night.

After almost a year of bombardment, Allied air raids became just another part of our daily reality, something to be worked around as we got on with life. One afternoon as I was walking with my mother, the warning siren climbed to its tension-inducing crescendo and was followed almost instantly by the deep boom of nearby explosions. The only shelter at hand was the insubstantial canopy of a young tree. I was terrified. I cried out, "Mother, can you pray standing?" My mother squeezed my hand and nodded her head, and the absolute trust that I had in her flooded me with well-being. I knew in my heart that we would survive.

In January 1945, a few of our Japanese neighbours moved out.

In February 1945, Uncle received a phone call from a friend with a long-awaited message: "The wounds are healing." This was code for indications that the war might soon be over. There was no sign of that in Hong Kong, however, where Allied air raids were intensifying and we no longer felt safe living so close to our remaining Japanese neighbours or to the vacated houses that were now a target for local gangsters and thieves. Once again, it was time to move back to Ning Yeung Terrace.

The Japanese who had commandeered our landlord's ground floor flat at Ning Yeung Terrace had left, enabling Mr. Ng Wah and most of his family to move back in. He offered Uncle and Aunt a bedroom. Second Uncle and Second Aunt generously invited the rest of us to live with them in their flat on the third floor, in spite of the overcrowded situation this created.

With the many people that now had to be fed, we began a self-imposed regime of even more restrictive rice rationing and had almost no access to fresh protein or vegetables. Flavour was added to our meals through the addition of small portions of preserved foods such as salted eggs, marinated tofu, pickled cabbage or dried sausage. After their meagre dinner, my uncles and aunts often passed the time playing mah-jong or dominoes with neighbours at Mr. Hui's second floor flat. Curtains would be drawn tight and the lighting – electric when available, candles when not – was kept dim as air raids and blackout curfews were ongoing.

Then one day, the Allies mistakenly bombed the medical clinic operated by Second Uncle's brother (also a doctor originally from Singapore), taking his life. I happened to be in Second Aunt's living room when she broke the news to his wife. We were devastated by the shocking accident, made all the more poignant by our anticipation that the war might end in the not too distant future.

Once again, Uncle resolved our overcrowded accommodation problem, this time by renting a two-bedroom flat for my grandparents, my parents, my brother and me. Our move was not at all arduous as what remained of our household items fit easily into the two-wheeled cart which a couple of hired hands pulled to the new flat just a short distance along Bonham Road from Ning Yeung Terrace. Our new home was on the fourth floor, with easy access to a roof deck offering a commanding view of Victoria Harbour. From the front balcony we could see Ning Yeung Terrace, where Uncle and Aunt continued to live in Mr. Ng Wah's flat, though they joined us each evening for family dinner.

On August 6, 1945, the United States Army Air Force dropped an atomic bomb on Hiroshima. On August 9, a second atomic bomb was dropped, this time on Nagasaki. The tremendous psychological shock of the devastating effects of these bombs, combined with the Soviet Union's entry into the war on the side of the Allies, left Japan with no choice. On August 14, Emperor Hirohito ordered Japanese troops to lay down their arms. We knew nothing of this until noon the next day when the Emperor's speech was broadcast on the radio and over the public address system in Hong Kong. My father told of seeing Japanese soldiers standing motionless in the street, heads bowed, eyes tear-filled, listening to their Emperor's words, then silently returning to their barracks.

It was exciting to me to hear the newly animated conversation of the grownups around our family dinner table over the next few days. But in the midst of their happy anticipation, I could sense anxiety related to some discussions involving China, which I could little understand.

What they were worried about was the fact that with the end of hostilities, the British government found itself in an awkward situation. It had previously accepted that Hong Kong lay within the operational sphere of China under Chiang Kai-shek – indeed the first order issued to a defeated Japan by the Supreme Commander of the Allied Powers, General Douglas MacArthur, required all Japanese forces in the region to "Surrender to Generalissimo Chiang" – however Britain now saw this arrangement as being harmful to its interests. A British naval contingent was dispatched to Hong Kong, seeking to be the first to re-enter the region and accept the surrender of the Japanese themselves. This would avert the necessity of having to ask China for the return of Hong Kong to British jurisdiction.

News of the British action created enormous international tension. However the Chinese Nationalist government, busily engaged in attempting to control the spread of Communist forces under Mao

Zedong, finally agreed to a compromise in which Britain would represent both itself and China when receiving the surrender of the Japanese occupying forces.

One late evening as I stood on our front balcony, I thought I could hear the sound of marching feet in the distance. It was too dark to see anything, but gradually the sound got louder and closer until finally I could make out a loose formation of armed soldiers marching past our building, whistling as they went. I recognized the tune as one that Fourth Aunt liked to sing – a British tune – and so I knew they had to be British soldiers. Several weeks of uncertainty followed, during which my brother and I were kept indoors although there were no soldiers to be seen anywhere, British or Japanese. Then, on Thursday August 30, I was wakened early by my mother and taken to a window. I could not believe my eyes. Sailing into Victoria Harbour was a large convoy of warships and I could tell that the sight made my mother – and therefore me – happy, in spite of the fact the leading vessel was flying the Japanese flag.

It was the Royal Navy fleet under the command of Rear Admiral Sir Cecil Harcourt. The Japanese ship, like the proverbial canary in the coalmine, had been ordered to lead the convoy to ensure safe passage for the British vessels through the potential minefield of the harbour. By mid-afternoon, friendly warships and numerous cargo vessels were anchored from one end of Victoria Harbour to the other. Three years, eight months and five days after Black Christmas, the Japanese occupation of Hong Kong was over. Seventeen days later, on September 16, we were formally once again under the auspices of the British Empire.

Return to Empire | 2

A New Life (1945-1949)

COLONIAL RULE – LAW AND ORDER

I turned eight in the fall of 1945, continuing to accept without question the fact that the colour and tone of my daily life as a Chinese boy was largely determined by other nationalities, first the British, then the Japanese, and now the British again. The British colonial system no longer discouraged us from feeling proud to be Chinese, however, openly acknowledging China as being one of the Allies who made the defeat of Japan possible. Victory commemorative pins became very popular, especially the version imprinted with the American, British and Chinese flags. It felt good to see China represented on an equal footing with the two most powerful Western nations and I wore that pin every day, though secretly I considered America to be the only nation to help China overthrow the Japanese.

After Rear Admiral Sir Cecil Harcourt had formally accepted the Japanese surrender on September 16, Hong Kong entered into another period of military rule, this time under Harcourt. Although merely a transition period, a period of preparing for the restoration of civil rule some eight months down the road, history has shown that this was not just a time of 'muddling through' by career soldiers who knew little about good governance. On the contrary, the military administration functioned remarkably efficiently in extraordinarily difficult conditions and by the end of December domestic banks were once again in operation, public utilities were running, and the colony had reopened for trade. However, many serious challenges lay ahead for the civil government upon the return of Governor Sir Mark Aitchison Young at the beginning of May 1946.

One of the greatest challenges was the maintenance of law and order among a population that had more than doubled to over a million people within six months, largely due to the return of many who had fled the Japanese occupation. The city's narrow streets were crammed with thousands of hawkers, and thieves could dispose of stolen goods to a stallholder with great ease. In addition, organized crime had flourished during the occupation and now triads – Chinese criminal organizations – were running drug, vice and gambling rackets with seeming impunity. The Hong Kong Police Force, meanwhile, had to be built anew, after being decimated by the Japanese. This led to even more problems.

The expatriate police officers who emerged from the internment camps were in poor health and many subsequently left Hong Kong to return to Britain. Former Chinese constables and sergeants reported back for duty, however their pay rates and employment benefits were so far below those of new recruits brought in from the United Kingdom and other British colonies that morale among the ranks plummeted and the chances of corruption were high. I had no idea how greatly this would soon affect the safety of our own home.

Though it was very different from the spacious house where we had lived during the later part of the Japanese occupation, our new flat on Bonham Road was adequate for our needs. My parents, brother and I shared the master bedroom and the second bedroom was assigned to my grandparents. With both my parents now working again, they could afford to hire a live-in servant whom we called *À Saam* ("Number

Three", as she was the third child in her family). Her job description came under the heading *Yat Keùk T'èk* ("One Foot Kick"), meaning that, for forty Hong Kong dollars a month (about five Canadian dollars), she was responsible for just about everything: cooking, cleaning, laundry, shopping and even helping me with my bath. She slept in the corridor on a foldable canvas cot and Aunt would often drop in to check that our home was being run properly.

One early summer evening, À Saam was instructed to hang the ladies' mink coats, including one belonging to Aunt, out to air overnight on the balcony before putting them away for the season. I was awoken next morning by cries of distress from my mother. The furs were gone, and so too were handbags and other precious pieces left out in the dining room. We discovered that the steel security bars on a window had been bent, enabling someone to gain entrance and take what they wanted. The police were called. Two plainclothes officers arrived and began questioning us in a harsh manner, scaring and confusing me. I knew that at least one robber had been in our home while we slept and now it felt as though the very people who should be protecting us were instead interrogating us. I remember Aunt telling them that the flat was the home of Dr. Wong Tse-chuen, as indeed Uncle had rented it for us.

A few weeks later, the doorbell rang when my father was out and Aunt was again visiting. I saw À Saam checking through the security hatch before announcing that it was the electric company and unlocking the door, whereupon she was violently propelled backwards as three men burst in, the first one waving a revolver and the other two brandishing knives. I remember hearing my mother and grandparents screaming. Within seconds, we were all herded together in the dining room and the man with the gun demanded to know the whereabouts of Dr. Wong. When Aunt said that her husband was at work, he ordered her to take him to her jewellery, so she told him that neither she nor her husband actually lived there. He then turned to my mother and repeated the command. My mother told him she did not have a key to the jewellery drawer and he immediately threatened to shoot "one or two" of us unless she cooperated. Believing that my family was about to be murdered, I yelled, "They're in there!" and pointed towards the master bedroom, whereupon, to my horror, the knife-wielding men grabbed my mother and disappeared with her into the bedroom. It was perhaps the worst moment of my life. I was sure they were about to kill her.

The man with the revolver sat down at the dining room table and began repeatedly emptying and reloading the bullet chamber of his weapon, nervously telling my grandparents that he and his cohorts were doing this only because they needed to *shik faân* ("feed themselves with rice"). After what felt like an eternity, the others came back into the room, pocketing the few pieces of jewellery and small amount of cash that had been in the drawer. To my indescribable relief, my mother also returned, looking distressed but unharmed. The three men then left the flat, warning us that anyone who went out on the balcony to watch their getaway would be shot.

Aunt ignored this warning. Instructing À Saam to lock and bolt the front door, she dashed onto the balcony and yelled down at passers-by for help. The gang leader was racing along the street, hesitating only long enough to assure the passers-by that he was chasing the thieves for us! Later, I heard Aunt tell Uncle that she had recognized the gunman as one of the plainclothes officers who had come to our flat in response to the fur burglary. We never recovered any of our losses from either incident.

FAMILY REUNION AND CHURCH OUTREACH

I was wearing my favourite quilted Chinese jacket while riding my tricycle around and around the dining room table when an unexpected visitor arrived. It was almost Christmas, the first Christmas after

Victory Day 1945. My mother greeted the beautiful lady with a warm handshake – kissing or embracing was uncommon among the Chinese in those days – and excitedly told me, "*Sź K'aŭ-mŏ* ('Fourth maternal uncle's wife') is back!"

With her mink coat, high-heeled shoes and fine makeup, Auntie Wan-fun looked like a movie star to me. It was hard to imagine that she had ever succeeded in disguising herself as a boy in order to escape from Hong Kong to China with her husband. After arriving there in early 1942, she and Uncle Wah-chiu had met up with a friend who, like them, was active in the sports community and who also happened to have connections with the Chinese Nationalist government. With his assistance, my uncle and aunt had travelled to Chungking (present day Chongqing) where Chiang Kai-shek had established his wartime capital and which had a strong American military presence. Uncle Wah-chiu's background in athletics and his outgoing personality earned him a position there as head of the American forces' hospitality centre, while Auntie Wan-fun was taken on as a liaison officer and became very popular. They both enjoyed all the benefits given to Allied military and diplomatic personnel. Then, with the war's end, the British government provided Uncle Wah-chiu, a veteran of the Hong Kong Volunteer Defence Corps, with passage back to Hong Kong.

All my mother's brothers were now returning to Hong Kong under the same government arrangement, with the exception of Uncle Wah-leung who instead went off to university in Pennsylvania after receiving treatment for his facial paralysis in Calcutta. And just like she herself had done, my mother's Hong Kong brothers also became very active in the Hop Yat Church.

Hop Yat Church had become more than a place of worship; it had become a gathering place in which those who had been separated by war could reconnect with one another. The Rev. Cheung Chuk-ling was no small part of the reason for this. Though still regaining his health after being interned and tortured by the Japanese, he was an inspiring preacher and gifted hymn composer who attracted a large congregation of Chinese of diverse backgrounds. As a nine-year-old with a developing curiosity about the wider world, I was intrigued to learn about some of them and to experience how the church was reaching out beyond the Hong Kong community.

Mr. Ngan Shing-kwan was an influential member of the church council and the owner of the China Motor Bus Company Limited. According to my father, Mr. Ngan began his transportation career as a rickshaw puller in Kowloon Peninsula in the 1920s and established his company in 1933, receiving exclusive rights to the operation of bus routes on Hong Kong Island. After the war, the network of CMB's routes expanded with the exploding population, necessitating the purchase of new buses from England. While waiting for their delivery, Mr. Ngan arranged with the government for a fleet of military lorries (trucks) to serve temporarily as buses, modifying them with the installation of steps at their rear so that passengers could access long benches that had been fastened onto the platform. It was incredibly exhilarating to a young boy like me to be able to ride in a genuine military lorry, all the sweeter when it was provided free of charge for some of our church outings.

Then there was Mr. Ng Wai-kee, a quiet man with a dry sense of humour who had become a close friend of my parents. At the end of a church event one evening, he took me by complete surprise when he pulled me aside to show me a revolver that he slipped discreetly out from his pocket. I was enthralled. I asked why he was carrying it, and he just smiled. He was simply a kind bachelor doing his best to entertain a young boy. I later heard that Mr. Ng had been a spy for the British during the Japanese occupation, allegedly reporting to Sir Jack Cater, who was to become Chief Secretary of Hong Kong. Mr. Ng himself became a senior official in the Hong Kong Fisheries Department, an important government entity in the colony while it was recovering from the shortage of food supplies.

Major Mok Man-lit was another church member who impressed me very much in his beige uniform resembling that of the U.S. marines. He was an officer of the New 1st Army of China, reputed to be the most elite military unit of the Chinese armed forces. He had the use of a jeep, which made him very attractive to the young women of the congregation and a hero to every young boy. I very much wished I could be like him, wearing an American-style uniform, driving a convertible jeep and sporting General Douglas MacArthur-type sunglasses, When he retired from the military to a job at the Fisheries Department, I was deeply disappointed as I felt it was the end of me ever getting a chance to ride in a jeep, however something even more exciting was just around the corner.

There was a lot of musical talent in the Hop Yat Church congregation and our choir soon earned a high reputation in Western choral performance. My mother, Uncle Wah-chiu, Auntie Wan-fun and Uncle Wah-cheung were all singers. For months after the Japanese surrender, Victoria Harbour was full of Allied ships and the choir was often invited to give onboard performances. Beyond my wildest dreams, my mother was sometimes permitted to bring my brother and me with her.

I was beside myself with excitement when we boarded an enormous navy landing craft at Queen's Pier and then headed out into the harbour at surprisingly high speed, creating large waves in our wake. Within a few minutes, we were alongside a towering battleship and were asked to proceed up a set of very steep gangway stairs to the main deck. To my dismay, an American soldier picked me up and carried me up those stairs, fearing that I might fall as I was so young, however my embarrassment was far outweighed by my eagerness to set foot on a real battleship.

The deck was filled with soldiers in uniform, most of them standing but some in wheelchairs or leaning on crutches. Against a backdrop of big guns and lifeboats, these *gweilo* (slang for Caucasian male, literally "ghosts" or "pale fellows") appeared to be quite enthusiastic about our visit. The ship's captain and chaplain formally welcomed us and then our accompanist, the son of Rev. Cheung, was escorted to an upright piano and the service began. The whole thing – prayers, hymns and sermon – was in English, a striking first-time experience for me. But the highlight of the visit had to be the refreshments that our hosts offered afterwards: a 'heavenly' spread of ham sandwiches, cakes, lemonade and ice cream – a feast the like of which I had never seen, a sharp contrast to four years of rationing and shortages.

That feast, however, delicious as it was, could not match a later memory of another visit, this time to a hospital ship. We were invited to tour the wards below the main deck and as we walked past a bearded soldier lying in bed propped on his side, he beckoned to me, the little boy of the group. Encouraged by my mother, I nervously approached and he handed me a small object from his bedside table. It was a coin. My mother explained to me afterwards that it was a Canadian coin and that the man was offering me his good wishes and his hope that I might get to see his "big and beautiful country" some day.

His out-of-the-blue wish for me was to come true twenty-one years later.

CATCHING UP AND CANTON EXPERIENCE

During the three years and eight months of the Japanese occupation, I had received no formal education, only English lessons from my mother and Chinese calligraphy instruction from my grandfather. Now, just like thousands of other Hong Kong children, it was time to catch up on my schooling. Choices were limited. Most schools were facing the challenge of recovering from wartime damage and of chronic staff shortages.

Hong Kong's education system was based largely on the British system, consisting of two years of kindergarten, followed by six years of primary school, then six years of secondary-level education. Schools were divided into two streams. The first stream, the Anglo-Chinese schools, was the most popular as the subjects were taught mainly in English and there was very little Chinese study. Within this stream there were government schools and grant schools, the latter run by various Christian missionary groups who received financial subsidies from the government.

The second stream consisted of Chinese schools that were privately run and mostly affiliated with a parent school in China. With the emergence of modern Western culture in post-war Hong Kong, however, these schools were declining in popularity. The teaching of Chinese culture and tradition was considered by many to now be outdated.

St. Stephen's Girls' College, a grant school under the Hong Kong Anglican Church, was just a short walk from our flat on Bonham Road. While openings for admission were limited, applications from both girls and boys in the neighbourhood were welcomed. In the fall of 1945, I sat the exam for entrance into Primary 3, along with my cousin Choong-ching (Second Aunt's younger daughter) and Mr. Ng Wah's youngest son and oldest grandson. The four of us sat together at a table in a big room filled with many other tables of candidates. Lists of questions written in English were placed in front of each of us, but there was next to no supervision so my dear cousin was able to help me with the answers. Consequently, next day our families were informed that their children had passed with flying colours.

Right from my first day at St. Stephen's, I knew I was out of place. Miss Atkins, the English headmistress, intimidated me, and the teachers, mostly Chinese, seemed to favour the girls, showing little patience towards the few boys in my class. My command of English was sufficiently limited that I had difficulty understanding much of what was being taught and was occasionally made to stand outside the classroom door for daydreaming during lessons, to the amusement of some of the girls and my own bitter humiliation.

Music should have been one area that I could manage well, however I found the part-time music teacher uninspiring compared to our church music leaders and I also had difficulty understanding his accent – he was a British officer from one of the battleships parked in the harbour and had been hired only because of the shortage of local music teachers. Even his crisp white naval uniform failed to excite or motivate me.

I did so poorly at St. Stephen's that my mother decided to withdraw me halfway through the school year. By this time, my brother was a boarder at the Lingnan Middle School, a well-known Chinese school affiliated with a parent school and university in China, and it did not take long for my mother to accept my grandfather's advice that Chinese education would do me a lot of good as well. I would lose face not being able to master our own language, he counselled.

And so it was that I found myself enrolled again into Pui Ying Primary School where I had started kindergarten almost five years before. The principal, Madam Au-Yeung, was a member of the Hop Yat Church and agreed to accept me into Primary 3 in the middle of the school year. Though it was technically the same level as I had been placed in at St. Stephen's, I now found myself studying a very dissimilar curriculum in a totally different cultural environment.

Dressed in green and white school uniforms, we began each morning's outdoor assembly with the raising of the Nationalist Chinese flag and the singing of China's national anthem followed by a recitation of the last will and testament of Dr. Sun Yat-sen, founding father of the Republic of China. Our teachers regularly preached the virtue of the republic's Nationalist government, encouraging us to be proud of China as a world power.

I was soon to see for myself what that power looked like on the ground.

Negotiations between Chiang Kai-shek's Nationalist government and the Chinese Communist Party under Mao Zedong took place in Chungking for six weeks in the autumn of 1945. Even while both were at the table stressing the importance of peaceful reconstruction in China following the ousting of the Japanese, active conflict between the two sides continued. The United States backed the Nationalists with military supplies and equipment, however the Communists trumped this military superiority with their land reform policy, a policy that few among the landless and starving Chinese peasants could resist: the promise that by fighting on the side of the People's Liberation Army they would gain control of the farmland they slaved on. This strategy gave the Communists an almost unlimited supply of manpower for both combat and logistical support, despite heavy casualties at the hands of the better-equipped Nationalist forces. Full-scale war between the two sides broke out in June 1946, plunging China into a state of civil war that was to last more than three years.

In Hong Kong, the Chinese Civil War was thought of merely as unrest in faraway northern China, nothing to be too concerned about. For some, the reports of Communist victories were considered the propaganda of leftist media, as surely the Nationalist government would eventually be able to get things under control, given America's support and the presence of the U.S. Seventh Fleet in the South China Sea. And so it was that when my father came home one evening early in the

conflict and announced that, as a member of the Hop Yat church council, he had been invited to attend a church conference in Canton (also
known as Guangzhou) and would take us – my mother, brother and
me – with him, I jumped for joy. Finally I would get to see China and
experience for myself everything I was being taught at Pui Ying School
about my motherland.

We left for Canton in the summer of 1946.

The true origins of Canton are lost in the mists of time but the most
popular legend tells of five celestial beings carrying sheaves of rice arriving on rams, blessing the land and offering the grain to the people as
a symbol of prosperity. When the celestials left, the rams turned into
stone and Canton developed into an influential and affluent city. There
is a renowned Chinese saying, "Hong Kong is the place to live; Canton
is the place to eat."

We boarded a train in Kowloon for the one hundred and forty
kilometre journey north to Canton (about eighty-five miles), a journey
which took almost six hours as the train kept stopping after crossing the
border into China so that villagers could sell local products such as fresh
fruits and dried meat. Our travelling companions were Mr. and Mrs.
Lee, close friends of my parents from Hop Yat Church, and their two
children, both younger than me. We had been invited to stay at Mrs.
Lee's brother's home in downtown Canton. Before we left Hong Kong,
my mother had said that it was important for me to memorize our host's
address by heart so that, if I got lost, I could seek help to get back there
and avoid being snatched by kidnappers. Not a particularly encouraging
indication of conditions in my motherland, I thought.

Upon arriving at the Canton railway station, we were picked up by
a friend of our host in a run-down sedan. To start the engine, the driver
bent down and connected the ends of two cables dangling below the

instrument panel, while Mrs. Lee told us that it was a luxury to own a vehicle so soon after the war with Japan. My father and Mr. Lee followed the overflowing car on pedicabs.

As we crossed the city on roads pitted with potholes, the scenes we encountered bewildered me. Everywhere I looked, there were swarming masses of pedestrians, bicycles, hawkers and pitiful beggars and a great deal of filth. The smell of open sewers made me feel ill in the stifling summer heat. I was greatly relieved when our ride in the "luxury" sedan came to an end. We had arrived at 21 Cheung Hing Street, Third Floor. Duly committed to memory.

The flat we stayed at for the next four days was quite dilapidated, as indeed were most buildings in Canton at the time. To my dismay, its bathroom featured a squat toilet, which I was told was quite common in China, and the plumbing was not connected to a sewage system, with sanitary waste disposal undertaken by hired crews during the night. I was so appalled by these facilities that my parents had to take me for a hasty visit to the only hotel in the city with modern plumbing fixtures, the Victory Hotel on Shameen Island (now Shamian Island), a formerly-colonial section of Canton bordering the Pearl River and featuring elegant Western-style architecture.

I was enthralled, however, by the flat's ingenious cooling device that served in place of electric fans. It was a huge screen made of bamboo and straw that was strategically placed close to the doorway opening onto the balcony so as to divert evening breezes into the bedrooms. It worked. As the partitioning walls did not extend all the way up to the flat's high ceiling, the breeze was indeed thus enabled to flow right through.

Though disappointed with the living conditions, I was soon taking pleasure in other aspects of Canton. We climbed to the top of *Paâk Wān Shaan* (White Cloud Mountain) to enjoy a panoramic view of the city. We visited the stone sculpture of the five rams, and the *Nğ Ts'āng Laū*

("Five Storied Pagoda") built in 1380 during the Ming Dynasty. And we paid tribute at the *Wŏng Fà Kong* ("Yellow Flowers Hill") memorial to the seventy-two martyrs who sacrificed their lives during the uprising of 1911 that led to the establishment of the first Chinese republic under the leadership of Dr. Sun Yat-sen.

I was also delighted by the diversity of fresh fruits that our generous host served while we relaxed in the evenings on the large front balcony. Along with watermelon, pummelo and tangerine, I was amazed at the number of varieties of lychee offered. Our host told us that the fruit was most famously grown in a suburb of Canton called *Lychee Waan* ("Lychee Bay", now called *Ly-waan*), a recreational area of parkland and canals. We decided to visit the area and that decision gave rise to my most pleasurable experience of the holiday, an enchanted evening spent aboard a small sampan navigated along a canal by a woman with the assistance of her children. The woman helped us choose freshly prepared seafood from various floating food stands, and as we dined on the delicious treats a refreshing breeze brought the faraway strains of Cantonese opera to our ears. It was an unforgettable experience, a glorious contrast to the noise, heat and challenges of the urban city.

On the slow train ride back to Hong Kong, I brooded about the fact that the living conditions in Canton were so far behind those in Hong Kong. I was trying hard to reconcile what I had seen with what I had been taught about China being a proud member of the great and victorious Allies. My young heart hoped that this pride would soon take on a more concrete form, literally, in my ancestral motherland.

MOVING FORWARD – CHINA, SCHOOL AND HOME

I was eager to start Primary 4 after my firsthand experience of China. My mother told me that I should now focus hard on my studies, however I found myself still drifting off into daydreaming in class even though language was no longer an excuse. My list of favourite subjects dwindled to one: Arts and Crafts. When I moved on to Primary 5, two additional things became my focus in school: Boy Scouts, and girls. As a result, two experiences – one with a scoutmaster and the other with a female classmate – offered me my next lessons in life.

By the age of eleven, I was feeling more sure of myself and participated enthusiastically in sports and school theatrical performances. The school also had a Boy Scouts program based on the English model and the scoutmaster was our physical education teacher, a man in his early thirties with a lean but strongly built body. À Kwok, one of my close friends in class, was a scout captain and so I too became an English Boy Scout – rather odd for a Chinese school. I enjoyed the training and soon became involved in organizing troop activities and outings. This seemed to impress the scoutmaster. It did not take long for me to be promoted to the rank of deputy captain and I found myself one of a small group of students who were treated as his favourites, being given first pick on interesting assignments or extra drinks and snacks during outings.

One of our favourite summer scouting activities was to spend the day at Shek-O, a beautiful white sandy beach on the south-eastern shore of Hong Kong Island. We used a handy cave as our changing area and on one occasion I was designated to guard the clothing while everyone else went swimming. While I was alone in the cave, the scoutmaster returned, approached very close and put his arms around me, saying how much he would like me to call him *Kái Yē* ("Godfather"). I was totally taken aback. When he then suggested I change out of my clothes and into my bathing trunks, I was stunned and suddenly scared. At that moment, to my immense relief, a few swimmers came back into the cave and the incident was over almost as quickly as it had begun, leaving me confused and unhappy and then angry.

During the week after this happened, I related my experience to my friend À Kwok and a few of the scoutmaster's other "favourites" and was shocked to learn that most of them had gone through a similar or worse experience with him. I asked why they had kept their terrible secrets and not reported him, but no one could give me a straight answer except to suggest that I should be the one to do it. And so, gathering all my courage, I walked into the office of Mr. Lee, my class teacher, and told him the stories. He brought the matter to the principal's attention and was assigned by Madam Au-Yeung to conduct an investigation, subsequently questioning each of my fellow "favourites". But after all that, absolutely nothing changed except that the scoutmaster now treated me with great animosity during physical education classes, the only time I now came in contact with him.

When I completed Primary 5 and entered my graduating year, Madam Au-Yeung appointed me Head Prefect on the recommendation of Mr. Lee. I considered that to be my consolation prize, a trade-off for the scoutmaster being retained on the school staff. As a neophyte Chinese philosopher, having absorbed at least a little of my grandfather's Confucian sensibility, I accepted the job.

As Head Prefect, I was in charge of a team of student monitors who reported to me early each morning for assignment to various duty posts. One of them was Mok Chor-fong, a top student in my class and a very attractive girl. I had a secret crush on her. However, something began to trouble me.

Chor-fong and her younger brother, who was also in our class, became active members of a supposed social group headed by Mr. Ho, a Primary 3 teacher known to support the Chinese Communist Party and the People's Liberation Army. With Mr. Ho's encouragement behind the scenes, Chor-fong hosted class picnics during which the "social group" raised money for the cause by selling a popular snack, dried olives, wrapped in 'Communist red' paper. Having been taught that the Nationalist government was the legitimate government of China, I considered what she was doing to be unpatriotic and began to openly criticize what was going on. Mr. Ho summoned me to his classroom and gave give me a lecture on the corruption of the Nationalist government, and then dismissed me with a firm warning to stop interfering. I decided to use my power as Head Prefect to make my own feelings clear once and for all. When Chor-fong reported to me for duty one morning, I assigned her to the worst possible post: in front of the men's toilet. My secret crush was over.

Not that my personal opinion made a difference. By late 1948 the Communists had seized control of the northeast of China and the capture of large Nationalist formations provided them with the tanks, heavy artillery and other combined-arms assets needed to execute successful offensive operations.

Not long after my family's return from Canton, there was an interesting change in our lives at home. My mother decided to take two years off from teaching to study at the Northcote College of Education and was awarded full financial support for this endeavour by the Ying Wa Girls' School,where she was a highly respected teacher even though she lacked formal training. Her students always treated her with esteem and affection, demonstrated in part by the fact that they never gave her a nickname, a derision most teachers had to endure.

This was a wise decision on her part as after graduating with a teaching certificate her salary would increase by fifteen hundred Hong Kong dollars a month (about two hundred Canadian dollars). Besides, at the age of thirty-five, she still had sufficient energy for all the roles she now performed: student, "rice earner", homemaker and mother.

She began to be very busy when she was at home, taking care of her own studies and assignments on top of helping me with my homework and helping my brother too when he came home at the weekends. My father also was busy, not getting home until late most nights from his work at the King's Theatre. Aunt began to be concerned about my parents' relationship. True to her spirit as matriarch of the family, she came up with a plan, suggesting to them that it was time for them to have another baby.

Our apartment was totally reorganized. The living room was converted into a bedroom for my parents, while my brother and I remained in the bedroom that we had shared with them but now the dining table was moved in with us and the former dining room became the new living room. It turned out to be a brilliant rearrangement, providing my parents with some precious privacy. I began to notice that my father was a happier man.

On February 22, 1948, my sister was born at the Tai Wor Hospital, delivered by Uncle, Aunt having retired from midwifery. She was a beautiful baby, weighing in at eight-and-a-half pounds (almost four kilograms), and was named *Siu-dong* ("Little Bell-shaped Jade Stone") by my grandfather. It wasn't long before we started calling her Dong-dong.

Along with my delight in becoming a big brother, I was suddenly conscious of the responsibilities that came along with the role. It would be seventeen years before I finally felt I could perform those responsibilities anywhere close to my satisfaction.

Growing Up | 3

Unique Environment (1949-1957)

A FUSION OF THREE WORLDS

I graduated from Pui Ying Primary School in the summer of 1949. I was eleven, fast closing in on twelve. Four years had gone by since the end of the Japanese occupation and Hong Kong's gradual economic recovery was helping its people to rebuild their lives.

According to my grandfather, there were four essential elements in a good life: shelter, food, clothing and freedom of mobility. Education, recreation and fine dining, he added, were the extras that could make a good life even better. It was incredibly fortunate for me that various members of my family collectively provided me with both the essentials and the extras. Their involvement and support transformed my adolescence into a fusion of three worlds, each giving me a distinct perspective that broadened and deepened my outlook and my life.

The first world was the one formed by my mother, my primary caregiver and moral compass. She gave me a wonderful start in life, teaching me about integrity and never doubting that there would be a better tomorrow. She herself epitomized these ideals and a great deal more.

When she graduated from the Northcote College of Education and returned to teach at Ying Wa Girls' School, my mother was given an advancement in seniority as well as in salary. She now earned more than my father and this allowed her to hire a nanny for Dong-dong. À Ìn ("Swallow") came from the same village in southern China as À Saam, who no doubt was grateful to have another pair of hands. For doubling as a domestic helper, À Ìn's pay started at thirty-five Hong Kong dollars a month (about six Canadian dollars). Like À Saam, she too slept on a foldable canvas cot in the corridor, and together they made a great team, conscientious about their work, loyal to our family, and caring for us children as though we were their own.

Besides teaching five-and-a-half days a week – there was school on Saturday mornings – my mother continued to give private English lessons to make extra money. This allowed her to arrange for music lessons for my brother from Ms. Mah, a piano teacher living close by. I was disappointed not to be included, but I accepted the fact that she could not afford lessons for two of us. Young though I was, I was keenly aware of my mother's numerous responsibilities. In addition to everything at work and at home, she often officiated at the Sunday service at Hop Yat Church and would spend a good part of Saturday evening preparing. As well, she was a popular amateur actor in parish-produced plays. I loved watching her in all her public roles and hoped beyond hope that one day I might become capable of following in her footsteps.

To help out, I sometimes took on handyman jobs around our home, once painting the body of our old refrigerator a brilliant white to make it look more like Uncle's new Frigidaire, and another time attempting some electrical work by installing a switch on my mother's desk lamp. After completing such tasks, I was given copious praise and encouragement, especially by my grandmother. Grandmother was a tiny person with bound feet, conditioned all her life to the role of a subservient housewife, but she never ceased to amaze me with her liberal outlook.

Her warm acknowledgement of my willingness to help others and of my innovative ideas helped me gain self-confidence.

This was quite in contrast to my grandfather, in whose opinion I was a rebellious child who showed little interest during his lessons in calligraphy or in Confucian virtues – especially the cardinal virtue of filial piety, which I often breached even as he was teaching it, debating vigourously with him or simply gazing into space while he spoke. For this behaviour, my father once ordered me out of the house. Being a stubborn twelve-year-old, I ran as far away as I could, determined never to go back, so my mother had to send À Saam to find me, much to my covert relief. My father did not utter a word on my return.

I had learned to compromise in my relationship with my father, but my mother wanted more from me and for me. On my thirteenth birthday in 1950, she gave me an English bible in which she had written in Chinese an inscription based on St. Paul's first letter to the Corinthians: "Love is not easily provoked, hopes all things, endures all things. And now abide faith, hope, love, these three; but the greatest of these is love."

There was also a fun side to my relationship with my father. He was an ardent football (soccer) fan, frequently invited to weekend matches by his boss. My brother and I were sometimes included and enjoyed the events almost as much as he did, the ride to the grounds in the back of the boss's Buick being the icing on the cake for us boys. I also got to see movies at the King's Theatre for free and my father sometimes even got me passes to other movie theatres.

The most important Chinese holiday is Chinese New Year, late January or early February on the Western calendar but marking the beginning of spring in China. New Year celebrations last for almost two weeks and are a much more serious affair than in the West. After dinner on New Year's Eve, families go to an outdoor market to purchase a cherry tree to bring home for good luck in the coming year. On New Year's Day and throughout the following two weeks, families visit one another, with the grownups handing out *Lai Si* ("lucky money") in a red envelope to the young people. It was particularly exciting when an envelope was left for my brother and me by some of Uncle and Aunt's wealthier friends with the money being divided equally between us. After Dong-dong's arrival, however, there was a notable change to this accounting. My mother began to split the money into five equal parts, with each of us boys receiving two parts and our sister one, as was the Chinese way. Dong-dong was too young to complain.

There was also a change in our sleeping arrangements following Dong-dong's arrival. She joined us boys in the dining/bedroom, taking over my bed while I inherited my brother's bed and he, being the eldest, got a new one. That too was the Chinese way.

The second world that I experienced was an enriched one that opened windows onto expanded possibilities. It was shown to me by Uncle and Aunt.

Aunt once explained that while she and Uncle could not have a child of their own, they had chosen to assist with my brother and me rather than adopt because of her love for her own brother, our father. She hoped her involvement would help us become the pride of our paternal grandparents' male blood line, and we in turn would become capable of taking care of our sister down the road.

As the firstborn boy and the future head of the family, my brother received special attention from Aunt. She would personally take him shopping for clothes and shoes on his birthday, ensuring that he would be well dressed while accompanying her on visits to her friends. I had to be content with inheriting his clothes when he outgrew them. However, she bought me a bicycle of my very own, which was kept at her house so that I could ride it around her garden – she and Uncle had moved back into their spacious property at Pokfulam in the summer of 1948.

It rarely bothered me that my brother received so much attention from Aunt because I suspected that it was me who was Uncle's favourite. I felt this in part because, though usually of rather serious demeanour, he would show amusement rather than annoyance at some of my 'mischievous' ways and he also went to the trouble of selecting gifts for me. I vividly remember him teaching me how to use one of those gifts, an Eastman Kodak Brownie Hawkeye camera, patiently introducing me to a hobby that I was to enjoy throughout my life.

As a filial daughter, Aunt always gave precedence to my grandfather's well-being, even assisting discreetly with his financial support of relatives in our ancestral village in southern China. When it came to his eightieth *taaî tsaú* ("grand birthday"), she made sure that the celebration was indeed grand. Invitations were issued in the names of my parents even though she and Uncle were footing the bill, and numerous gifts began to arrive at our Bonham Road flat: gifts such as gold *tsaú t'ò* (pear-shaped mementos engraved with the word 'Longevity') and *tsaú cheúng* (bolts of fine woollen fabric suspended from rods by clips featuring that same word). Over the span of two consecutive evenings, more than six hundred guests enjoyed an elaborate nine-course dinner ("nine" having the same sound as "long lasting" in Chinese) at the famed King Wah Restaurant in the King's Theatre Building. Each family group, in descending order of seniority among my grandparents' five children, bowed three times in front of my seated grandparents and a professional photographer took photographs. My brother, Dong-dong and I were filled with pride at our high position on the family tree.

Aunt's generosity also extended to taking us for English afternoon tea in elegant establishments like the Repulse Bay Hotel, where we were treated to delicious finger sandwiches, waffles and ice cream sodas. From time to time, she and Uncle also took us to other fine Western-style restaurants, teaching us table manners such as waiting until grown-ups had started before beginning to eat ourselves and how to properly place our cutlery during and after a meal. They also exposed us to live music, taking us to concerts by recording artists like Benny Goodman and Xavier Cugat – I distinctly remember being completely bowled over by the glamourous Abbe Lane, Cugat's wife and his orchestra's featured singer.

Often while Uncle and Aunt visited at the homes of their socially elite friends, my brother and I were taken along. When talk turned to overseas vacations and the prospect of schooling in America or England, I began to experience discomfort about my own identity, knowing that I was just Uncle and Aunt's nephew and could not hope to enjoy the same advantages as the actual children of our hosts. I cheered myself up by remembering that Uncle himself had been raised in impoverished circumstances by a widowed mother, however determination and hard work had brought him to the respected position he now held in Hong Kong society. I felt very grateful to have him as a role model in my life.

I also began to worry that someday soon I might lose him.

Already in his sixties, Uncle's irregular hours of work as a busy obstetrician had given him a stomach ulcer that took its toll on his energy level and well-being. Aunt must have shared my concern because she decided that it was time for him to take a break. Along with two fellow doctors and their wives, they set sail for the United States on the SS *President Cleveland* in the summer of 1953.

I was amazed by the huge array of elegant *Cheong Sam* (traditional Chinese gowns) that Aunt packed for their first-class trip, until Uncle explained that he and his colleagues would be representing professional

Asian society to Americans and Europeans who had largely encountered Chinese people only as waiters or laundry workers.

Every day throughout the two months duration of their trip, we eagerly anticipated the arrival of the mail at our Bonham Road flat. We were not disappointed. There were regular postcards depicting such thrilling landmarks as the Golden Gate Bridge, Yellowstone National Park, Niagara Falls, the Empire State Building, and then London's Big Ben – after crossing the North American continent, Uncle and Aunt had gone on to cross the Atlantic on the RMS *Queen Elizabeth*.

They arrived back in Hong Kong filled with exciting stories and with many souvenirs including recordings of Broadway musicals they had attended – *Annie Get Your Gun* and *Oklahoma* – and for me, a much-coveted Roy Rogers cowboy belt and gloves. Their holiday photos and movies took us weeks to fully peruse and gave me my first physical glimpse into other worlds, other possibilities. I was deeply affected.

I was also relieved to see that Uncle's health had clearly improved after this well-deserved vacation, though he and Aunt no longer engaged with us children in outdoor activities as they used to do. However, my mother's favourite brother, Uncle Wah-chiu, and his wife, Auntie Wan-fun, stepped in to fill that gap.

The third world that I experienced, thanks to Uncle Wah-chiu and Auntie Wan-fun, showed me the power of motivation and self-confidence. They were a fun loving, outgoing couple who taught me about community involvement, networking and succeeding in reaching goals.

Upon his return to Hong Kong after the war, Uncle Wah-chiu was employed by the Hong Kong Urban Council as a health inspector, enjoying job security and good benefits. Auntie Wan-fun became a Form Mistress at Sacred Heart School, a Catholic secondary girls' school, though she herself was an active member of the Hop Yat Church.

The two of them quickly re-established their network of friends and colleagues in Hong Kong's sports community and became actively involved as players, coaches and umpires in volleyball, badminton and tennis leagues. As well, they had many friends in the hospitality industry and led active social lives.

The urban council owned a holiday house at Middle Bay, a beautiful beach near Repulse Bay in the southwest of Hong Kong Island, and Uncle Wah-chiu had occasional use of it. One of the highlights of summer was to be picked up in his car and taken there for the day. While teaching me how to swim at the beach, Uncle Wah-chiu also conveyed the importance of coordinating mind and body in order to succeed, and the role of self-confidence in achieving success. He once told me the secret to winning a sack race – run in quick tiny steps with toes stretching the two bottom corners of the sack – and I was overjoyed to discover that indeed this 'coordination of mind and body' gave me the 'confidence' to leave all competitors in the dust.

Uncle Wah-chiu and Auntie Wan-fun often took us to restaurants for dim sum and I couldn't help but notice that everywhere we went they seemed to know the proprietors and were given special treatment. As well, when they came across anyone they knew, which was often, they invariable engaged in genial conversation. In this way, I learned powerful lessons in networking.

All three of these lovingly- and generously-shared life perspectives made my adolescent experience truly rich, like a vibrantly complex jigsaw puzzle, with each piece falling into place for my personal growth and inspiration.

CHINA AND THE CHANGING FACE OF HONG KONG

During 1949, my last year in primary school, Chiang Kai-shek resigned as President of the Republic of China when his Nationalist forces suffered bitter losses and numerous defections to the Communists. Vice-President Li Zongren took over the presidency but conflict between him and Chiang led to further deterioration of Nationalist strength. In October of that year Mao Zedong proclaimed the People's Republic of China with its capital at Beiping, which he renamed Beijing ("Northern capital").

On December 10, Mao's troops laid siege to the last Nationalist-controlled city in mainland China, Chengdu. By the end of the day, Chiang Kai-shek had been airlifted to Taiwan, where he would eventually be joined by some two million Nationalist Chinese including many of his senior government officials. A number of cabinet ministers had already left for the United States or Hong Kong, among them Uncle's paternal-uncle, Dr. Wang Chonghui.

After earning his doctorate at Yale University, Dr. Wang had worked in the Judicial Yuan, the highest judicial organ of the Republic of China, on the revision of the 1936 Republic of China draft constitution. He was aided in this endeavour by American advisors including the Dean of Harvard Law School, Roscoe Pound. The National Assembly had promulgated the new constitution in the spring of 1948 and Dr. Wang then became the presiding judge of the Supreme Court and Minister of Justice in the government of Chiang Kai-shek. With the fall of Chiang's government, he decided that it was time to retire from public life and came to Hong Kong with his wife, staying with Uncle and Aunt at their home at Pokfulam.

Dr. Wang was Cantonese, a mild-mannered person with glasses and a well-trimmed moustache. To me, he looked like a typical scholar. Mrs. Wang was quite different. She was an outgoing and sociable lady from Shanghai, a little on the plump side, who seemed to enjoy chatting with us children in spite of having to struggle with her Cantonese. Following Chinese custom, my brother and I addressed them as *Sź Shuk Kung* ("Fourth paternal-granduncle" or "Granduncle") and *Sź Shuk P'öh* ("Fourth paternal-grandaunt" or "Grandaunt") even though we were not actually blood relatives.

From time to time, they received visitors at Pokfulam. I was astonished one evening to see a pile of American dollars at the centre of the card table where an after-dinner game was in process, and was later to hear that a former Chinese minister of finance, a person subsequently labelled as having been corrupt, was at the table that evening. Granduncle Wang, however, enjoyed a reputation as a *ts'ing koon'*("pure official" or "uncorrupted").

Granduncle and Grandaunt Wang brought very little with them to Pokfulam, indeed their bedroom – Uncle's converted study – appeared to be adequate for all their possessions. I couldn't help but wonder how long they would be staying. Then one day about six months into their visit, some well-heeled gentlemen arrived and met in private with Granduncle, and within days he and Grandaunt were bidding us goodbye. They were on their way to Taiwan. I never had a chance to see them again.

I was to learn that Chiang Kai-shek needed the support of Granduncle, a respected constitutional expert, in order to be proclaimed President of the Republic of China once again. That proclamation occurred on March 1, 1950, just a few weeks after Granduncle's departure from Pokfulam.

Hong Kong's population grew rapidly from about two million in 1950 to almost three million less than a decade later. People came in droves from China as refugees and economic migrants. The immigrant nature of the Chinese population and their lack of ability to influence the colonial administration on policy matters combined to make important marks on the business culture of Hong Kong.

It seems to me that during that time and for many years after, Hong Kong Chinese people were a unique composite: philosophical about British rule of law, constantly searching for their Chinese identity, and greatly influenced by American culture. Under the British, they were not taxed too highly and were provided with justice via the courts and so, reasonably satisfied, they devoted their time to making money. They were very successful at this, thanks to their entrepreneurial spirit and determination to survive against all odds. Notwithstanding their lack of representation in government, the Chinese people brought stability and financial prosperity to the colony.

In spite of this, their Chinese identity made them automatically suspect in the eyes of their British overlord, Governor Alexander Grantham, who ran Hong Kong from 1947 to 1958. As Professor Steve Tsang notes in *A Modern History of Hong Kong*, Grantham believed that their affinity with China prevented most Hong Kong Chinese from developing loyalty to the colony, let alone allegiance to the British Empire. Consequently, he brought in changes to citizenship regulations. Anyone not born in Hong Kong would not be recognized as a British subject, and in order for such a person to obtain a passport, they would have to apply for one from the Republic of China in Taiwan (getting one from the mainland People's Republic of China was out of the question after the closure of the border in 1949). Having been born in Hong Kong, I however was eligible for a British passport, had I wanted one.

In 1949 when I turned twelve, I was issued a Hong Kong Identity Card. The photo on it, taken against a vertical scale bar, shows a serious boy, four feet and eleven inches in height (one hundred and fifty centimetres) and wearing glasses. Under 'Race', I was identified as 'C' (meaning "Chinese"); under 'Nationality Claimed', I was identified again as 'C' (meaning "Chinese"). I found this very confusing. Was I British? Or was I Chinese?

Whichever I was, it was American culture, not British or Chinese, that had the greatest impact on my adolescent years.

Most observers expected Chiang Kai-shek's new government to be defeated by a Communist invasion of Taiwan, and the United States showed no interest in supporting Chiang in this anticipated final stand. However things changed radically with the onset of the Korean War in June 1950. At that point, allowing a total Communist victory over Chiang became politically unacceptable to the U.S. and President Harry Truman ordered the Seventh Fleet into the Taiwan Straits to maintain neutrality of those waters and prevent any spread of the conflict – or of Communism.

This led to thousands of American soldiers coming to Hong Kong from Korea for off-duty recreation throughout the years 1950 to 1953. They filled restaurants, bars and movie theatres with their larger-than-life presence. Hollywood movies in English with Chinese sub-titles now dominated the entertainment scene and thanks to my father's position as House Manager at the King's Theatre I saw many first-run movies for free, some of them over and over again. My record was MGM's *Bathing Beauty* starring Esther Williams, which I watched no less than eight times over the course of a couple of weeks.

MGM, Warner Brothers, 20th Century Fox, Columbia Pictures, Universal Pictures, United Artists and RKO were the main distributors of movies to the King's Theatre and to its across-the-street competitor, the Queen's Theatre, as well as other cinemas such as the Lee Theatre, the Roxy Theatre and the new Hoover Theatre owned by a family from Shanghai. It was customary for the feature presentation to be preceded by cartoons and by dramatic newsreels. I remember stirring black-and-white footage of the Korean War that depicted American soldiers firing powerful anti-tank bazookas against the Communists – the American and UN allies were always portrayed to be winning, though in reality of course the conflict was to end in a tense stalemate.

I particularly enjoyed action movies: cowboy, pirate and swashbuckler box office hits starring Gary Cooper, Tyrone Power or Errol Flynn. Johnny Weissmuller, as Tarzan, became my hero. Jane Russell, whose provocative costuming in Howard Hughes' *The Outlaw* made her an instant Hollywood icon, was my favourite pin-up star. Then there was the unforgettable *International Burlesque* incident. This was a black-and-white documentary featuring a series of striptease shows across America, and someone at the King's Theatre had come up with the advertising slogan: "Enjoy ice cream with your eyes while sitting on a comfortable sofa." It worked at the box office and it certainly worked for my brother and me. We sneaked in unseen, or so we thought, after the lights were dimmed and the film had already begun. Half an hour into it, we became conscious of a man standing in the aisle next to our seats. It was our father. He silently walked away after a few seconds, leaving me shaking with trepidation throughout the remainder of the screening, almost afraid to go home. To my utter surprise, however, he never said a word about our escapade, possibly because censorship ensured that no full frontal nudity had been shown on the screen.

The American influence bombarded us through radio airwaves as well. *Voice of America* was broadcast in Cantonese and in English, constantly reminding listeners of the hardship of the Chinese people living "behind the Bamboo Curtain", and of the existence of "Free China" (meaning Taiwan under Chiang Kai-shek) which would one day "liberate the mainland with the support of the millions of unhappy people living there."

The airwaves were also full of American popular songs and swing music. I saved up every dollar of my pocket money to spend in the few stores in town that sold imported records, starting with 78 rpm singles, eventually advancing to 45 rpm extended plays, and finally to 33 rpm long playing records. Influenced by my older cousins at Ning Yeung Terrace, I preferred swing music over pop and rock and roll. My favourite bands were the Glenn Miller, Tommy Dorsey and Artie Shaw orchestras, and my idol vocalists were Frank Sinatra, Jo Stafford, Dinah Shore and the Andrews Sisters. I particularly enjoyed songs with a romantic theme, the ones that were good for slow dancing.

Even the clothes I wore were influenced by America, especially Hollywood. Cowboy jeans were not available locally, but a store named Evergreen in Kowloon handled mail orders from the United States and I was thrilled when my mother agreed to order me a pair of Levis. They took a month to arrive from Hawaii, having been made to measure with allowance for shrinkage after the several washes required to make them look fashionably 'old'. I bought a heavy belt to go with them. The belt was intended to also serve as a weapon of self-defence, as depicted in the movies, though I never had to put it to that use. Proud as I was of my 'cool' outfit, however, I did not wear it in Uncle and Aunt's presence. They considered jeans to be un-gentlemanly.

To augment my trendy American aspirations, I drank Coca Cola, which had now flooded Hong Kong's soft drink market, the runner-up being 7 Up. And to add to my burgeoning social persona, I would eventually experiment with cigarettes, sampling Lucky Strike, Camel and Chesterfield, all unfiltered and all of them American brands as I considered English brands to be too 'square' for my newly sophisticated lifestyle. Fortunately, I did not become addicted.

THE REBELLIOUS STUDENT AND INSPIRING JESUITS

My mother was a strong believer in the Chinese proverb "Learning is a treasure that will follow its owner like a shadow everywhere." It was important to her that her sons have a good secondary school education.

She further believed that receiving that education in English would lay a particularly solid foundation for our future. In this, she was fully supported by Aunt.

Wah Yan College was – and still is – an eminent secondary school for boys operated by the Society of Jesus, a Roman Catholic religious order, with English as the language of instruction. The school had been shut down during the Japanese occupation but reopened on September 8, 1945 in an old low-rise building on Robinson Road in Mid-levels, with the senior classes spilling over into a three-storey annex. Because of the unique mixture of well-qualified local Chinese teachers and Irish Jesuit priests on its staff, Wah Yan was recognized for its rigorous academic standards and enjoyed a reputation as the best English secondary school for boys in Hong Kong.

Though double the cost of government-run schools, Wah Yan's fee of thirty-eight Hong Kong dollars a month (about five Canadian dollars) was affordable for many families at a time when other privately run schools were charging double that amount again. For many years after the war, hundreds of applicants competed for the limited number of openings available at Wah Yan. As I would be switching from a Chinese school curriculum to an English one, my chances of being accepted were questionable. My brother faced a similar challenge since he too had been attending a Chinese school. However, my mother would not give up without trying. It was time for Aunt to exercise her influence.

Mr. Ng Wah, our former landlord and a good friend of Uncle's, was a prominent benefactor of Wah Yan College. Ping-kin, one of Mr. Ng's older sons, was already a student there and some of his younger sons were about to join their big brother. When Ping-kin brought his younger brothers to meet the principal, my brother and I went along as well. It was a very short interview. In the eyes of Father Cooney, we were all Mr. Ng's children and were therefore duly admitted. In my case, however, there was an unexpected twist to the outcome. The class I had applied to enter was full and so I was placed in the next class up, for which, as I soon discovered, I was academically unprepared.

I was admitted to Class 7 (Grade 6 in Canada). In theory, it was to be a repeat of my graduating class at Pui Ying Primary School and should have made life easy for me. In practice, however, it was a substantially higher level. My academic challenges were compounded by the fact that I had been placed in Class 7A, the 'A' signifying academically gifted students, rather than 7B or C which were for the more average. And so I had a poor start at Wah Yan, ranking close to the bottom of the class at the end of the school year. I still managed to advance and that fall found myself promoted to Class 6 (the lower the class number, the higher the grade level, so I was now in the equivalent of Grade 7 in Canada). Fortunately for me, it was Class 6C.

During that next school year, a major change took place at Wah Yan. Due to the heavy influx of immigrants from China, particularly Shanghai, and the shortage of schools in Hong Kong, most schools were required to double up their enrolment capacity by establishing a dual system comprised of morning classes for one group of students and afternoon classes for a second group for a period of two years. This resulted in a slight reduction of class time and a somewhat compromised curriculum. I was part of the morning group and was fascinated by the sight of the modishly dressed and coiffed students from Shanghai on their arrival for afternoon classes. Hollywood had influenced the youth of Shanghai long before those of us in Hong Kong, and it showed.

In 1951, I successfully advanced from Class 6C to the next higher class, which had been reclassified and renamed as Form 2B at the direction of the Hong Kong Department of Education. Father Cooney had just retired and was replaced by Father Carroll as school principal. Father Cooney had been very cheery and approachable, but Father Carroll was stern looking, with a firm upper lip and scholarly glasses perched atop a pointed nose. He turned out to be a 'no nonsense' principal indeed, but one with a kind heart.

In the fall of 1952, I advanced to Form 3B (Grade 9 in Canada). After three years in the English system, I felt that I had finally adjusted, thanks to my mother's encouragement and after-school instruction, plus extra tuition in Physics and Chemistry, something for which she had carefully budgeted. Contrary to my experience at Pui Ying Primary School, no one at Wah Yan was interested in Chinese politics or in discussing mainland China and Taiwan, however they also paid little attention to the conventions of the British Empire, including the coronation of Queen Elizabeth II on June 2, 1953. Instead, the emphasis was on academics and religious instruction in Catholicism.

In the Religious Knowledge class, we were taught about venial and mortal sin, purgatory and hell, and remedies through confession and the recitation of prayers using rosary beads. Our Religious Knowledge teacher once suggested that if we did not know the answer to a question in an exam, we could write "God is supreme" in the blank space, and that would be acceptable enough to make the grade. I had difficulty absorbing much of this. As the speaker for my confirmation class at the Hop Yat Church, I took offense every time the teacher spoke of "Protestant errors," however I managed to focus my mind on the end goal of successfully graduating from this prestigious school. The fact that many of my classmates, even the Catholics, did not seem to take Religious Knowledge too seriously helped.

I was under the illusion that the Irish background of the Jesuits would make them the more inspiring teachers, however they taught mostly in the senior forms, with lower forms like mine having mainly Chinese teachers and so I became an uninspired student. My attention span in class was short and the class size – thirty-four – made individual attention by the teachers difficult. Nor were we encouraged to ask questions or to have class discussions. Furthermore, I sat in the back row next to someone who turned out to be a big distraction, but who also soon became my close friend.

His name was Tang Man-chan, though we called him by his nickname, *À Mǎ* ("Horse"), as he had somewhat equine facial features. He was at least three years older than me, having had his education disrupted by the war. On our first day of school, other students beat me to the 'good' desks closer to the blackboard and I felt disappointed and nervous at having to share a double desk at the back with someone so much older and rather tough looking. On the other hand, I was impressed with his trendy crew cut hairstyle and tight jeans and tee shirt with rolled-up short sleeves. To my surprise and delight, he turned out to be very amicable.

We soon developed an easy friendship and chatted about everything that was on our minds, not just outside of class but also during. À Mǎ particularly liked to demonstrate his knowledge of the female anatomy by surreptitiously showing me explicit photos accompanied by his own graphic commentary. During recess, I would tag along with him to the convenience store down the street so he could buy a pack of Lucky Strikes and it was he who gave me my first lesson in smoking. Under his tutelage I quickly advanced from choking on the first puff to inhaling down my throat, and finally to releasing perfectly formed rings of smoke from between my pursed lips.

On one unforgettable occasion when we were near the store, we spotted a student from a nearby school who looked like an immigrant from Shanghai. We Hong Kong students were somewhat jealous of the fact that many of these Shanghai students appeared to be wealthy and so we consoled ourselves by looking down on them because they could not get into a school of high academic standing like Wah Yan due to their lack of English language skills. That day, À Mǎ yelled at this unlucky target, "Why are you staring at me?" The student yelled back in Cantonese with a strong Shanghai accent, "I am not staring at you. You are the one staring at me!" À Mǎ then retorted, "If you were not staring at me, how would you know I am staring at you?" and before he finished speaking, he was across the street and throwing punches. The fight came to an end only when the sound of our school bell summoned us back to the classroom.

Street fights among youths were not uncommon in the 1950s, as immigrants from mainland China poured into Hong Kong. Confrontation not being my style, I was content to remain a bystander in À Mǎ's altercations – but I sure felt safe when hanging out with him. Without losing sight of my school studies or my peaceable upbringing, I greatly enjoyed my friendship with À Mǎ, my real-life teenage idol.

Reward and punishment played a very important role in my education at Wah Yan. There was a test on a selected subject every Monday and Father Carroll would personally drop by our classroom on Saturday mornings to present the reward certificates to the three students with the highest grades in ascending order: blue for third place, pink for second and beige for first. Another form of reward was related to sports. Wah Yan had the strongest secondary school basketball team in Hong Kong, consisting of high calibre players recruited from other schools. From time to time they were challenged by a basketball team from a visiting American ship and in spite of the American players' greater height, our school team usually triumphed. At the end of each winning match, Father Carroll would make the 'surprise' announcement that the following day would be a school holiday, just as he also proclaimed following any similar victory by our top-notch swimming team.

When it came to punishment, the methods used varied between the Irish Jesuits and the local Chinese teachers. When I was caught yawning in class one day, I was ordered by the teacher, Father McAsey, to spend the remainder of class time on my knees on the hard tiles that overlay the concrete balcony outside the classroom. On the other hand, when Mr. Wong, the Physics teacher, spotted me playing with turpentine too close to a Bunsen burner, my punishment was to write "Turpentine is inflammable" one thousand times, to be submitted to him in one week. I considered both of these to be moderate punishments. The punishment that would break Wah Yan's all-time record was just about to land on me.

In Form 3B, Mr. Lo Kwok-yuen was my Form Master as well as being the History and English Literature teacher. His appearance as a mild-mannered and easygoing person disguised his toughness and firm character. Students at Wah Yan had given him the nickname *Shē Wŏng Ló* ("King of Snake", indicating a lazy man), probably due to the fact that he was always in a hurry to end Saturday classes because that was race day at the Hong Kong Jockey Club. Along with a few other of our Chinese teachers, he was a regular patron at the Happy Valley racecourse – something that was acceptable to the Jesuits because the Jockey Club was one of the main sources of financial support for education and health services in Hong Kong.

I was not a fan of Mr. Lo and particularly did not enjoy his teaching of History, in part due to the fact that the curriculum chronicled only the history of Britain and its colonies, which I did not consider to be useful, particularly when taught by a Chinese person who had never been to England or other parts of the Commonwealth. One Monday morning – Black Monday, as it turned out to be for me – I decided to make fun of him in class, taking advantage of his habit of beginning each lesson by writing on the blackboard.

Before Mr. Lo entered the room, I covered his chair with a film of chalk dust shaken from the blackboard eraser. When he arrived, we all stood to attention and greeted him with the customary, "Good morning, Sir," after which he took off his jacket, as usual, and took his seat, as usual. When he then rose and turned his back to begin writing on the blackboard, the seat of his dark pants was covered in white chalk and the whole class erupted in raucous laughter. It did not take him long to realize that someone had played a trick on him, and with his face turning red, he "invited" the person who had committed "the crime" to stand up and be "recognized". When the room went silent, he issued the ultimatum that if no one was willing to come forward, the entire class would be punished – an effective measure taken by an experienced teacher. The last thing I wanted was to let down my classmates, so I stood up and confessed. Without hesitation, as if he had been prepared, he handed down his punishment: I was to write "I must not play in class" thirty thousand times, to be submitted to him in one week. It was a punishment that shocked everyone. No one in the room, Mr. Lo included, expected me to be able to fulfill that punishment within such a short time, and yet I did not dare to think of the possible consequences of failing to do so – perhaps expulsion from school.

My mind quickly turned to one of my grandfather's Chinese proverbs, "The greatest victory is the battle not fought." By the end of class on that Black Monday, I had come up with a plan. I was not the brightest student of mathematics but I was able to figure out that if I could reduce the workload of thirty thousand lines by one-third, and be able to further divide the task of writing those ten thousand lines, I could perhaps meet the deadline. First, I invented a multiple writing device by taking three ballpoint pens and binding them together at an inclined angle with elastic bands. A test confirmed that every line written would immediately become three, which marvel met with À Mǎ's praise and approval. With his assistance, I then proceeded to Phase Two of my plan and persuaded two more classmates to join the production team. And thus my own workload was reduced to five thousand lines, which instantly became fifteen thousand thanks to my new writing device, while À Mă and the other two team members shared the remainder of the workload between them, also using versions of my invented writing device.

A critical part of Phase Two was to find a sufficiently enticing compensation package for each team member. For this, I drew on my special connection with the King's Theatre. Thanks to my father, who had no idea of my dilemma at school, I was able to fulfil my promise of two coveted Dress Circle movie tickets for each of them.

Upon Mr. Lo's arrival for our morning class the following Monday, I presented him with a thick pile of handwritten lines. He could hardly believe his eyes, even saying out loud that he had not expected me to be able to fulfill the punishment. But that was not the end of the story. I now felt that I needed to make peace with Mr. Lo before our thorny relationship affected my future standing in class. At À Mă's suggestion, we made a courtesy call to the teacher's home in Kowloon the following week and I presented two VIP passes for the King's Theatre as a gift for Mrs. Lo. Mr. Lo served us tea and cakes and we chatted as if nothing untoward had ever happened between us. Two weeks later, following a test, Father Carroll delivered the results on Saturday morning and I found myself the happy and relieved recipient of a blue reward certificate for History.

Mr. Lo was to become my caring teacher and friend, true to the Chinese saying, "A good fight makes good friendship." Thanks to him, at the age of sixteen I learned a lesson on innovation. And on diplomacy.

Few Chinese students in Hong Kong spoke English outside of the classroom and the resulting lack of practice in English conversation meant we were not very good at it, indeed we were labelled as speaking 'Chinglish'. The language teacher who provided me with the solid foundation in English that would take me through my senior school years was Mr. John Fung, who was also my 4B Form Master. He distinguished himself by adopting a Queen's English accent, which was quite a contrast to the Irish accents of the Jesuits. He paid a great deal of attention to pronunciation, grammar and spelling, which I found most helpful.

Regardless of the challenges – and maybe also because of them – I continued to develop self-confidence, academically and socially. My classmates gave me the nickname *Paan Chué* ("Team Manager") because I organized football (soccer) matches and I was described in our Year Book as "a sociable person and leading member of the Debating Team." The Year Book did not mention that I also organized dance parties, very important because they enabled us boys to meet girls. The dances were held in students' homes. At times I needed to be a skilful promoter of the event so as to collect sufficient financial contributions to cover the cost of refreshments and to do this I would promise dim lighting and music that ensured slow dancing – my schoolmates wanted results for their investment. The most important trick for making any dance a success, however, was to ensure a sufficient supply of girls, and thanks to the help of À Mă and his own steady girlfriend, I earned a reputation as a capable supplier and matchmaker.

I was sad when I learned that À Mă was leaving school once we completed Form 4 (Grade 10 in Canada). His father was in poor health and needed his help running the family business. We continued our relationship, however, getting together after school or on weekends and a year later I felt honoured and grown-up to be invited to my best friend's wedding banquet. At the age of 20, À Mă was marrying his long-time sweetheart.

His older brother was being married at the same time. Their twin wedding banquet was a very significant event, as their mother believed that a happy family occasion would restore health to À Mǎ's father and by having two sons marry at the same time the chances were doubled. There were hundreds of guests and the atmosphere was festive and noisy, the clack of thousands of mah-jong tiles during pre-dinner games resounding like exploding firecrackers. The two bridegrooms and their brides visited each table in turn, toasting everyone with brandy and whiskey. À Mǎ was smart enough to keep sober on his wedding day by filling his glass with Chinese tea while a trusted friend engaged the guests in the traditional alcohol-based *yám shing* ("bottoms up") for luck on his behalf.

I advanced to Form 5B (Grade 11 in Canada) in the fall of 1954. At the end of that academic year, I would be required to sit a weeklong series of public exams in order to graduate with a Hong Kong School Certificate. These exams were commonly known as O-Level (Ordinary Level) or School Leaving exams. Upon graduation, students could then choose to further their secondary school studies or to enter a vocational school or the job market. Those who decided to further their secondary school studies would apply for acceptance into Form 6, commonly known as the A-Level (Advanced Level) or Matriculation. Competition for A-Level places was stiff, as class sizes were much smaller and only those who had completed Form 5 with a sufficiently high grade average had any chance. They also had to have passed in English, a compulsory subject.

I was concerned about my prospects. Even if I did well in my strong subjects such as History and Geography, it would be difficult for me to achieve a high enough grade average compared to those who also did well in areas that I was weaker in: mathematics and the sciences. Wah Yan had earned its reputation as an excellent school partly because of its students' high achievements in both those areas. Fortunately, my 5B Form Master was Father Grogan, a gentle, cheerful and patient man with impressive qualifications and teaching experience. I considered him the ideal person to guide me through this critical year and indeed two other key things happened during my Form 5 year that offered me the green light for my academic future.

First, I became fast friends with a very bright and kind-hearted classmate, Raymond Hung. Raymond had come from a government school that excelled in mathematics and science and his excellent academic background in those areas made him a top student in our class. Typical teenagers, always hungry, we spent a lot of time together hanging out at coffeehouses, noodle shops and hawkers' food stands. He was one year older than me and had taken out a learner's driver's permit, so we often ventured out at night with the requisite L-plate fastened to the tail bumper of one of his family's cars – he came from a wealthy family – with him as the student driver and me posing as the instructor, though I'd never yet been behind the wheel of a car. This went on for almost a year until he passed the driving test and became a qualified driver. Fortunately, the police never stopped us during that year. Apart from having fun together, Raymond also became my tutor in mathematics and science, a real blessing for my School Certificate exams.

The second advantageous thing that happened that year was the reorganization of the secondary school structure by the Hong Kong Department of Education. An extra year was added to the A-Level program, requiring students to now complete two years in Form 6, the first in Lower Form 6 (Grade 12 in Canada) and the second in Upper Form 6 (Grade 13 in Canada). The program was also divided into two streams, one being Arts, the other being Science. Arts students would study subjects such as History, English Literature, Chinese Literature and

Art, while Science students would focus on subjects like Mathematics, Physics, Chemistry and Biology.

A decent number of distinctions ("excellent" marks in a subject), credits ("good" marks) and pass marks had to be achieved at the end of Form 5 in order to obtain the School Certificate and to be competitive for acceptance into A-Level, however the pressure on me to do well in mathematics and science was now lessened as I could focus on doing well enough in my better subjects to get into the Arts stream of Lower 6. Father Grogan devoted a great deal of time to planting the seeds for his students' successful adaptation to the two streams, focussing on each individual's strengths, and Raymond Hung continued to be a great help with my weaker subjects.

Throughout School Certificate exam week in the late spring of 1955, I studied hard and kept myself in the best physical and mental condition I could. I suspected I would actually fail in one subject, Civics, a division of political science dealing with the rights and responsibilities of citizenship – a concept that was foreign to my life under colonial British rule. The exam included some interesting non-political questions, however, a few of them relating to urban development and traffic issues on Hong Kong Island. I found it difficult to express all my ideas on these topics in writing and so I instinctively began to sketch them instead with accompanying explanatory notes. It hit me that this was probably an unorthodox way of answering the questions, and I was now even more certain that I would fail the subject.

Two weeks later, the School Certificate exam results were published in the *South China Morning Post* for all to see.

I jumped for joy when I discovered that I had received a 'credit' in Civics – and I had no way of knowing then that, some twenty years later, something resembling my sketches would indeed take shape along the Hong Kong harbour front. Thanks to Raymond, I was also successful in the dreaded Mathematics and Science exams, earning a 'pass' in each, and so I achieved a sufficiently decent grade average to enable me to advance to Lower Form 6 in the Arts stream.

To my great dismay, however, Raymond did not. In spite of good marks in most subjects including Mathematics and Science, he failed in the one subject that was compulsory, English, and so his family decided to send him to London to complete his secondary school education. It was difficult to say goodbye to such a good friend.

My mother used to tell me, "Teachers open the door, but you must enter by yourself." During my A-Level years at Wah Yan, two inspiring Jesuits opened doors to my future. Father Terence Sheridan, my Form Master in Lower 6 Arts, was the first.

He was a man of great intellectual gifts, friendliness and energy. A writer and a lover of drama, he initiated an annual series of Chinese operas performed in English – a daring and successful venture into Anglo-Chinese cultural relations back then. He also produced plays and edited a lively cultural review. I was indeed fortunate to have such a versatile and gifted person as my English Literature teacher, particularly when it came to the study of Shakespeare. Father Sheridan was so animated that I could visualize the action in each play as he read it aloud to us. When he clearly defined the difference between Romeo's 'romantic love' of Rosaline and his 'true love' for Juliet – something I found rather amusing coming from a Catholic priest – I remember thinking that he must have had a romantic past.

He was also my History teacher. Though still disappointed that Chinese history was not part of the curriculum, I was impressed with the way Father Sheridan could analyse the political significance of the historical events that we did cover. His inspirational teaching of both literature and history showed me the depth of complexity in relationships, both personal and international, and also showed me the power of effective communication.

When I moved on to Upper 6 Arts in the fall of 1956 at Wah Yan's brand new, state-of-the-art campus located at Mount Paris in the East-Central District of Hong Kong, Father Albert Chan was my Form Master and became the second Jesuit at Wah Yan to open a door to my future.

Born in Peru of a Chinese father and Peruvian mother, Father Chan was passionate about everything Chinese. He had a doctorate in Chinese history from Harvard University and was considered the foremost credentialed historian in Hong Kong as well as one of the most important Ming historians in the Western world. I was indeed fortunate to have him as my teacher of Chinese Literature. For the first time in my life, I heard my ancestral culture articulated with scholarly insight and clarity, and my understanding and appreciation of it deepened. He also opened my eyes to the correct forms of vocabulary, speech and written characters in the Chinese language, and how they had lost some of their authenticity in Hong Kong after a century of British influence. His teachings gave me a clearer understanding of where I had come from and of who I was.

He was also wise to the ways of adolescent boys and their need for adventurous activity. He took us for outings to some of the offshore islands where we discovered him to be just as fit physically as he was intellectually: he was a strong swimmer and expert diver.

In Father Chan, I had finally met the Chinese philosopher who touched my heart and soul, preparing me for the next phase of my life.

THE ENTERTAINER AND FIRST TASTE OF MONEY

I had a habit of belting out hit tunes in the bathroom at home, mimicking crooners such as Nat King Cole and Frankie Laine, so when I auditioned for the Hop Yat Church choir, my larynx was in good shape and I was noticed by Phoon Kwan-to, a distant cousin who often played swing tunes on the piano in the church hall. We called him *Sam Koh* ("Third brother", his ranking in his family). Sam Koh decided he was going to help me develop as a singer.

Radio Rediffusion was a successful radio station in Hong Kong run by the Rediffusion Company, which provided subscribers with an affordable and simple speaker box with volume control and selection switch for the English and Chinese channels. Its broadcasts were part of the attraction in local teashops, surpassing the popularity of the government-run Radio Hong Kong. One of its well-known programs was *Listeners' Paradise*, a talent competition on the Chinese channel, and Sam Koh enrolled me for an audition in the Western popular songs category. I chose a Nat King Cole number, *Pretend*, and we began weeks of practice together in the church hall.

The program host was a woman with a Shanghai accent by the name of Madam Chong. Along with all the other candidates, Sam Koh and I were ushered into a soundproof studio equipped with a piano. The sight of a microphone hanging from the ceiling – an apparatus I had never yet used – and the presence of the other candidates began to bother me and I could feel tension overtaking my stomach and my throat, so much so that when it was my turn to perform I could barely sing. When I finished, Madam Chong suggested politely that I come back another time and try again.

To console me, Sam Koh treated me to an ice cream soda and a vigourous pep talk, telling me not to give up and to indeed try again. Two weeks later, I did. This time I was successful and made it onto the air. I had given my first live broadcast as an amateur singer. I was sixteen.

I now wanted to master a musical instrument. I found a piano accordion at Uncle's house and taught myself to play by ear in the key of C, one of the most commonly used key signatures in music. A year later I felt confident enough to perform in public and Sam Koh and I started a seven-piece band for church hall concerts. I also started a separate five-piece band with younger musicians who were into modern dance music like rumba, samba and cha-cha. We named ourselves The Moonlight Serenaders in homage to my idol Glenn Miller and made our public debut at a YWCA dance, thanks to the backing of Auntie Wan-fun.

I had long watched Auntie Wan-fun, Uncle Wah-chiu and my mother perform in dramas and comedies in our church hall. My mother was a popular actor usually playing the part of a mature person, while my uncle and aunt made their names in roles as a romantic couple. When I reached the age of seventeen in 1954, I had my first chance to follow in their footsteps.

I had inherited their passion for the stage and was delighted to find myself popular as a romantic drama actor, greatly enjoying playing at falling in love with older women. On several occasions, I also did the warm-up act as a solo comedian and then went on to perform in the featured drama. My amateur talent caught the eye of Milly Ko, my mother's goddaughter who was a manager at Hong Kong Commercial Radio. Thanks to her, I unexpectedly landed my first professional engagement as a performer.

Holiday on Ice was a family-oriented ice skating show that began in the United States in 1943. Its star performers were mostly former skating champions recruited from Europe and America, and a traditional element of each show was the precision number with its famous spinning wheel, in which the skaters linked arms with one another, one by one, gradually creating two lengthening 'spokes' which spun around a centre point. The show was making its Far East tour in 1955 and arrived in Hong Kong for a month-long engagement at the large open-air Hong Kong Football Club stadium.

The show had been promoted for months in advance and tickets were selling well. On the Friday of its opening, I was at school when I received an urgent message from my mother to contact her goddaughter Milly immediately. When I phoned, Milly told me that Holiday on Ice was in desperate need of a master of ceremonies for that evening's gala opening and she had arranged for me to meet with the show's business agent for an interview that afternoon.

Milly's exciting proposal caught me totally unprepared, however I was eager to jump on what sounded like the opportunity of a lifetime. After school, I hurried downtown to the offices of Peat Marwick and was quickly escorted into the presence of one of the Western partners. It turned out to be not much of an interview. We spoke only briefly – it was quickly evident that Milly had told him about my performance experience – before he declared that I would indeed be the emcee that night and also for the duration of the show's engagement. This took me by surprise as I had thought I would be needed for the opening performance only. A performance every weekday plus two on Saturdays and Sundays was a huge time commitment for a whole month, but at seventeen hundred and fifteen Hong Kong dollars a week (almost three hundred Canadian dollars), it was irresistible. I could not turn it down.

It was already after half-past five o'clock and I had to report to the stadium by seven, so I rushed home, donned my one-and-only suit and matching tie, passed up on dinner, and hurriedly filled my mother in on the thrilling turn of events.

At the stadium, a middle-aged American with a crew cut introduced himself as the show's manager. Quite clearly taken aback by the youthfulness of his new emcee, he hurriedly took me backstage to meet Walter and Sonja, a husband and wife team from Austria who had been with Holiday on Ice for many years. Sonja was to be responsible for me. She greeted me warmly and handed me a pile of cue cards inscribed with the show's announcements in English, while the manager instructed me to also make the announcements in Chinese (meaning Cantonese) as well. Then I was whisked onstage.

I found myself on a large raised platform festooned with curtains and flowers and equipped with a phalanx of sound and lighting systems. Walter, who was the show's music arranger, bandleader and pianist, took his place at the onstage grand piano while Sonya introduced me to the other band members. Looking out from the stage, I could see a large artificial ice surface surrounded by stadium seats set up in a U-shape and with VIP seating sections added ringside. Immediately below me at centre stage was the performers' access from backstage onto the ice. The audience was already starting to pour in and spotlights showcased the celebrity guests, including Hong Kong movie stars, as they were escorted to the ringside seats.

Uncle Wah-chiu and Auntie Wan-fun had often complimented me on my ability to improvise onstage and that evening, I knew, would be the moment of truth. I had less than fifteen minutes to read through the cue cards and familiarize myself with them sufficiently to superimpose the Cantonese lines. I knew I needed to apply a tasteful sense of humour and to switch smoothly between the two languages. To pump up my energy and confidence as the opening moment approached, my mind turned to lyrics from one of Uncle's favourite Broadway musicals, *Annie Get Your Gun*: "There's no business like show business!" Showtime arrived. I was as ready to roll as I would ever be.

The evening was a success. Afterwards, the manager approached me with a relaxed smile, giving me his one and only piece of advice, "Son, ya gotta speak *fester* . . . but you're *swell*." After a few days on the job, I felt comfortable enough to bring along school textbooks to study between making announcements.

By the end of the engagement, I had earned a princely seven thousand Hong Kong dollars (twelve hundred Canadian dollars). I felt I was now a man of some independence and decided to spend almost half the money on a second-hand Royal Enfield, a 350cc British-made motorcycle, along with a pair of leather boots and dark sunglasses. After I passed the driving test, my most frequent passenger became Norma, the adopted granddaughter of our church minister and my co-star in many romantic onstage roles even though she was a few years older than me. It was a thrill to finally experience for myself what Father Sheridan had spoken of as 'romantic love'.

PRAYING FOR THE FUTURE

While I had been in Lower Form 6 in 1955, our family life entered another new phase. My brother left home. After a year at the Hong Kong University Medical School, he had decided to continue his studies in Canada at the University of Manitoba in Winnipeg, with his tuition and living expenses largely funded by Uncle as Aunt firmly believed that upon graduation he would assist Uncle in his busy medical practice. My brother would eventually get married in Canada to the daughter of a Hong Kong Chinese family whose late father had been a close friend of both Uncle and Aunt. His future was set.

Meanwhile, I was somewhat frustrated by the uncertainty regarding my own future.

Aunt had noticed my keen interest in drawing and began taking me along on visits to her friends' homes, pointing out to me their varied and interesting range of contemporary design. However, unlike her explicit commitment towards my brother's career, there was no indication that she had any expectation regarding mine. I also realized that Uncle's health was deteriorating, which could affect his ability to support even my brother's education.

My good friend Raymond Hung had been writing to me regularly from London where he had completed secondary school and was now studying architecture. He suggested I join him and sent me the prospectus for the Architectural Association School of Architecture along with information on living conditions in London, assuring me that it would cost less than nine hundred pounds sterling a year (some fourteen thousand Hong Kong dollars/twenty-four hundred Canadian) to study and live there. At the same time, my brother was telling everyone how good life was in Canada and that it would be nice for me to join him at the University of Manitoba. He also suggested that I could support myself there by working part-time.

There was little I could do to cement my future prospects except for two things. First, every time I passed the Hong Kong University School of Architecture with Uncle and Aunt, I would conspicuously turn my head towards the building, hoping that they would interpret this as an indication of my desire to study architecture. Then, as that did not seem to work, I turned to my second option. I prayed for my dream to come true. Every night.

My mother always seemed to be able to read my mind. After dinner one evening, she telephoned Uncle and Aunt and arranged for us to meet at their house. She gently but clearly explained to them my hope of becoming an architect, the research I had done on the schools in England and Canada, the cost implications, and the fact that my dream would not be possible without their support. It was then Uncle's turn to respond. He began by explaining that due to having to slow down at work because of his health, the prospect of supporting both my brother and me was a difficult one. Then, quite suddenly, he changed his tone and with a big smile said, "I will now have to work harder to support this naughty boy."

My caring Uncle had already researched the two schools on my list. He said that even though the Architectural Association School of Architecture in London – known simply as the AA – did not offer a university degree, it was by far one of the most prestigious architectural schools in the world. The award of the Architectural Association Diploma (AA Dipl.) upon graduation and the passing of the professional practice exam would qualify me as an Associate of the Royal Institute of British Architects (A.R.I.B.A.), a highly prestigious professional qualification. He said he realized that it would be expensive to send me there, as the tuition fee of one hundred and twenty-five pounds sterling a year (about two thousand Hong Kong dollars/three hundred and fifty Canadian) was more than at a university, but he thought it worth the investment as some of Hong Kong's most successful architects were AA graduates and the school's patron was no less a personage than Her Majesty The Queen.

With Raymond's assistance, I submitted my application in the summer of 1956 along with a school transcript, my collection of design sketches and a reference letter from Father Barrett, who had succeeded Father Carroll as principal of Wah Yan College. And so it was that in the fall that I entered Upper Form 6, I was informed that my qualifications had been accepted, however admission to the AA was subject to an entrance exam and an interview. Father Barrett received the exam papers just before Christmas and locked me into the Jesuits' wine cellar to complete them. To my surprise, many of the questions were non-academic in nature, such as my knowledge of Mohandas Gandhi and Napoleon Bonaparte, of Israel and Palestine, and of Broadway and Hollywood. After two hours, Father Barrett sealed the completed papers and mailed them back to London.

Two months later, I was directed to attend an admission interview conducted in Hong Kong by Mr. Eric Cumine, an AA alumnus and one of the most prominent architects in the colony. When I arrived at his office, I was amazed to find Mr. Cumine sitting at a desk not far from the reception area, rather than in a private suite. The wall behind him was covered with a display of photos promoting many of the contemporary buildings in Hong Kong that he had designed. He was a tall man I guessed to be in his fifties, Eurasian, with dark-rimmed glasses and a bow tie, looking exactly as an architect should, I thought. He reached out his hand and greeted me warmly while Chinese tea was served. He asked why I wanted to become an architect and before I had a chance to answer, he added, "There is no money in architecture. If you want to make money, you should go and sell fruit." I understood right away that he was referring with a dry sense of humour to another architect in Hong Kong who had become a millionaire mainly by also running a chain of fruit stores.

Mr. Cumine did most of the talking and seemed to already know a lot about me, including my schooling and stint with Holiday on Ice. His final question was, "Which are some of your favourite buildings in Hong Kong?" Without hesitation I replied, "Those ones," pointing to the photos behind him. He bid me goodbye with a smile and wished me good luck.

The letter of my official acceptance into the Architectural Association School of Architecture arrived in the spring of 1957. I was overjoyed. In June, much to the pleasure of my family, I graduated from Upper 6 at Wah Yan College with distinctions in History and English Literature. When I went to say goodbye to Father Barrett, he mentioned that he was disappointed that I had not converted to Catholicism after eight years at the school, however he made me a generous offer, saying I would be welcome to use the facilities of the Chinese Catholic Students Hostel in London.

My prayers had been answered. I was ready for England.

I was born on the third floor of Ning Yeung Terrace, Bonham Road in the comfortable neighbourhood of Mid-levels, Hong Kong – the backdrop to my first memories of relatives and friends, warm memories of togetherness and security through the early years of my childhood.

(TOP): Almost from Day One, Uncle was my dearly-loved mentor and role model.

(BOTTOM): The youngest grandchild at the time, I proudly stood at my grandfather's knee as the whole family gathered to mark his 70th birthday in 1939.

(TOP LEFT): There was a four-year age difference between my older brother and me.

(TOP RIGHT, UPPER): Allied ships in Victoria Harbour after the Japanese were ousted from Hong Kong in 1945.

(TOP RIGHT, LOWER): The liberation of Hong Kong is celebrated at the cenotaph in Central in August 1945.

(BOTTOM): 116 Pokfulam Road, the longtime home of Uncle and Aunt.

(TOP LEFT): Skilled in the art of teaching, my mother's home tutoring often gave me the edge I needed during my schooldays.

(BOTTOM LEFT): Uncle Wah-chiu and Auntie Wan-fun were a fun loving couple who showed me how to succeed in reaching goals and to enjoy doing it.

(BOTTOM RIGHT): My goodbye-to-primary-school photo, taken in 1949.

(TOP): My father and mother cherished their late-arrival daughter – little Dong-dong, about four in this photo, had been born when I was ten and a half and my brother was fifteen.

(BOTTOM): Fourth Aunt (a nurse in Uncle's clinic), my mother and father, Aunt and Second Aunt pose behind my grandparents.

Besides being my home tutor, my mother – "Mommy" – was ever my staunchest supporter, loving guide and constant inspiration.

Uncle and Aunt had this photo taken in a New York studio in 1953 – their far-flung trip opened my teenage eyes to the expanse of possibilities 'out there' in the world.

(TOP): Riding my pride and joy, purchased with the earnings from my first show business gig.

(BOTTOM): My high school idol, À Mă.

(TOP): I thoroughly enjoyed the many carefree summer days spent at the beach at Middle Bay with the families of two of my mother's brothers, Uncle Wah-cheung *(first left)* and Uncle Wah-chiu *(middle back)*. My mother *(back row, third right)* was always pleased when her mother *(back row, third left)* also came along.

(BOTTOM): Just a few weeks before heading off to England, happy anticipation is written all over my face *(back row, first left)* in this photo of the Wah Yan College Class of 1957. Father Albert Chan, my Upper 6 Form Master and hero whose teachings stirred in me a deep sense of my own identity and potential, is seated centre front.

Eye Opener | 4
England and Continental Europe (1957-1964)

A SLOW BOAT TO LONDON

I sailed for London early in the summer of 1957. Travelling by ship was both cheaper and easier than flying, especially with the amount of luggage to hold the substantial array of heavy clothing and blankets considered essential armour against the notorious chill and damp of England. My 'armour' included a thick woollen overcoat for outdoors, a quilted jacket made by my mother for indoors, and long underwear sent from Winnipeg by my brother.

Aunt was intent on me dressing like an English gentleman. Two three-piece suits were made by Uncle's tailor from some of the fine woollen fabric my grandfather had received on his eightieth birthday, and my 'gentleman's wardrobe' was completed with a grey New Yorker fedora from Uncle's personal hat collection along with his umbrella.

My mother presented me with a portable Olivetti typewriter so that I could write home often and Uncle gave me his favourite Leica IIIf camera, the one that he had used on his trip to America and Europe, so I could include pictures along with my letters. I was also promised regular care packages of traditional Chinese foods such as dried mushrooms, scallops and cabbage, nutritional supplements for maintaining energy and good health during the coming years of 'exile' so far from home.

Uncle had booked me into a two-passenger cabin on the RMS *Corfu*, operated by the Peninsular and Oriental Steam Navigation Company (P&O), sailing to London in July via Singapore, Penang, Colombo, Aden, Port Said and Gibraltar. My family and several friends, including À Mǎ, came onboard at the Kowloon Wharf to give me a good send-off. À Mǎ introduced me to a fellow passenger he knew by the name of Li Chi-keung – *À Li*, as he preferred to be called (in Chinese culture, introducing oneself simply by the family name is a casual and friendly gesture) – who was, according to À Mǎ, a smart street fighter. I was touched that he wanted me to get to know someone who might serve as a good protector.

My true protector, of course, was Uncle. He escorted me to my cabin, where we were greeted by the steward, a man from Goa, to whom Uncle promptly gave fifty Hong Kong dollars (eight Canadian dollars) and with a warm handshake instructed him to "Look after the boy." When the happy steward had departed, Uncle handed me a bank draft for five hundred pounds sterling (a little over twelve hundred Canadian dollars), which was more than half the annual allowance of eight hundred and fifty pounds for which he had budgeted, and instructed me to open a bank account as soon as I arrived in London. "Though education is what I can give you, not money," he added. "Education is the most valuable thing in life." He completed his parting advice with a few gentle hints concerning safe sex.

Within minutes, the ship's horn blasted and it was time for my family and friends to disembark. With the sound of the ship's engines vibrating in my ears, I looked down from the deck and waved, holding back tears as the image of my loved ones became smaller and ever further away. At nineteen, I was on my own for the first time in my life.

As the ship headed east out of Victoria Harbour I bid a silent goodbye to the diminishing view of downtown Hong Kong and the Kowloon Peninsula and went below deck to my cabin. A young man with a crew cut was unpacking. Speaking Cantonese with a slight Mandarin accent, he introduced himself as Franklin Hsu, a seventeen-year-old student from Taiwan whose father owned a shipping company there. Franklin had been 'shipped' to Hong Kong in order to obtain an entry visa for England as a Hong Kong resident, he said, which I found rather intriguing. We hit it off right away and he kindly offered me the lower of the two bunk beds in deference to my more advanced age.

The cabin was small, with the bunks facing the door and a little desk in one corner next to a washbasin – the steward advised us to use the supply from the seawater storage tank for washing and only use fresh water for rinsing, as the vessel's access to fresh water was limited. A twelve-inch porthole let in natural light and a ventilation shaft brought in fresh air from the outside. Communal bathroom facilities were a short way away, just down the corridor. This was to be home for the next three weeks.

A distant gong sounded and the steward knocked on the door, announcing that dinner was being served. It was bad timing. The ship had entered the South China Sea and was rolling so severely that Franklin and I, attempting to make our way to the dining lounge, were cast from one side of the corridor to the other until a growing churning in my stomach forced me to dash through a door marked Gentlemen. I was just in the nick of time. There would be no first-evening-at-sea dinner for me. Franklin, however, did not seem to have any trouble. He sympathetically brought dry soda crackers and hot tea to my bunk later that night.

Next morning, the ship was moving calmly and I knew I would be able to face breakfast after a refreshing shower. In the dining lounge,

Franklin and I were escorted to a table of male Chinese students, including À Mǎ's friend À Li. Like Franklin, À Li was going to London to complete his A-Level high school studies, while our three other tablemates were heading to technical schools or universities in Britain. Half a dozen or so Chinese girls were sitting at a nearby table and we discovered that they were on their way to England to train as nurses or teachers. Our shared sense of travelling further and further away from everything familiar in our young lives soon bonded all of us into a tight-knit group.

The second day at sea went by very quickly and we arrived at the first port of call: Singapore. The daughter of one of the doctors who had travelled with Uncle and Aunt to the United States seven years earlier picked me up at the dock and treated me to lunch in her home, a beautiful modern structure designed by her husband, architect Ong Eng-hung. Then I was shown around the city by Dr. Phoon, an elder brother of Second Uncle and who, like Second Uncle, was also a physician, as were two more of his brothers, all of them from a prominent Singapore Chinese family. The first thing that struck me was the diversity of the city's population – Chinese, Malays, Indians, Asians of varying descent, and Caucasians – which was quite different from the predominantly Chinese face of Hong Kong. I also noticed very little sign of British colonial influence other than in the street names, perhaps evidence of the fact that after being repossessed by Britain following the Japanese surrender in 1945, Singapore had been granted self-government, with its own prime minister and cabinet overseeing all government matters with the exception of defence and foreign affairs. Again, quite different to how it was in Hong Kong. I got the overall impression that the Chinese were a driving force behind Singapore's business, professional and academic sectors.

Quite a large number of new passengers came onboard at Singapore. Many were Chinese students and I couldn't help but notice that though they dressed more conservatively than we did, they were much more assertive in the way they expressed themselves in both English and Mandarin and were openly proud of being Singaporean. The British expatriates who came onboard were also more open and friendly than those from Hong Kong and one of them quickly befriended our group. Fred was a recently retired Singapore government official and over the course of the trip he took it upon himself to initiate me into the world of specialty cocktails, introducing me to Tom Collins and Gin Gimlet in particular, with lots of lager beer and crisps (potato chips) thrown in for good measure.

The first mail from home arrived when we docked in Colombo. I was delighted to receive letters from my mother and from Aunt and Uncle, to which I responded via return aerograms (air letters) with accounts of the exciting happenings of my first week at sea, including the entertainment programs which had proven to be enormous fun. I had even been persuaded to enter a costume contest dressed as Hollywood star Ava Gardner in the 1954 movie *The Barefoot Contessa*. Clad in a sarong and brassiere, sporting face makeup deftly applied by the girls and strutting to a flamenco beat provided by the ship's band, this sultry Spanish dancer managed to capture the contest's top prize, much to the hilarity and delight of my new friends.

After brief stopovers in Colombo and Aden, we entered the Red Sea via the Bab el Mandeb Strait, the narrow neck of water separating Asia from Africa – this passage between continents where desert meets ocean offered one of the most exotic and fascinating natural landscapes I had ever seen. Shortly thereafter, now within the confines of the Red Sea, the air temperature began to rise dramatically, so much so that the ship's interior became very uncomfortable and passengers were encouraged to sleep on deckchairs in the open air. I continued to use my cabin but found sleep elusive during the two nights of the one-thousand-nautical-mile journey north to the southern entrance to the Suez Canal.

Once there, the *Corfu* lined up to take her turn going through the canal, only recently reopened following the removal of vessels that had been purposefully sunk in order to block passage through the waterway during the Suez Crisis of the previous year, a serious military conflict between Egypt – whose government wanted to nationalize the canal – and Israel, Britain and France, who opposed nationalization. Had the conflict still been underway, we would have been forced to sail all the way around the continent of Africa in order to reach England from Asia.

Our journey through the canal was uneventful and we arrived safely at its northern terminus, where our ship's captain advised passengers to be cautious of "unfriendly" Egyptians when going ashore in Port Said, explaining that many held a negative attitude towards the British following the conflict. Being Chinese, however, our little band of students managed to have a grand time in the port city, visiting a lively night market that offered cheap copies of high-end jewellery and watches. Several British passengers tagged along with us, hoping to be less conspicuous among a group of Asians, and I couldn't help but chuckle at the novel experience of being considered essential to the personal safety of any Englishman.

As we sailed west through the Mediterranean, I noticed that Asian and Middle Eastern influences gradually diminished. Onboard the *Corfu*, everything was becoming more British. The dance music played by the ship's band took on the predominantly 'slow, slow, quick-quick-slow' rhythm favoured by Victor Sylvester and his Ballroom Orchestra, and in the dining room we were treated to dishes such as Fish and Chips and Bangers and Mash (mashed potatoes and sausages).

Gibraltar, with its iconic Rock, was our last port of call. I was impressed that a great deal of Spanish cultural heritage was evident in that small country, in spite of two hundred and fifty years of British sovereignty. It made me realize that Chinese culture too had continued to flourish back home in Hong Kong, notwithstanding more than a century of colonial rule.

When we headed out into the Atlantic Ocean, I began to get a taste of what an English summer might be like: mild temperatures, windy conditions and predominantly grey skies. The water was rough in the Atlantic and also in the English Channel, however the excitement of knowing that I would soon set foot on British soil kept me too focussed to feel any seasickness, or perhaps I had earned my sea legs after twenty-one days afloat. I was eagerly looking forward to my new life with all its possible adventures starting with finding my very first home-away-from-home, a flat that À Li and I could share.

We arrived at the Port of Tilbury, forty kilometres (twenty-five miles) downstream from London Bridge, after breakfast on July 11. In deference to the occasion, I had donned a suit and tie and Uncle's fedora. The cabin steward came to say goodbye and following Uncle's instructions I gave him another tip: twenty pounds sterling (fifty Canadian dollars). He was very pleased and told me that my tagged luggage would be waiting for pickup after I had cleared immigration formalities and disembarked.

I was delighted to spot my old friend Raymond Hung waving exuberantly amidst the large crowd on the wharf and it wasn't long before we were greeting one another warmly after our two-year separation. He guided À Li and me to a grey Austin A30, a compact British car that he had bought second-hand, and we piled our luggage into the boot (British term for "trunk") and across most of the back seat. Very soon, we were heading into the city. It felt really good to be Raymond's passenger once again, just like in our days together at Wah Yan College – but we were now in London and things would never be the same again.

A TERRIBLE START – A FEW USEFUL LESSONS

Raymond was living in a rented house in Hendon, a residential area about eleven kilometres (seven miles) to the northwest of central London. He shared the house with Hobart Liang, a former classmate of mine at Pui Ying Primary School. Both of them had completed their first year at the Architectural Association School of Architecture and would be entering their second year in the fall. They generously invited À Li and me to sleep in their living room until we could find a place of our own.

My first experience of culture shock came when I realized that the blond German girl we were introduced to at the house was, in fact, Hobart's live-in girlfriend. Raymond later explained that it was not uncommon for Chinese boys to date European girls, of whom there were many working in England as *au pairs* (child care providers). German girls liked Chinese boys in particular, he said, because they paid for everything on a date, whereas British boys often expected a girl to share expenses.

That first evening in London, Raymond took À Li and me to a restaurant near Marble Arch to meet three of his other friends from Hong Kong – *À Ho,* Smoker (because of his ever-present cigarette) and *Tai Pan* ("The boss") – whom I was to come to think of fondly as The Gang of Three. I distinctly remember that first English meal. It was a plate of roasted chicken, leg portion, accompanied by a heap of mashed potatoes and a few overcooked Brussels sprouts. I had selected it because of its price: two shillings and sixpence (about forty cents Canadian). I noticed that everyone else chose more expensive dishes, evidence, I thought, of their families' greater ability to support them.

It was a fun evening, with each of them sharing humorous experiences and impressions of Britain along with tidbits of more serious advice, but my mind was only half present as I thought of the tasks I needed to accomplish the next day. I was anxious to get a hold of a map of the city with an A-to-Z street listing and another of the London Underground, the subway system known colloquially as the Tube. I also needed to open a bank account. And I could hardly wait to pay a visit to my new school.

The next day, my first full day in London, was indeed very productive, thanks to Raymond once again acting as chauffeur.

The Architectural Association School of Architecture – the AA – is one of the world's renowned and most influential schools of architecture, and so I was surprised to find it housed behind a rather understated dark brick facade, taking up numbers 34 and 35 in a row of three-storey houses on the south-western side of Bedford Square (it was only later that I came to know that this row forms one of the best preserved set pieces of Georgian architecture in London). However, once inside, I was amazed how spacious the interior appeared, with a full basement and the rear of the building extending back to an alleyway. When I looked down from the upper floor studios, I could see an outdoor courtyard full of tables and chairs, which Raymond told me was Chings Yard, a nucleus where students informally gathered to exchange ideas.

It was exhilarating to finally be standing inside my dream school. I was also a little confused at finding this legendary institution almost empty, until Raymond cheerfully advised me that in a few short weeks it would be very different due to the start of the hectic school year, and I should use the precious time until then for getting my bearings in my new city.

After I'd opened a bank account at the Midland Bank on Tottenham Court Road close to the school, Raymond and I met up with À Li and the Gang of Three for afternoon tea at the nearby YMCA. I was happy to discover that I could satisfy my hunger relatively inexpensively on sandwiches and cakes at afternoon teatime, saving money on dinner later on. The YMCA was to become my second home.

Raymond announced that evening that he would soon be leaving for a holiday in Germany. He then made me a very generous offer: the use of his car while he was gone. Since it meant driving on the left side of the road, just as in Hong Kong, and since I now had experience driving Uncle's standard gearshift vehicle, I gratefully accepted his offer, delighted at the prospect of the convenience of exploring London by car. When I dropped him off at the Victoria railway station a few days later, Raymond's parting words were simply, "Keep the car clean and fill up the tank for when I get back."

A few evenings later, I drove À Li and the Gang of Three to an espresso bar in Soho, a trendy area of central London that was particularly popular with students and other young people. One could spend hours very inexpensively at these new coffee houses (the first one had been opened by Italian movie star Gina Lollobrigida just a few years earlier), sipping on espresso and enjoying the passing parade of au pair girls. The five of us had a great time that warm summer evening, completely losing track of the hour until a server informed us that it was past midnight, closing time.

I offered to drive À Ho, Smoker and Tai Pan home to their flat in South London and the three of them piled into the back seat while À Li sat next to me in the front, helping with directions through the quiet night-time streets. Suddenly, like a bolt from the blue, as we were going through an intersection on a green light we were hit broadside on the passenger side and the car rolled over onto the driver's side, my side. The next thing I was aware of was the flashing lights of ambulances and police vehicles as I was being extracted from the overturned vehicle. I could see a large coach (bus) mere inches away and shards of shattered glass glistening on the ground. I had no idea how long I had been unconscious or the condition of any of my passengers.

As the ambulance deposited me at the hospital – it was St. George's Hospital at Hyde Park Corner – I spotted À Li also being carried into the Accident and Emergency Department, where we were immediately seen by separate medical teams. After a thorough examination, I was given an injection, likely a sedative, and a doctor began picking glass particles from the upper lid of my right eye, followed by another injection, this time of an antibiotic, and three stitches to close the wound. I was then handed my eyeglasses, broken but still usable, and was happy to see À Li standing close by sporting just a couple of stitches to a small wound on his neck. To our immeasurable relief, we were informed that our three other passengers had not required medical care and had gone home from the accident scene under their own steam.

As we were leaving the hospital, À Li and I noticed a man in a coach driver's uniform staring intently at us. We suspected that he was the one who had run the red light and hit us, and no doubt he would have been anxious to determine our condition. We were indeed alive, but quite sore and very shaken.

I decided to seek financial compensation from the coach driver or his company. Aunt had given me the name of a distant cousin who was a summer employee at a law firm in London, so I phoned her and she arranged for me to meet with one of the junior lawyers. His advice, however, was disappointing. It would be a waste of money and time to file a legal claim, he said, as there was no independent witness to verify how the accident had occurred, all my passengers being my friends and also victims of the incident themselves. It appeared that I would have to be philosophical about this dead end and just be thankful that we had all come out of the accident relatively unscathed, especially as there were no seatbelts or protective airbags in those days.

When Raymond returned to London a few days later, he was both sympathetic and shocked about the situation. He also revealed that he did not have insurance coverage for a second driver and the car's frame had been twisted so badly that it would cost a fortune to fix. I knew that the price tag was mine to pay. We headed to the repair garage, where a mechanic offered to purchase the damaged vehicle 'as is' for ninety pounds sterling – an offer that Raymond accepted – and to that ninety I added another two hundred and ten from my newly opened bank account, so that Raymond was reimbursed for the full amount he had paid for the car and my moral obligation was fulfilled.

Poorer but wiser, I now found myself with little money left to cover expenses, having given away one quarter of my annual allowance only weeks into my 'exile'. I had no choice but to write home about this misfortune and pray for Uncle and Aunt's understanding and forgiveness. I was also thinking about my mother – how embarrassed and disappointed she would be with a son who appeared to be so careless – but my family's reaction to the situation was better than I could ever have hoped. Uncle gave me a lecture about checking both ways before entering an intersection even on a green light, and then he promised that he would remit the balance of my first year's allowance earlier than planned.

The experience certainly taught me about not taking anyone's generosity for granted and about obligation and liability. I also realized that I really had to find a part-time job.

À Li and I moved into a place at Wood Green, close to a Tube station at the northern end of the Piccadilly Line. It was a furnished flat on the upper floor of a small house belonging to a retired Italian-British couple, right next to a fish and chips shop. We had a bedroom, a living room, a tiny eat-in kitchen and a bathroom. The kitchen stove and bathroom geyser (tankless hot water heater) were fuelled by a central gas supply system, and portable paraffin (kerosene) heaters were the source of ambient heat. We soon became accustomed to the smell of strong cheese (beloved by our landlord downstairs) and of hot grease (from the deep fryer in the 'chippie' next door) that often permeated the flat, but this was little to contend with when the only restriction imposed on us by our landlord was a firmly announced, "No girls allowed!"

Food parcels from Hong Kong made it fun to do our own cooking in the beginning. Pretty soon, however, we got tired of the chore of washing up and pots and pans often piled up in the sink. Taking pity on us, our landlady occasionally invited us downstairs for an Italian dinner. This was always enjoyable, as they were a friendly couple and seemed to have the same passion for eating as we Chinese did, preparing food in great variety and in large quantities. As well, the husband, Andrew, had a well-equipped carpentry workshop and kindly built me an adjustable stand for my newly acquired drafting board, a thoughtful gift I was to use throughout my student years in London.

To pass the time one afternoon, À Li and I decided to attend an orientation session for newly arrived Commonwealth students offered by the British Council. Participating in the session with us were students from Africa, Malaya and Singapore and the advice communicated included such things as how to clean the "ring of dark deposit" in a bathtub and how to remove stains from a shirt collar using a toothbrush and soap. The impression given was that we were somehow lacking in knowledge of basic hygiene practices. We were then invited to share presentations reflecting our various cultural heritages. A student from Ghana made a speech about his country's newly gained independence, followed by a Nigerian student's expression of hope for independence in the near future. Singapore's representative spoke about his political idol, Lee Kuan Yew, who would go on to become the first prime minister of the Republic of Singapore two years later. When it came to my turn, I simply went to the piano and played *Rose, Rose, I Love You*, the well-known English adaptation of a popular Chinese song. That was my way of indicating that freedom from colonial superiority was still a foreign concept in Hong Kong.

LEARNING TO BE MORE THAN AN ARCHITECT

"Architecture is an act of love." Those were the first words uttered by my first instructor at my first lecture on my first day of classes at the AA. September had come at last and I was now a bona fide student of architecture, finally living for real what had for so long been only a dream.

Our instructor that day – he was also my first year Studio Master – was John Dennis, a flamboyant English architect who was fond of wearing a threadbare jacket that was forever missing a button. After his provocative introductory pronouncement, he strode over to an old piano and began playing a few chords entirely off-key. This was his way of demonstrating that the human ear tends to be more sensitive than the human eye, he explained. It is much easier to notice off-key tones in a chord, he said, than to spot dissimilar dimensions in a row of equally spaced columns, proving that architecture is more than something that meets the eye and that an architect also needs to listen. This made a lot of sense to me. I was reminded of the Chinese word for 'listen', which is composed of a combination of four characters, the first representing 'ear', the second 'eye', followed by 'intensive attention' and then 'heart'.

Incredibly, at this first lecture, I found myself seated beside someone from home, someone I actually knew. Six years earlier, Freddy To had been one of my classmates at Wah Yan College until his family had sent him to England to a public school (the British term for a private school).

At first I thought him to be now rather British in his manner, however we were soon conversing companionably in Cantonese and discovered that we shared a lively interest in modern jazz music.

Our fellow first year students were mostly British, but a few came from Asia – the Asian Club, we called ourselves. There was Ong Chin-bee from Singapore, Cho Padamsee from Bombay, Kamal Muntaz from Lahore, and of course Freddy To and myself from Hong Kong.

During the Christmas break, À Li and I got jobs as overnight parcel handlers at Euston railway station in central London. We reported for work each evening after supper and finished ten backbreaking hours later at six the next morning. Huge volumes of parcels, crates of produce and other foodstuffs, and morning newspapers arrived on cargo trains from Birmingham, Manchester and Liverpool, and everything had to be transferred by hand to other trains or to storage depots.

À Li and I were not the only Commonwealth students on the work team, which was supervised by an Englishman who did not treat us very well. After he made some racist remarks, however, I told him that I was a Kung Fu master and he became less aggressive after that. When he was not around, À Li and I would sneak into the workmen's canteen to warm up with a cup of tea, or grab a quick nap on top of sacks of produce while waiting for the next train to arrive. At the end of each shift, we returned home for breakfast, slept until well into the afternoon, ate supper and then straight into the nightshift again. So much for a break from school.

Christmas afternoon, however, I spent at the home of Mr. Herbert Randall, an old Eurasian friend of Uncle's. After a traditional English Christmas lunch (dinner), the highlight of which was to see who would get the sixpence coin that had been hidden inside the plum pudding, we retired to the living room to watch Her Majesty The Queen deliver her annual Christmas message on television while Mr. Randall dozed by the fire.

I did not enjoy my first year at the AA as much as I had anticipated. I was surprised that we focussed more on art and drafting than on architecture, and the only assignment I took real pleasure in was the design and construction of a piece of furniture of my own choice – I created a bench, half of which was slatted with a cushion on top while the other half served as a coffee table. I later gave it away to a friend.

Throughout the year, I received help from several kind senior students. One of them was Chan, who, coincidentally, was a son of the wealthy fruit-selling architect to whom Eric Cumine had referred during my interview in Hong Kong. Then there was Tam, a final year student married to Kristel, who hailed from the same town in Germany as Hobart's girlfriend. I knew that the German influence was strong at the AA – its teaching philosophy was based on that of the iconic modernist *Staatliches Bauhaus* school of design – but I was beginning to suspect that German girls had probably also contributed significantly to that reputation.

What influenced me personally, however, was not so much girls as it was the burgeoning counterculture activities that were proliferating in London in the late 1950s. I became involved in the Ban the Bomb movement, a widespread campaign for nuclear disarmament. During street demonstrations, we sported a button featuring a brand new logo formed by combining the semaphore signals for the letters N and D, standing for 'Nuclear Disarmament', a logo that is now one of the world's most widely recognized symbols for 'Peace'. I also became involved in the Anti-Ugly League, which opposed the construction of massive office buildings of second-rate design in East End London, indeed some of us at the AA played a leading role in organizing the league's demonstrations. It did not take me long to pack away my English gentleman's suits in favour of corduroy pants, casual jackets and turtleneck sweaters. My new image, that of an artist, was topped off by a black beret and a pipe replaced my occasional cigarette.

My academic performance in that first year was mediocre but good enough for me to advance to the second year, a year I was looking forward to as the curriculum would finally begin to focus on building design. During the summer break, I was determined to get a taste of continental Europe.

Under normal circumstances I could not have afforded to travel to the Continent, however an opportunity arrived when À Li's father bought him a new four-door Ford Anglia as a reward for completing his A-Level courses and for being accepted into the University of Southampton. Like me, À Li was keen to visit that summer's Expo 58 in Brussels, the first World's Fair since war's end. In August, we boarded a car ferry to Holland and headed for Belgium in À Li's new vehicle, accompanied by Franklin Hsu, my RMS *Corfu* cabin mate.

Expo 58 was spectacular. The Atomium, the main pavilion and icon of the fair, was a one-hundred-metres-tall (three hundred and thirty-five feet) model of an iron crystal and would become a permanent symbol of the Belgian capital. And I was inspired by a second pavilion – the Phillips Pavilion – whose displays uniquely managed to meld architecture and musical composition, two of my greatest passions.

The expansive campground close to the Expo site was well equipped with washrooms and convenience stores, but our tent was a bit of a squeeze, only just big enough for the three of us to lie down in. This did not stop us from thoroughly enjoying each day's exploration of the fair's many exciting exhibits, though we could not afford to eat at its internationally themed restaurants, instead filling up on hotdogs and soft drinks. Pretty soon, of course, we were craving some good food and so we decided to try out a Chinese restaurant we had spotted in downtown Brussels.

The restaurant was on the upper floor of an aging commercial building and was almost empty when we entered, as most Europeans ate dinner quite late. We were warmly received by a young Cantonese waiter who introduced himself as *Mok* (his family name) and helped us select inexpensive items from the menu. Throughout our meal, he chatted about his experiences as a working student in Belgium and we agreed to get together for coffee after his work shift had ended. We felt lucky to have met someone 'local' who could give us suggestions for enjoying the remainder of our stay. When Mok heard about our congested tent, he suggested that Franklin could stay at his flat, which we all agreed was a generous offer and a great idea.

Next evening, we dropped Franklin off at the restaurant close to closing time and À Li and I settled down for a more comfortable night's sleep. It was still pitch dark, however, when we were awakened suddenly by someone crawling into our tent – it was Franklin. And he was very upset. Mok had made offensive advances towards him, he said, and in shock he had bolted and somehow found his way through the dark city streets back to the campground. We promised Franklin that we would not let the young waiter get off scot-free.

After daybreak, we knocked on Mok's door and ordered him into our car. Maintaining complete silence, we drove out of the city into the countryside, with our hostage looking very nervous, probably anticipating some form of underworld execution. After almost an hour, À Li stopped the car beside some woodland and we ordered Mok to get out, just as we had seen done in so many Hollywood gangster movies. He dropped to his knees on the ground and begged for forgiveness – and that was the last we saw of him as we sped away, back towards the city.

Shortly after our return to London, À Li moved to Southampton for his university education and Franklin became my new roommate. We lived in a flat in Hendon in northwestern London, within walking distance of the Hendon Central Tube station.

The new flat was on the upper floor of a two-storey house owned by a retired Jewish-English couple. It had its own entrance off a common vestibule and was much larger than my previous flat, though still with a geyser hot water heater and paraffin heaters for warmth. Instead of having a refrigerator – an unheard-of luxury for student tenants – we had a larder (a kitchen cupboard ventilated to the cool outdoors) in which we kept the bottles of Gold Top Guernsey milk that were delivered every morning by a milkman.

After more than a year in Britain, Franklin had mastered English and begun work on his A-Level courses. I was able to assist him from time to time and in return he offered me the larger of the two bedrooms so as to accommodate the drafting and layout tables that were necessary accessories to my own studies.

One of the early assignments of my second year at the AA was a rural planning exercise: the redevelopment of a village main street. I worked very hard on it and felt quite confident when the time finally arrived for presenting my plan to the jury, a panel of architectural critics headed by my second year Studio Mistress, Elizabeth Chesterton, who was later to be knighted by Queen Elizabeth for her contributions to architecture, planning and landscaping. Though it was my first time making such a presentation, I was not nervous. The jury's assessment of my work, however, turned out to be an important lesson for the remainder of my years at the AA, and indeed for all my future endeavours. My presentation was judged as being a disaster.

I had proposed a wide motorway cutting through the village, requiring the replacement of many buildings. Trees were to be removed, making way for signs and for street furniture. I had paid scant attention to the physical needs of village inhabitants or existing community traditions. Too much focus was placed on the 'how' and not enough on the 'why' or 'what' of the redevelopment. And to crown it all, my speaking style was deemed to be pretentious and my arguments unconvincing.

This painful failure marked the start of a substantial improvement in my work thereafter, bringing to mind my grandfather's wisdom, "A gem cannot be polished without friction, nor a man perfected without trials." That suddenly remembered and comforting phrase was like his parting gift to me.

In April 1959, just six months after my humbling presentation, I received the sad news that my grandfather had passed away in our home at the age of ninety-one. He had been baptised a Christian on his deathbed, I was told, and had been laid to rest in the Chinese Christian Cemetery near Aunt's house at Pokfulam.

During my second Christmas break in London, I found a two-week job as a relief postman for Royal Mail. My shift began at dawn sorting letters into pigeonholes and then, after the requisite cup of tea, sorting a large bag of mail into bundles before heading out with them onto the streets of Hendon. The first day on my route, I was accompanied by an experienced mailman who cautioned me in distinct Cockney tones that a dog could be lurking inside any house, just waiting to nip the fingers that pushed the letters through the slot in the front door. In spite of this risk, however, I found mail delivery to be an easier and more financially rewarding job than that of an overnight railway station parcel handler, and I especially appreciated getting home by early afternoon, with the rest of the day to be spent as I liked and the night to be spent in sleep as nature intended.

With the money I earned that Christmas, I was able to buy a second-hand scooter, an Italian-made Lambretta, for thirty pounds sterling (close to seventy-five Canadian dollars). It was in pretty poor shape but it freed me from overcrowded commutes on the Tube. Then, after completing my second year at the AA, I landed a summer job drafting school buildings for the Architectural Division of the London County Council and was delighted to be able to upgrade to a brand new Lambretta, one with a windshield, for a trade-in price of ninety pounds sterling (around two hundred and twenty Canadian dollars).

Of my five academic years in London, I found the third to be the toughest. Not only had the design projects become larger and more complex, but in addition the critics' expectations were very high, rightly so. Most challenging was the preparation of a complete set of construction working drawings for a major design project. This consisted of more than twenty sheets, all hand-drawn (computer drafting had not yet been invented), right down to details for components such as window frames and roof drains.

The drawings had to be based on the technical knowledge gained from lectures and from textbooks on structural design and building practices. Their production was both labour intensive and time consuming, taking a good part of the year to complete in pencil and ink on thin tracing paper. To erase a mistake made in ink required scratching at the error with a sharp razor blade, using just the right amount of pressure to efface the mistake without also making a hole through the fragile paper. No easy feat, and definitely conducive to attempting to get it right the first time.

The third year Studio Master was David Oakley, an experienced architect highly regarded in the profession and a 'no nonsense' teacher. He was the one responsible for meticulously scrutinizing the submitted working drawings and it was widely known that the percentage of students able to meet his high standards was low. Anyone who failed would be required to take a year off to gain practical experience in an architect's office and then submit a revised set of drawings the following year, necessitating an extra year at school. Successfully completing the working drawings assignment was compulsory in order to advance to the fourth year; it was also required by the Architects' Registration Council of the United Kingdom, the regulatory body for the licensing of professional practice.

To my tremendous relief and delight, I found myself among the fifty percent of my class who managed to pass, the only Asian student to do so. My friend Raymond, who had started one year ahead of me, had failed the assignment the previous year and never did return to the AA.

As a surprise reward for my academic success, my mother contributed half the cost of a return air ticket to Honk Kong and convinced Uncle to pay the other half. And so in the early summer of 1960, after three years in England, I excitedly boarded a de Havilland Comet 4 operated by the British Overseas Airways Corporation (BOAC) out of Heathrow for my first-ever flight. It was the early days of jet aircraft and I felt like a jet-setter. The journey lasted almost twenty hours, with stopovers in Beirut, Karachi, Bombay and Singapore, but the time passed very pleasantly as I was seated next to an attractive girl from Hong Kong and was only too happy to get to know her. Marianna told me her father was an obstetrician and gynaecologist of Indian origin and her mother was Chinese with one Belgium parent, which explained her own rather unique good looks. She seemed to be quite mature and even sophisticated, so I was surprised to discover she was only seventeen, returning home for the summer from a private school in England. We agreed to meet again while in Hong Kong.

I was thrilled to find my family waiting to greet me at the Kai Tak Airport. Uncle was in good health, although he and Aunt had noticeably aged since I'd last seen them. My mother, however, was just as cheerful and energetic as ever and my little sister Dong-dong had grown into a pretty twelve-year-old. My father, no longer working at the King's Theatre, was now a sales agent with the China Underwriters Insurance Company, and my grandmother was still able to be active at home, indeed she even accompanied me on an emotional visit to my grandfather's grave.

The trip home was intended to be a holiday with family, but I also wanted to find a short-term job in an architect's office and to find inspiration for my still-one-year-away fifth year graduating thesis, hopefully a design project with a Hong Kong theme. I was delighted to be hired for the summer by Clifford Wong, a respected architect who had qualified at McGill University in Montreal, and it was particularly satisfying to be given a good deal of freedom and responsibility in the design of several large projects. It was also a new and welcome experience to be treated as a real architect by the firm's technologists.

Best of all, I indeed hit upon a graduating thesis, one that seemed perfect on so many levels: the redevelopment of the maternity wing of the Hong Kong Sanatorium and Hospital. Uncle was a director and shareholder of the hospital, one of the most prestigious internationally-accredited private health facilities in Asia, and it was compelling to me that I would be able to dedicate my graduating thesis, the ultimate work of my professional education, to him, my benefactor and himself a maternity specialist. Uncle was very pleased. He promised to provide me with all the background that might be helpful, including the technical and medical requirements of such a facility.

As the summer went on, however, I was surprised to sense some disapproval emanating from both him and Aunt. It began when they found out that I was dating Marianna and it soon became very evident that they considered her an inappropriate match for me. In turn, their disapproval made my mother unhappy, as she feared that I was demonstrating ingratitude towards them by continuing the relationship. Uncle and Aunt or Marianna? Though she was captivating, there was no real competition for my loyalty.

My fourth year at the AA was a year for delighting in the opportunity to study the discipline I loved, with the pressure of the compulsory working drawings a thing of the past and the graduating design thesis still a whole year away.

My flat-mate Franklin chose to further his studies in the United States and I decided to find a room of my own so my late hours working on school projects would not disturb anyone else. I acquired the services of a real estate agent and was shocked to overhear some of his telephone conversations with potential landlords, conversations in which he described me as "a pleasant Oriental" and then being told there was no vacancy. Eventually, however, he managed to find me a room in a renovated house at Finchley Central, located between the more affluent areas of Swiss Cottage and Hampstead in northwest London. It cost five pounds sterling a week (fourteen Canadian dollars), a bit higher than the going market rent, but I took it because it was just a fifteen-minute scooter ride from school and from my favourite Soho coffee bars.

My Studio Master was John Winter, an English architect with a Masters degree from Yale University in Connecticut. The project that I enjoyed the most was the design of a travelling theatre, which excited me because of my personal love of acting. It was thrilling to be able to go behind the scenes, literally, in renowned West End theatres in order to gain technical knowledge for the project. Mr. Winter also introduced some fresh American ideas on teamwork in architecture and my team included Jim Farthing, an English student, and Alan Bradshaw, who hailed from Northern Ireland. We soon became fast friends.

Jim and his charming wife Alison invited me to spend Christmas with his parents in Totnes, Devon, and I thoroughly enjoyed their warm hospitality, fun family traditions and good food, all set in beautiful country surroundings. Alan also invited me to his home in Northern Ireland and I had my first experience of that country's rolling landscape, its ubiquitous churches and weathered tombstones, Mooney's pub and dark Guinness and, yet again, warm hospitality towards a student far from home.

The year passed very quickly and the fifth and last school year was just a few months away. I was determined to gain some professional experience in Europe during this final summer break.

The *Staatliches Bauhaus* school of design existed in Germany for a brief fourteen years prior to World Ward II but its influence was enduring. Its teachers and students continued to have major impact not only on the AA but on architectural trends across Western Europe, the United States, Canada and Israel throughout the following decades. I was convinced that my education would not be complete without gaining some first-hand European perspectives on my chosen profession. The opportunity arrived when senior students were invited to compete for the Henry Jarvis Scholarship, a bursary for summer travel-study awarded by the AA. I knew that could be my ticket to Europe.

Applicants had to submit a proposal outlining an objective and including a final design product. Knowing that precast concrete construction was now widely recognized as being efficient and economical for major housing projects in Europe, I took on the challenge of coming up with a method of improving the visual aesthetics of such mass-produced buildings – the 'Why' of my proposal. I submitted working drawings for a building formed by precast hexagonal modules – the 'What' of my proposal. And I consulted with Arthur Kohn, a senior Studio Master at the AA, who kindly provided me with contacts in Stuttgart and Paris who would be willing to assist with my study and travel logistics – the 'How' of my proposal.

I won the competition and set off for two weeks of travel-study in Germany and France.

My hosts in Stuttgart were Walter and Hede Munz. Mr. Munz, in his early sixties, was an editor and writer for several architectural journals, while his wife was a teacher of music and singing. They welcomed me warmly, insisting I call them by their first names, and escorted me to a *pension* (bed-and-breakfast guesthouse) close to their home before taking me out for a Chinese dinner with some of their in-the-business friends. Walter was determined to make my week in Germany fruitful, introducing me to engineers and architects who might be helpful.

Dieter Gertz was one of those professionals. In his thirties, he was both an architect and an engineer and had designed a number of precast concrete buildings – he also drove a Porsche, an Opel and a Fiat and lived in a strikingly modern home, all of which impressed this twenty-three-year-old greatly. He showed Walter and me around several of his projects including a church in precast concrete near the Swiss border, leading to my first exhilarating ride along a speed-limit-free *autobahn* (expressway).

Thanks to another of Walter's contacts, I also had an eye-opening visit to a plant in Frankfurt that manufactured prefabricated buildings. Dwelling units were mass-produced in cubic modules complete with plumbing fixtures and mechanical and electrical services, enabling the lightning-fast construction of multi-storey structures. Though the architectural design quality of the buildings was sorely lacking, I could appreciate that the process provided an efficient way of filling the serious housing needs of post-war West Germany.

My next destination was Paris, where my contact was to be a Madame Bougiere of *L'architecture d'aujourd'hui*, a respected magazine of modern architecture. I went into the bookstore on the ground floor of the building housing the magazine's offices and asked, in English, for Madame Bougiere. This was met with an uncomprehending stare and I began to worry about the second half of my summer studies, as I was unable to speak any French. Then a miracle happened.

A man appeared from behind a row of bookshelves and spoke to me in English. With him as my interpreter, I discovered that Madame Bougiere was on holiday and that August is a bad time to do any business in the French capital, it being the month when Parisians traditionally vacate the city. My rescuer introduced himself as Paul Bossard, architect. He was an intellectual-looking man of middle age, wearing glasses with a light silver frame and speaking English with a heavy French accent. I found myself telling him of my interest in precast concrete construction and he enthusiastically informed me that he had designed several buildings in that medium and offered to show me the drawings of his current project. Taking a leap of faith, I accompanied him in his Mercedes to his offices on the ground floor of a classical building where he and his wife, Renée, also an architect, ran their professional practice and lived in a loft overlooking the design studio below. They proudly showed me the working drawings for their latest precast concrete project, a series of medium-rise residential buildings with articulated facades. The structural forms were unconventional and sculptural, in complete contrast to many of the unimaginative developments I had seen in Germany. I was fascinated and eager to see the project for real.

Paul picked me up early the next morning for a visit to the site where a few of the buildings were already complete and others were still under construction. I learned that all the precast components were produced on-site under the supervision of the architect, enabling a vast range of interesting forms and shapes to meet the project's aesthetic as well as functional requirements, just like a suit that is made-to-measure rather than mass-produced. That totally unanticipated and unplanned site visit became a highlight of my travel-study experience, opening my eyes to new structural possibilities.

It was already past midday when we left the site and Paul suggested lunch. We were soon seated on the patio of an elegant restaurant and he ordered for both of us, knowing that I was unable to read the menu and probably hungry enough to eat anything. First came a bottle of wine, then a green salad and a generous portion of pasta with cheese. I was not yet really a wine drinker, but the wine that I sipped that day was so smooth on the palate that it quickly became an inseparable part of the pleasure of the meal. In spite of our language barrier, I learned over lunch that Paul, clearly a respected architect, contributed articles to *L'architecture d'aujourd'hui*, but what was more important to me was his demeanour: that of a sincere, intelligent and generous person who treated a young stranger in need of help with generosity and kindness, even going so far as to refer often to a French-English dictionary to facilitate our communication.

After our plates had been cleared away, to my utter surprise another course – the *plat principal* of veal and potatoes – arrived at the table, to be followed later by cheese, grapes and espresso. It was past three in the afternoon when we finally finished eating and I knew I had had the good fortune to experience the French way of approaching a meal: relax, socialize and enjoy. It was certainly time for Paul to drop me off at my hostel, as so much relaxation and enjoyment had made it impossible for me to resist the call of an afternoon nap.

Next day, Paul showed me a number of precast concrete residential projects built by the government. Just as in Germany, they were of high density and architecturally unimpressive, speed and efficiency of construction being essential in France also in order to ease the shortage of affordable housing.

I spent my last evening in Paris with Paul on a patio on the *Avenue des Champs Elysées* in sight of the monumental *Arc de Triomphe*. I was a willing student as I learned to take sufficient time to appreciate the aroma as well as the taste of an espresso and to indulge the tradition of dipping a cube of sugar into a fine *apéritif* before placing it in the mouth and slowly washing down its sweetness with that same espresso. When I departed for London the next day, Paul's many good-hearted *"Santé!"* toasts became a deeply treasured memory.

My travel-study report on precast concrete buildings in Germany and France was well received – it seems I had successfully fulfilled my role as a Henry Jarvis Scholar. In appreciation, I sent copies to Walter and Hede Munz and to Dieter Gertz and Paul Bossard, and later received a letter from Walter expressing interest in seeing Paul's unique residential project and requesting an introduction to the French architect, which I was more than happy to provide. It pleased me greatly to eventually hear that my two European mentors had gotten along extremely well together, both professionally and personally.

I was determined to make the most of my fifth and final year at the AA. What I did to achieve that can best be described as 'Three for the price of one,' perhaps an echo of the triple-line writing instrument I had invented at Wah Yan College almost a decade earlier. At the start of the academic year, I became aware of two other study opportunities that could support and inform my graduating design thesis and also add extra authority to my AA Diploma. I grabbed them both.

The first opportunity was a one-year graduate program at the AA School of Tropical Architecture (later renamed the Department of Development and Tropical Studies). It was offered primarily to graduates and practising architects from Africa and Asia and covered such topics as solar control, natural ventilation, geographical conditions and local social development conditions. Fifth year students in good standing could apply for admission, and apply I did, the only one of my classmates to do so. I looked forward to establishing contact with architects from other countries and learning from their experiences as well as from the experiences of the program's director, Dr. Otto Königsberger, a German architect who had worked in urban planning in Asia, Africa and Latin America. I was very happy when my application was accepted.

The second study opportunity was a yearlong program offered in the evenings by the Royal Academy of Arts. Called the School of Advanced Architectural Studies, it was intended to be a forum for discussing and debating architectural issues. The size of the forum was limited to ten young architects and graduate students selected by a panel of architects and artists. I sent in my application and was invited for an interview at the academy in Burlington House on Piccadilly in central London.

I vividly remember the weight of my portfolio getting heavier and heavier as I was escorted along the cold, shadowy, endless corridors of the historic building and up several stone staircases to emerge in a large portrait gallery with a long table at the far end. Sitting behind the table were three interviewers including Sir Basil Spence, the head of the program and most notably associated with the winning design for the new Coventry Cathedral that replaced the one destroyed during WWII, and Mr. Bill Howell, a program instructor who also taught at the AA and was considered to be one of a "dynamic trio" of architects responsible for many of the London County Council's higher quality housing developments. I had researched their backgrounds and so was prepared for the topics raised in the interview, and they in turn showed genuine interest in the various ideas I was developing for my graduating thesis. And so it was that I came to be admitted to the School of Advanced Architectural Studies and looked forward to earning a postgraduate certificate from the famous Royal Academy at the end of the year.

My primary focus during this final academic year at the AA, however, had to be on the design for the new maternity wing for the hospital in Hong Kong, and producing that design would consume the majority of my time. My fifth year Studio Master, Robert Maxwell, encouraged me to augment what I had learned over the past four years by consulting with local obstetricians and gynaecologists – the people on the job – and by checking out several bricks-and-mortar maternity facilities. This I did. In addition I received many valuable comments from Uncle, to whom I mailed copies of my preliminary sketches on a regular basis.

Mr. Maxwell's style of teaching was refreshingly modern. He encouraged discussion and debate in class, focussing on substantiveness of content and clarity of language, which proved to also assist my successful participation in the forum at the Royal Academy. He went on to become Dean of the School of Architecture at Princeton University and internationally known for critical writings on modern architecture in relationship to contemporary art, literature and music.

One evening, several days before my final thesis presentation, I took a break from the drawing board for a drink in a nearby pub, where I unexpectedly ran into Mr. Maxwell and we had a good conversation that included some details of my thesis preparation process. I considered buying him a friendly drink but decided that might look like an attempt at bribery – he would be chairing the design jury the following week – so I headed home and got back to work instead.

By now, I was living in a rooming house not too far from Hong Kong House, a hostel near Hyde Park that served good Chinese food in its canteen. I had become a frequent patron of the facility and made friends with one of its residents, Dr. Haroon Abdullah, a physician from the Queen Mary Hospital, just up the hill behind Uncle and Aunt's house in Pokfulam, who was in London preparing to take the membership exam of the Royal College of Obstetricians and Gynaecologists (MRCOG). He became a very important part of my thesis preparation, adding to my knowledge of pre-natal, post-natal and delivery facility requirements.

The five-man design jury included Mr. Maxwell and Dr. Abdullah, who, at my suggestion, had agreed to serve as an expert medical critic on the panel, complementing the roles of the other four jurors who were all architects. There was a good-sized audience including several classmates who were curious about what I had been working on. Flanked by twenty carefully detailed drawings, I gave my hour-long presentation as cogently and professionally as I could, keenly aware that this was the moment of truth. Without the approval of my thesis, I would not graduate as an AA architect.

After an animated exchange of questions and answers between the jurors and me, Mr. Maxwell pronounced the verdict in words I will never forget: "I commend the author for his thorough research and creative design and for the clarity of his presentation. I recommend 'Stored' for the project." I was ecstatic. 'Stored' indicated special recognition of achievement, an endorsement that the project had distinct quality and that the school wanted to put it in storage for future exhibition.

And so, after five life-changing years, I traded my graduating thesis for an Architectural Association Diploma (AA Dipl.) and shortly thereafter augmented that diploma with an AA Tropical School Certificate (AA Trop.Cert.) and an RA School of Advanced Architectural Studies Certificate (RA Cert.).

The best reward of all, however, was the smile on Uncle's face when next I saw him.

ACTING AND MUSIC – SWINGING LONDON

During my studies in London, I began to realize that architecture embodied many of the same elements as acting and music, my two favourite pastimes. Each possessed emotion, theme, structure, rhythm and delivery and all were subject to the interpretation of the beholder. I found that acting and music added dimension to my professional training.

During my first year at the AA, I heard that Twentieth Century Fox Film Corporation was shooting a movie just outside London and was looking for Chinese people to audition, as the story – *The Inn of the Sixth Happiness*, featuring beautiful Hollywood star Ingrid Bergman – was based on the experiences of a British missionary living in China. An agency in Soho was responsible for the hiring. By the time I got there, only non-speaking roles were left but I happily signed on as an extra for three pounds and ten shillings a day (about nine Canadian dollars) plus lunch, and was instructed to report to Pinewood Studios the following week.

With high expectations for my first taste of Hollywood, I arrived at the studios early on Monday morning. In the parking lot, I noticed a young Chinese man getting out of a four-door Morris and subsequently discovered his name to be Burt Kwouk. He had a speaking role in the movie and was to go on to perform in many big screen and television productions, perhaps most famously as Cato Fong, Inspector Clouseau's faithful manservant in all but one of the Pink Panther comedies starring Peter Sellers.

I was directed to an outdoor set resembling a Chinese village street, where I was given a bamboo pole and two basket bundles plus a traditional Chinese hat and sandals and a set of peasant garb for pulling on over my own clothes. I then joined a line to receive a dab of makeup – a quick brush with charcoal powder – before someone briefed me on my role: I had the part of a villager balancing heavy bundles on a pole across one shoulder while running down the street in the midst of a Japanese air raid. On the cue of "Action!" from the assistant director, I was to start running from one end of the street to the other, along with a crowd of other 'villagers'. We went through two rehearsals before the final shoot began later in the morning.

Immediately next to the street set was another set depicting a village temple in front of which there was an open carriage with horses. A camera was aimed towards the temple and the director was seated behind it, a graceful blonde woman standing at his side – none other than the legendary Ingrid Bergman, looking a lot smaller than my impression of her on the big screen. Before long, she took up a position in front of the temple and as soon as the director called "Action!" an explosion sounded, smoke and fire billowed from hidden canisters and several young children ran out of the temple towards Ms. Bergman, who hurried them through the smoke and into the waiting carriage. Then came "Cut!" from the director, immediately followed by the cue of "Action!" for those of us on the adjacent street set. I ran with my heavy bundles, along with the other 'terrified villagers'.

We repeated the take three times and I was impressed by Ingrid Bergman's disciplined approach, performing and repeating on cue like a well-oiled machine. At the break for lunch, I quite happily downed two fried eggs – they had run out of chicken – and a pile of Brussels sprouts and boiled potatoes. After all, it was not about the food; it was about being in a movie with a major Hollywood star, one who was to win a National Board of Review of Motion Pictures award as Best Actress for her performance.

Upon the release of *The Inn of the Sixth Happiness* in Hong Kong, Uncle bought tickets for an entire row of seats in the Roxy Theatre so my family could see me in my Hollywood debut. To my surprise and great disappointment, however, he wrote to say that they could not find me in the movie. When I finally saw the film myself, I discovered why. My scene had been shot in broad daylight but had been transposed into a night scene by the use of lens filters and it required a great deal of concerted effort on my own part to spot myself running in the dim background of a very brief 'night-time' shot of Ingrid Bergman and the children. So much for my big movie career.

Dabbling in amateur stage production proved to be more rewarding. The opportunity came about during my fifth year at the AA when the warden of Hong Kong House, the hostel near Hyde Park, wanted to fundraise for Chinese refugees in Hong Kong. Building on my stage experience back home and the knowledge I had gained from my fourth year theatre design project, I convinced the warden, Miss Turner, that a play performed on a stage set up in the hostel's expansive lounge could draw a good audience, including Westerners, as long as it was in English and incorporated modern theatre techniques. She bought into the idea.

I was introduced to a professional actor by the name of Bill Cartwright, whose girlfriend was Michelle Mok, Miss Hong Kong

1958 and also an actor. Bill told me about the English script for a play depicting the love life of an ancient Chinese hermit, which we rewrote to include the addition of a storyteller. Bill agreed to direct the play, the beautiful Michelle agreed to take on the pivotal role of the storyteller, and I selected nine Chinese students living in the hostel to complete the cast. One of them, a music student named Alannah, became a Hong Kong television actress some years later.

A scaffolding company was hired to build an open stage in the lounge – I chose an open stage, without the traditional curtain, so the audience would feel closer to what was happening onstage: the live action, the photographic projections depicting the dream of the hermit, and even the changing of sets and props by discreet stagehands dressed in black. Professional theatre lighting and sound systems were installed and a team of women volunteered to make the costumes.

Bamboo Shelter sold out all three hundred seats for each of its three evening performances and so my first attempt at amateur stage production became a much more satisfying experience than my performance in a professional Hollywood movie.

The friend in London who most passionately shared my taste in music was Freddy To, the 'surprise' classmate from Hong Kong I had sat beside for my very first lecture at the AA. I frequently dropped into his north-west London home to enjoy his extensive collection of ballads and Latin jazz records played on a quality hi-fi (high fidelity) sound system. Freddy was a gifted pianist and I admired the way he struck out the jazz chords on his sister's grand piano (she was studying at the Royal Academy of Music) and would sometimes join him at the keyboard for an impromptu duet. It was so much fun we began to think of forming a band and once again Hong Kong House provided the creative opportunity.

While at the hostel one evening, the sound of live music – I remember it was a swing version of *September in the Rain* – drew me into the lounge where I introduced myself to a group of Hong Kong students in the midst of band practice. The pianist and leader of the group was Albert Fung, a classical music student, and he was accompanied by guitarist K.K. Wong, bassist and trumpet player *Seefu* (nickname for "Master") – also a classical music student – and drummer Clarence Chang. Together the foursome made up the Hong Kong House Band and they were preparing to perform at an upcoming dance.

When I spotted an accordion lying nearby, I mentioned my days of playing the instrument in a band in Hong Kong and Albert invited me to jam with them. By the end of the evening, it felt as though I had been part of the group for years. I told them about Freddy, a versatile flutist as well as keyboardist, and that was the beginning of the newly expanded Hong Kong House Band.

The six of us were soon accepting paid engagements outside of the hostel and so had to join the Musicians' Union. We added a vibraphone to our pool of instruments and Freddy eventually took over the accordion as well as doubling as flutist, freeing me to become the vocalist, the role I most enjoyed. We performed together for two years before Albert Fung and Seefu moved on and we were joined by bassist Albert Poon, another AA student from Hong Kong. We renamed ourselves The Oriole and adopted *Yellow Bird* as our signature tune. One of our most memorable engagements was playing for a romantic dinner dance hosted by the Japanese Embassy on a riverboat cruising along the Thames. They paid us very well too. The Oriole eventually cut a 33 rpm record in an Oxford Street recording studio, just for the thrill of it – I would later have it re-recorded onto a compact disc – but ironically swing music was dying in the "Swinging London" of the 1960s, quickly being replaced in popularity by rock. The Beatles, The Rolling Stones and Jimi Hendrix had burst onto the scene.

Freddy To was not only my class- and band-mate, I could easily describe him as my soul mate in music. When we performed together, his chords and infill melodies and my vocals seemed to be in natural harmony and there was little need for us to rehearse. He also served as something of a matchmaker for me.

He introduced me to my first girlfriend in London. Thorunn Johannsdottir – we called her Dodie – was a classmate of Freddy's sister at the Royal Academy of Music and was frequently invited to their house parties. She was a beautiful blond with Icelandic parents and the made-in-Hong Kong cheongsam she often wore set off her looks to perfection in my eyes. I had the pleasure of dating her on several occasions and she accompanied me to the annual AA carnival. Her world of music, however, was far above my own. She was top of her class and destined to become a successful concert pianist, leaving London for Moscow on a music scholarship, where she met and married the celebrated conductor and pianist Vladimir Ashkenazy,

Another classmate of Freddy's sister came into my life one evening at a London coffeehouse. Patsy Toh was an attractive Chinese girl and we hit it off right away, talking easily and discovering we had a lot in common including a love for the music of Debussy and Ravel. I was disappointed to learn that she was just visiting from France, where she was now studying at the Paris Conservatoire. Several months later, however, she phoned to say she was back for another visit and we met for dinner. We began dating each time she came to London, sometimes hanging out at the all-night fruit and vegetable market in Covent Garden and pretending to be hippies. We had fun and developed a special relationship, even though the time we spent together was sporadic and limited.

Eventually, however, we decided to go our separate ways, knowing her world was to be one of music in Europe while mine would be of architecture in England and then, most likely, in Asia. Patsy went on to perform professionally in Europe, China and the Americas and to serve as a professor of piano at the Royal Academy of Music. She married Fu Chong, a fellow concert pianist respected for his authoritative interpretations of Chopin.

FAITH, HOPE AND LOVE

My graduation from the AA in the summer of 1962 signalled the beginning of my life as an architect, however I still needed to pass the professional practice exam required by the Architects' Registration Council of the United Kingdom in order to be registered as an Associate of the Royal Institute of British Architects (ARIBA). Two years of professional experience with a firm of chartered architects was required prior to taking the exam, so I needed to find a job right away – and ideally a job that paid well so that I would not have to continue looking to Uncle for financial support.

I applied to a number of reputable firms in London. Two responded. The first firm was not impressed by the fact that my thesis project had been for a facility in Hong Kong rather than in Britain. The second firm, however, specialized in hospital design and offered me a junior position paying eight hundred and fifty pounds sterling a year (two thousand Canadian dollars). Hungry for the work though I was, I did not have a good feeling about this offer as the associate who interviewed me had left me with the impression that he was doing a 'foreigner' a favour. With only two days to respond, I went home desperately hoping to find alternative opportunities. By sheer chance, I came across an advertisement for architects in a newspaper and made an appointment for an interview the following day.

The offices of Booty, Edwards and Partners, Chartered Architects, were on the top floor of 24 Portland Place, a three-storey Victorian building right across the street from the Chinese Embassy where Dr. Sun Yat-sen, founding father of the Republic of China, had spent some time in 1896. A good omen perhaps, I thought. I could not have been more right. Another miracle was about to occur.

A friendly receptionist escorted me to the principal of the firm, Peter Merer, an English gentleman in his early fifties sporting a polka-dot bow tie, red suspenders and a genial smile. He explained that this was the London office of an international company with its head office in Kuala Lumpur and other offices in Kuching and Sandakan in eastern Malaysia, as well as in Singapore and Brunei. It was one of the leading firms of architects in Southeast Asia with three British and two Chinese partners. He casually enquired if I might know of the Chinese partners: Ong Eng-hung in Singapore, and Kington Loo in Kuala Lumpur. I nearly jumped out of the chair. Mr. Ong was the architect married to the daughter of Uncle's friend and I had lunched at their home during the port-of-call visit to Singapore; and Mr. Loo was married to the daughter of Second Uncle's older brother, a doctor practising in Hong Kong. Mr. Merer and I were both amazed by the coincidence.

He examined my portfolio and was delighted that I had chosen a hospital project for my thesis, as their London office had been set up precisely because they had been commissioned to design a geriatric hospital northwest of London and they were in need of an assistant architect with hospital design experience. It seemed I was a perfect fit. I was hired as a consulting architect, meaning that I would be collecting a fee – twelve hundred and fifty pounds sterling a year (three thousand Canadian dollars) – rather than a salary. I was starting to feel like a professional.

I had only one week in which to organize my new life. I quickly found an unfurnished studio flat in the basement of a renovated building at Leinster Gardens in central London, within walking distance of Hong Kong House and its delicious Chinese food. Rent was six pounds ten shillings a week (about sixteen Canadian dollars) plus the cost of electricity, but there was free parking on the street for my newly-acquired third-hand Austin A40. I furnished the flat with a new bed, the drafting board table that had been built for me by my first landlord, some bookshelves I had built myself, and a rented black-and-white television that worked by feeding coins into a meter. Then, satisfied that my housing needs had been taken care of, I boarded a BOAC VC10 airliner for a brief trip home to Hong Kong, a big-hearted graduation gift from Uncle.

When I spotted him sitting apart from the crowds in the Kai Tak Airport, Uncle's face creased into a great smile – the most gratifying reward possible for my years of study. I went over to him right away and uttered a heartfelt "Thank you!" He shook my hand without a word, appearing to be holding back tears. I could hardly wait to show him my graduation diploma and certificates and to present him with a copy of my design thesis for 'his' maternity hospital. Aunt told me later that he had said to her, "The naughty boy has grown up."

My brother had joined Uncle in his medical practice, having returned from Winnipeg with his wife and their children – two of them at that time, a son and daughter; another daughter was later born in Hong Kong. My grandmother, at ninety-one years of age, continued to amaze me with her level of energy. My father, meanwhile, was now working as the manager of the Star Theatre in North Point, a densely populated area of Chinese immigrants, and my mother remained as busy as ever at Ying Wa Girls' School, where my sister was doing well in her studies. I suddenly realized that the time was quickly approaching when I would need to do what I could to assist with my no-longer-so-little sister's higher education.

My two weeks in Hong Kong went by very quickly. Uncle Wah-chiu and Auntie Wan-fun took me to nightclubs, sometimes surprising me with pre-arranged requests from the resident bands to go onstage and sing with them. It was all tremendous fun. Everything in Hong Kong seemed to be evolving at a fast pace, not unlike in Swinging London.

Shortly after my return to England I received a letter from Dieter Gertz: the Stuttgart architect-engineer was coming to London for a visit. I was excited at the prospect of being able to return a little of his hospitality of the previous summer and reserved a room for him at a little hotel close to where I lived. He arrived at my door looking slimmer than I'd remembered and carrying a small suitcase, which he could not wait to open to retrieve two bottles of white wine – not just any white wine, he enthused, but a Liebfraumilch of the exceptional 1957 vintage, "The best year of harvest!" His ensuing description of its flavour introduced me to the fact that there are many nuances to wine and its appreciation, opening a door into another world of taste for me.

I happily took him on an architectural tour of London and to the newly constructed modernist Coventry Cathedral, some one hundred and sixty kilometres (one hundred miles) away in the West Midlands. I was greatly relieved that my old Austin survived the journey, which no doubt was quite a change of transportation for a lover of luxury cars like Dieter.

I thoroughly enjoyed every moment of our time together, and it was with tremendous shock that I received the news of his death from cancer just a few months later. From that moment on, Liebfraumilch became my drink of choice when remembering my generous mentor and dear friend.

Reporting for work on my first day at Booty, Edwards and Partners, I was introduced by Mr. Merer to David Blatchford, an English AA graduate who was the senior assistant architect in the drafting office. His work-station was in front of a bank of windows overlooking Portland Place and I was assigned the workstation in front of him, indicating that I, the rookie architect, ranked next to him. In front of me were the work-stations of two draftsmen (architectural technologists), one of them a Greek by the name of Dimitri and the other Ken from Czechoslovakia. Occupying a small front corner desk was Phillip, a young Chinese man from Singapore who was the office clerk, looking after printing and stationery supplies and running errands as they were needed, and ably supported by Joan, the friendly English receptionist-secretary. It was indeed very much an international team.

The firm was banking its reputation in the United Kingdom on the design of the Amersham Geriatric Hospital, which was scheduled to be completed within two years. Its success could lead to other jobs in Britain. Our structural engineering consultants and quantity surveyors occupied offices one floor below us, though their headquarters also were in Asia. Such collaboration between related professional disciplines was common among former colonial Southeast Asian companies.

David Blatchford, my immediate superior, was a relaxed and patient person who usually met his fiancée at the end of the formal working day. Dimitri always went home in time for dinner with his wife, while Ken had a date with his girlfriend most evenings. Without a female companion of my own, I frequently stayed at the office and worked late. This unplanned scenario resulted in me contributing positively to the hospital project – and thus being noticed by Mr. Merer.

When it was announced that David was being transferred to Eastern Malaysia to run the Kuching office, Mr. Merer asked me to take over the position of senior assistant architect, taking charge of the hospital project right up to its completion. I was delighted to move to David's workstation, not least because there was an electric heater mounted on the wall immediately behind my new seat. I now had the warmest workstation in the office.

On evenings off and on weekends, I entertained myself by indulging my childhood passion for movies. I was at the Leicester Square Theatre (now called the Odeon West End cinema) one evening when something unusual happened: the American national anthem was played over the sound system at the end of the film. Outside the theatre, taxis and cars lined both sides of the street, many with their doors wide open, and people were standing around or aimlessly wandering. The atmosphere was tense and London appeared to be almost at a standstill. I overheard someone say that President Kennedy had been shot. I rushed home to watch in horror the repeating television footage of the motorcade in Dallas, the President being hit and Mrs. Kennedy's piteous reaction, and the limo speeding to the hospital. Over and over the images played until finally the devastating news: the President was dead. It was Friday, November 22, 1963.

I suddenly became aware of how far I was from those I most loved.

For me, the best sanctuary from sadness and loneliness was my faith. Having been brought up in a Protestant family and educated in a Catholic school, my faith was not so much based on religious tradition as on something deeply personal. I had tried the Chinese Christian Church at the YMCA but it did not resonate with me, then by chance one Sunday evening I ventured into an Anglican church near where I lived. Instantly I was drawn to the minister's decidedly untraditional preaching style which included references to artists such as Picasso. After the service, he introduced himself as Antony Bridge – Tony – and I discovered that he had been a professional artist before becoming a minister. He took a genuine interest in my cultural heritage and my architectural profession and made me feel very welcome, and I soon became quite active in his Christ Church congregation, reading scripture from the pulpit and participating in the Christmas processional. Besides providing spiritual strength and guidance to me, Tony and his wife Brenda also contributed to my social life by hosting friendly wine-and-cheese gatherings for young members of their congregation.

In the summer of 1964, I had completed the requisite two years of professional experience and was ready to sit the professional practice examination. I came out from the all-day exam with a good feeling – and I did indeed pass. At 26, I was finally in a position to take charge of my future.

I had a decision to make: to continue working in London where I might always be considered an outsider, or to return home to Hong Kong, which was facing political uncertainty under the shadow of Communist China and was affected by the escalation of the ongoing war in Vietnam. An unexpected answer was, once again, handed to me.

Back at the offices of Booty, Edwards and Partners, the working drawings for the Amersham Geriatric Hospital were almost complete and in my spare time I had entered an Ideal Home design competition, winning first prize and gaining good publicity for my firm. One Friday afternoon in late summer, Mr. Merer asked to see me in his office. He informed me that he was returning to the Kuala Lumpur office and that an associate from that office would be coming to London to take his place. I immediately became worried about my future prospects but then, to my surprise, he asked, "Would you like to move with me to KL?"

I instantly felt excitement and requested more details. He explained that he would need a right-hand man in Kuala Lumpur and I would fit in well because that city had a vibrant Chinese community that was considered to be the engine of the Malaysian economy. He further indicated that I would be hired as a British expatriate on a three-year contract, with an attractive salary, housing allowance, return passage for annual leave back in England, and a car loan that could be paid back over the duration of my contract.

Several happy thoughts jostled for attention in my mind: I would be able to purchase a brand new car in London tax-free because it would be taken out of Britain; my chances of meeting some nice Chinese girls would be much greater in Malaysia than in London; and – the icing on the cake – my earnings would not just make me self-sufficient but also enable me to help support my sister's higher education. Weighing all these pros, it was obvious to me that the attraction of Kuala Lumpur surpassed that of London or even, at this time, of Hong Kong.

I accepted Mr. Merer's offer, to take effect after I had completed the working drawings for the geriatric hospital and passed the project along to my successor for the construction stage. I wrote to my family about this exciting turn of events and began to shop for a car, soon settling on a new Austin Mini. It was the cheapest model and did not include a radio or heater, but I upgraded it by installing a sports steering wheel and gearshift handle in a wood finish plus a pair of sporty wing mirrors, trading in my old Austin A40 to pay for them.

My mother answered my letter. I anxiously ripped it open, hoping for my family's approval of my coming move. Approval was given, but was accompanied by shocking news. Uncle had just passed away.

After years of enduring the increasing pain of a peptic ulcer, he had died in 'his' hospital – the Hong Kong Sanatorium and Hospital – cradled in Aunt's arms while she sent him off with gentle hymn singing. His ashes had been scattered in the western inlet of Victoria Harbour, in view from his house at Pokfulam. He had not wished to be buried, as he said he had no children of his own and did not want to burden others in the family with the task of grave tending.

I was flooded with the immensity of knowing that whatever I was or would become was due in large measure to him, my surrogate father, my mentor and my truest friend, the man who had unfailingly shown me faith, hope and love throughout every day and every situation of my life. I could not begin to repay what I owed him and I knew that the best reimbursement possible was for me to resolve to always treat my family and friends the way Uncle had treated me. Crying at his loss seemed a totally inadequate response.

But even as his bright presence in my life was suddenly dimmed, a new light was being lit.

As I prepared for my upcoming move, my good friend Freddy To invited me to accompany him to the home of four Chinese sisters from Hong Kong. They were all under twenty, a little too young for me to take any romantic interest in, but Freddy mentioned that their eldest sister would soon be visiting from Hong Kong. When we went back a week later, she was there. Loretta was warm, unpretentious, cheerful, engaging, attentive, caring and stunningly beautiful, her dark hair piled on top of her head like a little crown.

We all sat comfortably on the heated floor – Loretta, her sisters, Freddy and me – enjoying conversation over multiple cups of tea. I soon discovered that Loretta and I had mutual friends in Hong Kong and that before moving to London to train in Home Economics she had been a classmate of my cousin Choong-ching, Second Aunt's younger daughter, at the Diocesan Girls' School. We found ourselves chatting happily until two in the morning, long after Freddy had gone home and Loretta's sisters were asleep. I could not take my eyes off her.

I began to take Loretta and one of her sisters for drives in my new car. I learned that she, like me, enjoyed musicals and dancing and dining out. Finally, I thought, I had my perfect date companion. Over dinner one evening at The Guinea and The Piggy restaurant in Leicester Square, I introduced her to a bottle of vintage Liebfraumilch 1957 and after dinner offered her a Benson & Hedges cigarette (having heard that was the brand favoured by the Royal Family) which I lit with a gold Dunhill lighter, considered a luxury brand. I was trying very hard to project the image of a sophisticated architect. And I was on cloud nine.

Over the next several weeks, our thoughts often appeared to be totally in sync – whenever one of us said something, it seemed to have been already in the mind of the other. The chemistry between us was potent, but there was one major fly in the ointment. She would shortly be returning to Hong Kong – and to an unhappy marriage.

We left London together, sharing precious time in Barcelona, Capri, Sorrento, Rome, Pisa and Florence before parting when I got off the plane in Kuala Lumpur and she continued the journey home to Hong Kong. All we could do was place our trust in destiny.

I quickly adopted the relaxed 'Continental' fashion of my fellow students who hung out in the trendy coffee houses of Soho in the late 1950s, abandoning my 'English Gentleman' wardrobe of three-piece suits.

(TOP LEFT): The new student at his dream school – the Architectural Association School of Architecture in London (1957).

(TOP RIGHT): My band, The Oriole, was engaged for parties and dances in London and we even cut a record in an Oxford Street studio. After Freddy To *(front right)* took over the accordion, I became the vocalist, the role I most enjoyed.

(BOTTOM): The cast and director of *Bamboo Shelter* made my first venture into stage production very rewarding (1962).

Loretta – my love at first sight, my forever love.

Lost Years | 5

Malaysia, Singapore and Brunei (1964-1966)

THE WRONG PLACE AT THE WRONG TIME

I was twenty-seven and full of high hopes and happy expectation when I arrived in Kuala Lumpur in the fall of 1964. Just like my professional self, Malaysia too was a brand new entity, born out of years of effort. Surely this fledgling federation of the former Malaya, Sarawak, Sabah and Singapore held the promise of regional harmony that could only lead to prosperity after decades of colonialism, uniting, as it did, the inherent strengths of the Malay, Chinese and Indian races.

Thian Oon-kim, a local Chinese architect who had worked with me briefly in the Booty Edwards office in London, met me at the Sungai Besi Airport. As we walked past the terminal's open-air restaurant, I was particularly struck by the multi-ethnicity of the people relaxing together around tables laden with satay, hot pot and beer, the warm evening illuminated by lanterns hanging from palm trees – so very different to London and indeed to Hong Kong.

We drove through quiet streets lined with low buildings – again, quite a contrast to the larger cities I was familiar with – to the Majestic Hotel, a modest hostelry where a room had been booked for me. Thian (it was the custom for local Chinese to address one another by last name) promised to pick me up next morning. Alone in my room, exhausted after the long flight, I was suddenly overwhelmed by the unfamiliarity of everything around me and began to wonder if it had been a mistake to move to a place so very different from anything I'd ever known.

Peter Merer's genuinely warm welcome at the office next day did much to relieve my apprehension. It was good to see him again and I had to smile at the fact that though his familiar jacket and red suspenders had been abandoned, he still wore a long-sleeved shirt and his trademark bow tie in spite of the tropical heat. Kington Loo, his co-partner in Kuala Lumpur, was dressed more casually, however I was somewhat taken aback when he turned only briefly from his drafting table to offer me the most cursory of acknowledgements – not quite the greeting I had expected from the son-in-law of Second Uncle's older brother.

Mr. Merer introduced me to my new colleagues. With the exception of Doug Sanger from England and Ron Pratt from Australia, the dozen or so architects were all Chinese, and so too were the technologists other than the head draftsman. Space in the office was tight but I was assured that we would soon be moving to larger quarters in a modern high-rise that our firm was in the process of building for the Chartered Bank right next door to our current location on Ampang Road, a grand boulevard lined with mature trees and a mixture of stately mansions and commercial buildings.

There were two teams in the KL office. The Australian Team was headed by Mr. Loo, a graduate of the University of Melbourne, and included Ron Pratt along with two local Chinese architects who had also graduated from Australian universities, Alex Foo and Seto Kwok-yin. They mainly handled projects from local clients, including the national zoo and the new airport, Subang International, which would very soon replace the one I had so recently arrived at. The English Team, headed by Mr. Merer, included Doug Sanger, Thian and now me, and our primary responsibility was for the projects of Western corporate clients such as the Chartered Bank, the Hong Kong and Shanghai Bank, and the Esso Petroleum Company. The office's junior architects, all graduates of either English or Australian schools, fell in line behind their respective alma maters, so to speak, and both teams shared the common pool of draftsmen.

I was put in charge of designing the layout of our new offices which would occupy a whole floor of the under-construction high-rise. It proved to be an exercise in diplomacy as well as in design. I very quickly became aware of a lack of cohesive spirit bordering on rivalry between the two office teams – which probably went a long way towards explaining Mr. Loo's coolness towards me – and so assigning space was a task that required infinite tact so as to avoid upsetting anyone. The layout that was finally approved by the two partners made perfect sense from a practical point of view but did little to ameliorate the polarization within the firm: Mr. Merer and Mr. Loo would occupy corner offices at opposite ends of the building, with their respective team members close by and the large drafting office occupying the 'neutral territory' in the middle section.

I soon became quite content with my working life in Kuala Lumpur, thanks to the fact that I continued to be Mr. Merer's trusted lieutenant and enjoyed having a pleasant office, a small team of dedicated assistants and a decent salary. My social life too began to take shape, expedited by the convenience of my newly-arrived tax-free Austin Mini. The evening that Thian invited me to join him and some friends at a Chinese restaurant was a particular turning point, however, as that was when I was introduced to a local custom that made me uncomfortable, a popular drink that left me cold, and – most fortuitously – a young accountant who was to become my best friend in KL. I also became the unwitting victim of a friendly practical joke.

When the soup course arrived, the large tureen was placed at the centre of the table and I was horrified to discover that each person was expected to eat directly from this communal bowl, dipping our sipping spoons repeatedly into the liquid. Having been indoctrinated in good hygiene habits around food all my life, this was one local custom I never did get used to. I found myself unable to go back for a second taste. I had no trouble, however, enjoying the diverse array of hot and spicy dishes that followed, each with a serving spoon for loading up our individual plates, much to my great relief. The meal was accompanied by many bottles of Tiger beer and ended with glasses of Brandy Ginger, a highly popular local concoction of Cognac and ginger ale that I secretly decided was really rather a waste of good brandy.

Thian's friends were all young local Chinese professionals and I particularly connected with one who, like me, had received his professional training – he was an accountant – in England. Tham Yap-sang and I swapped tales about our British experiences and I enjoyed his forthrightness and dry sense of humour. When the conversation around the table turned to badminton, one of Malaysia's most popular sports, I mentioned that I'd practically grown up with the game, coached by an expert, my Uncle Wah-chiu, at which point Tham suggested I demonstrate my skill by playing against a mother of four that he knew. Spurred on by the group and uplifted by the beer and Brandy Ginger, I cheerfully accepted the challenge, betting a nice seafood dinner for everyone to be paid for by the loser.

An evening match was arranged for the following week and I arrived at the outdoor badminton court feeling confident and looking forward to an easy victory. Tham volunteered to be the umpire and the competition began with me winning the draw for first serve. The remarkable skill of my opponent, Eng-lui, very quickly became obvious as her lightning-speed wrist shots continuously landed the shuttlecock at spots just beyond my reach. It turned out to be an effortless victory for her and a total embarrassment for me, until eventually Tham let out the truth: Eng-lui was in fact a Ladies Badminton Champion and he had suggested the match for a laugh, sensing that I was a good sport.

I happily hosted the promised seafood dinner a week later for everyone including Eng-lui and her husband. I'd passed a rite of passage and was admitted into their good-natured social circle, with Tham soon becoming my closest friend. Over numerous family meals with him and his wife Elsie and their two little daughters, I began to feel very much at home in my new city.

I moved out of the Majestic Hotel and had been living at the Hotel Malaysia for several months when one of our social group, Wong Yoke-meng, offered to rent a spacious furnished flat to Thian and me at a moderate cost. As a senior official with the Malaysian Ministry of Finance, Wong was provided with the two-bedroom flat in a prestigious central location of the city, however he and his family were living instead in a house in a trendy new neighbourhood called Petaling Jaya (commonly known as "PJ"). It was an extraordinary offer that Thian and I gladly accepted. Now I not only had a pleasant place in which to entertain friends, but I also was able to save some money, thanks to the two of us sharing living expenses. Indeed, we were even able to hire a live-in Chinese servant to take care of the cooking, cleaning and laundry for us.

Now well settled in KL, it was time to visit my family in Hong Kong. I was particularly anxious to see Aunt.

My mother had taken time off from her teaching duties to meet me at Kai Tak Airport. I was delighted to see that she looked and sounded as healthy and energetic as ever, but everything else felt so very different – the absence of Uncle's physical presence was painfully tangible to me, his smiling greeting having always been a huge part of my pleasure at returning home. I was grateful that Uncle Wah-chiu and Auntie Wan-fun had accompanied my mother that afternoon, just a few days before the start of Chinese New Year in 1965.

We chatted incessantly on our way to Hong Kong Central, where Aunt was attending a close friend's birthday banquet in a restaurant and awaiting my arrival. I spotted her across the room, dressed in mourning black, a white flower in her hair, playing mah-jong with friends at a corner table – a Chinese way of relieving sorrow for a little while. My heart was in my throat as I approached and gave her a loving hug.

I stayed close to Aunt throughout the evening and we went home to Pokfulam together by taxi – she no longer had a chauffeur. Times had indeed changed. The house had been converted into a duplex, with the upper floor providing living accommodations for Aunt and a self-contained flat on the ground floor rented out to a Chinese-American family. Aunt needed the rental income, as her inheritance from Uncle was limited due to the fact that he had supported both my brother's and my own education overseas. Forever the filial first daughter, she was still providing financial assistance to my grandmother and to distant relatives of my late grandfather in our ancestral village in Zhongshan. As well, she was paying the salaries of an aging housekeeper, a young domestic helper and a gardener who kept the property in good shape.

We had a lot to talk about. My brother had taken over Uncle's medical practice and was doing well, he and his family living in a nice flat and driving an American car, a classic symbol of success. Aunt shed a few happy tears that I too was at last able to stand on my own feet: her final mission had been accomplished.

Aunt had kept Uncle's old Mercedes in the garage, still carrying the historic "24" licence plate. She no longer liked to drive, she said, not without Uncle; however I managed to convince her to let me take her for a ride the following day. It took a while to get the old diesel engine started, but we finally set out to retrace the familiar route to Repulse Bay that we had enjoyed so often with Uncle during my growing-up years. It was truly a sentimental journey, and one I was grateful to be reliving with Aunt.

I took another sentimental journey during my seven-day visit home: I reconnected with Loretta. It had been almost six months since we had parted and she had finally left her unhappy marital home and moved in with her supportive parents. Our little time together was precious. I told her of the many things I enjoyed about Kuala Lumpur, hoping that one day she might join me there, and she was excited by the idea. That, however, was the extent of our dream. We both knew that the seeds we each had painstakingly planted – she in Hong Kong and me in Malaysia – still needed to be attended to and cultivated, so our future was unknowable.

The great majority of my time in Hong Kong was divided between Aunt and my mother, some nights spent at Pokfulam and others at the flat on Bonham Road with my parents, my grandmother (now an amazing ninety-five-year-old) and my sister. One evening, my mother pulled me aside to make a request. Dong-dong would be finishing secondary school the following year and was then to be admitted to an interior design school in London; my mother's savings would cover half of the travel, tuition and living expenses – could I help to cover the remainder?

Just as I too had done nine years earlier, Dong-dong had researched her best educational possibilities, and just as for me back then, financial uncertainty stood between her and her dream. I knew exactly the anxiety she was experiencing. Now it was time for me to deliver on my promise to Uncle's memory by showing my sister the same faith and hope that he had shown in me. Without hesitation, I said yes.

Back in Kuala Lumpur, tension had been building within the office over the disparity of salaries and benefits between expatriate and local architects, all of whom might be doing the same amount of work but the locals were not given any housing or car allowances or paid passages for home leave. At the same time, Malaysian corporate culture was rapidly transforming from colonial dominance to domestic self-sufficiency. The senior management of Booty Edwards – all five partners – now established a new policy on employment equity and incentive. Junior partnership positions were offered to three of us in KL – Doug Sanger, Alex Foo and me – and also to another senior architect working in the Singapore office. Doug turned down the offer, preferring to continue enjoying the benefits he received as an expatriate, but I could not resist the prestige and perceived reward of becoming a partner, even a junior one.

Within hours of formally accepting the offer, my expatriate pay, my housing and car allowances and my home leave privileges were discontinued and a five percent share of the firm's monthly profits took their place. Of course, there was always a risk of profits turning to losses, but at twenty-eight I felt that was a chance worth taking.

To further cut costs, the firm also decided to change the status of our branch office in Ipoh, a city some two hundred kilometres north of Kuala Lumpur (one hundred and twenty-five miles). It would from now on be operated by an independent agent and the contract was offered to Thian, an offer he accepted. After his departure, I continued living in the flat alone.

With my new status as a partner of Booty Edwards, my community of friends in KL began to expand. Aunt connected me with Pearl Eu, the elder daughter of one of her close Hong Kong friends who had married into the influential Eu family of Malaysia and Singapore. Pearl and her husband John kindly welcomed me into their social circle which included such people as Ong Hock Thye, the first ethnic Chinese to be appointed Malaysia's Chief Justice, and Yong Pung-how, who was to become the Chief Justice of Singapore.

I felt honoured to be accepted by these distinguished people and enjoyed numerous informal dinners in their unpretentious company, many of our evenings ending in friendly competition at a ten-pin bowling alley. I had the feeling too that those with marriageable daughters were interested in my status as a single, Chinese, British-educated professional who was associated with a respected firm in KL. They had no way of knowing that this bachelor's heart was already spoken for back in Hong Kong.

John Eu invited me to join the Royal Lake Club, of which he was a board member. This long-established social institution had successfully transitioned from an exclusive colonial clique into an open multi-racial club in keeping with the changing environment of an independent Malaysia, and I particularly relished the opportunity to re-ignite my love of performance by playing the piano at social events and helping create lively entertainment evenings at the club. Within months, I was invited to join the board of governors myself.

Less than a year after arriving in KL, I felt pleasantly secure, both professionally and socially. I did not see what lay ahead.

The creation of Malaysia by the merger of Malaya, Sabah, Sarawak and Singapore in 1963, just two years earlier, had been a marriage of convenience to free their respective peoples from British colonial rule. It did not take long for the marriage to turn sour. After much heated ideological conflict between Malay and Chinese interests, the Malaysian parliament voted to expel Singapore from the federation in the summer of 1965 and Singapore's secession and independence became official that August.

This schism had a negative effect on the political stability of the region. That, along with Indonesia's continuing opposition to the very concept of Malaysia, led to an economic slowdown and a number of Booty Edwards' major projects, including a new Hilton Hotel, were put on hold. With the completion of the Chartered Bank high-rise and several minor projects for other banks, there was no new work on the horizon for Mr. Merer's team. The office in nearby Brunei, however, was busier than ever following the recent discovery of a major oil and gas field, and so, within a few weeks of the Singapore secession, Mr. Merer departed for Brunei.

I was left to attend to the completion of a small list of projects, with no mentor and with no support from Mr. Loo. My future prospects with Booty Edwards in KL were suddenly in question. Mr. Merer had indicated that I might be needed in Brunei, but my instincts told me that I should start exploring other options as well, after all I had a sister to support and needed to be prepared for potential rainy days ahead.

Wong Yoke-meng, whose flat I was renting, suggested that I consider starting my own practice as he and many of his civil service colleagues were planning to build new homes, thanks to generous financial assistance from their employer, the Malaysian government. Though my loyalty was to Mr. Merer, I did not see any harm in taking a few exploratory steps. Thian, already operating the independent practice in Ipoh, was keen on joining forces with me, believing that our mutual friend Wong might be able to open even more doors for us with the government. We had business cards printed and I set up meetings with Wong's house-planning colleagues, soon discovering that dealing with a group of clients, each of whom has his own unique design requirements but no independent financial resources, was a time-consuming and unprofitable business. However, I was willing to be patient and to keep my options open.

Then the riot occurred.

Even after the secession of Singapore, racial tension still existed between the Chinese and Malay in Malaysia and things came to a head towards the end of 1965 in the form of a riot in central Kuala Lumpur. Curfew was imposed and things calmed down within two days, however it was a frightening experience. The homes of the Agong (head of state) and many senior government officials were in my neighbourhood and so it was cordoned off by the military, stranding me in the flat. My confidence and hope for a bright future in Malaysia was shaken. That's when Mr. Merer called and asked me to join him in Brunei.

It was difficult to think of leaving my many good friends in KL to start over in a new country. It was difficult to give up on the potential business partnership with Thian. But for earning my "bowl of rice", what other choice did I have?

I left Kuala Lumpur in early 1966 on a Malaysia-Singapore Airlines Fokker F27 Friendship airplane, catching a connection to Brunei in Singapore.

THE LAST STRONGHOLD OF THE EMPIRE

For some unknown reason, though Booty Edwards had been executing architectural and engineering works in Brunei since the early 1900s, even working on the original Istana Nurul Iman (Sultan's Palace) and the landmark Omar Ali Saifuddin Mosque, no office had been established there until very recently, things having been run from Kuching in Sarawak instead. Peter Merer, with his engaging personality, was the ideal person to now cement our firm's physical presence in the oil-rich sultanate.

Mr. Merer greeted me as warmly as always on my arrival at the airport in Brunei Town (renamed Bandar Seri Begawan just a few years later). He was accompanied by David Blatchford, whose transferral to the Kuching office four years earlier had led to my being promoted to senior assistant architect in the London office. David was in Brunei to assist Mr. Merer only until my arrival, as he and his wife had "fallen in love" with Kuching and had no intention of leaving that city. I sensed right away that there was important work to be done in Brunei.

A room had been booked for me at a hotel favoured by expatriates and nicknamed The Brunei Hilton, no doubt in derision of the fact that it was rather dated and gloomy. It was conveniently located, however, and within easy walking distance of the Booty Edwards office. I reported for work bright and early next morning.

The office was on the upper floor of a two-storey building overlooking the Padang (open square), with other offices in an adjacent wing on the same floor occupied by firms of engineers and quantity surveyors, the same ones that had been associated with us in London. The ground floor was home to the city's only branch of the Hong Kong and Shanghai Bank. Directly across the square from us, colonial-style buildings housed key government departments, evidence that we were strategically located to give the impression of a strong presence in the country.

I was introduced as the "Visiting Senior Architect" to the staff, all of them Chinese including the office secretary, Mrs. Fong, who was originally from Hong Kong. Mr. Merer explained that the small size of the office was due to the fact that few qualified people wanted to transfer to Brunei because it was still considered a developing country and it would be too costly to lure them with expensive benefit packages. His intention was to have the designs and drawings physically produced back in Kuala Lumpur and for me to travel back and forth between the two offices as needed in order to supervise the various projects on hand.

That first morning, he took me to a meeting with a senior government official in one of the offices across the square, introducing me as his right hand man. Booty Edwards had been commissioned to do Brunei's parliament building complex, for which preliminary drawings had been produced a few years earlier. The government official, an Englishman, assumed that I had already been involved with the project and instructed me that the seating layout in the main chamber should be modelled after the British House of Commons. Knowing that the Sultan of Brunei had supreme power and presided over the legislature, I as tactfully as possible raised the point that the configuration of Westminster is designed to facilitate a ruling party and an official opposition. Without blinking, he smiled and said, "Build it anyway."

For the next few months, I was kept busy working on the parliamentary drawings and overseeing the conceptual designs for a school and a hospital in Tutong, about forty kilometres (twenty-five miles) to the west of Brunei Town. When Mr. Merer went back to England on holiday, I was left to manage all the projects during his month-long absence.

Living in Brunei as a single person was a lonely affair, even with a car for getting around in – Mrs. Fong had helped me find an old Toyota to lease. A dreary bedroom in the 'Brunei Hilton' and that hostelry's dated restaurant were my home territory, quite a contrast to the comfortable flat and personal cook I had enjoyed in Kuala Lumpur. Fortunately, there was a tiny bookstore in the hotel lobby and I filled many an hour immersed in its stock of Ian Fleming novels, devouring all fourteen in the James Bond series.

Most Saturday afternoons I went straight from the office – we worked half a day on Saturdays – to the Royal Brunei Yacht Club. This was where the elite of the expatriate community socialized, including Brunei's chief of police (a retired Scottish officer from Rhodesia), the head of Radio Brunei (a retired American radio broadcaster), the head of Brunei's Finance Department (a retired British accountant), and John Gray, manager of the Hong Kong and Shanghai Bank who was later to become executive chairman of the HSBC Corporation. As a junior partner in Booty Edwards, I was included in this expatriate circle. In spite of the club's name, there was a great deal more drinking than boating going on there most weekends in 1966 and so within mere months my waistline had expanded by several inches, thanks to too many Tiger beers downed over copious games of Liar's Dice.

On Sundays, I was often invited to brunch at the home of one expatriate acquaintance or another. Traditional curry dishes were served by their Malay household staff, the meal always preceded by sherry, accompanied by beer and concluding with port – oh the waistline! Sunday afternoon was family time for these married friends, usually involving a trip to the beach or shopping at the Royal Dutch/Shell Petroleum company store in nearby Tutong. As for me, Sunday afternoons were for napping, frequently followed by a movie at a cinema near my hotel.

Not all my recreational life was quite so sedentary, however. I joined the local chapter of the Hash House Harriers, a non-competitive running and social club for expatriates with branches in many countries. The running part involved a version of a paper chase, with participants tracking a trail laid by a front runner and ending up at a finishing point where liquid refreshments ensured some good-natured socializing. We met once a week, usually on a country road, and started off at the blow of a whistle by our leader, a British Gurkha officer, following a newly-laid trail through wooded areas and often through a kampong (a Malay village) or two.

This weekly event was physically demanding, thanks to my expanding girth, and I often had to struggle to keep up. It was also quite intense, as I had been fed stories of machete-wielding villagers threatening intruders who accidentally trod on their vegetable plots, so I was extremely nervous about being left behind and getting lost in a kampong as evening darkness was falling.

The consolation of the chase, however, came at the end of the trail. A jeep was always waiting for us, loaded with cases of chilled beer that were served out by the Gurkha officer's men. After quenching our thirst with these 'military supplies', we usually then made our way to the only decent Chinese restaurant in town, where the regular patrons had become used to the weekly scene of a bunch of rowdy Westerners in sweat-soaked tee shirts and shorts taking over the place. No doubt my Chinese features made me a conspicuous member of the intrusive group.

One day, this restaurant, along with all other eating facilities in Brunei Town, was shut down without notice by the Health Department because of a cholera alert. I suddenly found myself with no access to cooked food. Once again, Mrs. Fong helped me out. She invited me to her home to share her family's meals, turning a difficult situation into a delightful one as I now enjoyed some delicious Hong Kong-style home cooking. This was one of many kindnesses I experienced from the Booty Edwards office staff during my time in Brunei, possibly in part because they appreciated the experience of finally working for someone who spoke their Chinese dialect.

The tactics for dealing with Brunei government officials at that time were an eye-opener for me. One of our projects was ready for construction and only required approval from the Department of Electrical Services, the head of which was an Englishman notorious for his 'collaboration' with local electrical contractors. Asked to give the green light to our project, he instead insisted that there was insufficient power supply on the site and imposed the requirement for an electrical substation to be built at a cost of many thousands of dollars. Our own electrical engineer,

who was Indian-Malaysian, disagreed, pronouncing the demand prepos-
terous as the project required very limited power. Mr. Merer brought in
an electrical engineering consultant all the way from London. When
the three of us got together with the demanding government official,
the matter was quickly settled "between Englishmen", with the official
now agreeing that an electrical substation was indeed not required.

This incident with the Department of Electrical Services turned out
to be relatively minor, however, in comparison to my encounter with
the Chinese building contractor who had been awarded the contract for
the Brunei parliament building complex.

My review of the preliminary drawings had caused me a good deal of
concern, as I considered the design not up to the standard appropriate
for such a prestigious project. As well, many construction details were
lacking and would certainly give room for the contractor to lay claims
for extra costs due to required changes during construction. Some dras-
tic revisions were needed. I made the necessary improvements and then
called in the contractor for a meeting, with the intention of negotiating
needed changes to the technical requirements in the contract that had
already been awarded to him. Recognizing that he was an influential
person in the Brunei business community and probably well connected
with government authorities, I was cautious and tactful in my approach,
but he did not take it at all well, even threatening that I should "watch
my back" in Kuala Lumpur. I did not think too much of this at the time.

I was in KL a few weeks later to continue working on drawings. Mr.
Merer was also there. One afternoon, he called me in for a meeting in
Mr. Loo's office, which was rather unusual as I had very few dealings
with Mr. Loo. Fleetingly, I wondered if it could be something about
my junior partnership – perhaps I was being considered for a promo-

tion. The grim expression on their faces as I entered the office, however, immediately indicated otherwise.

I was told to sit down and it was then that I spotted lying on the desk one of the business cards that had been printed for my potential joint venture with Thian some months back. Mr. Loo began accusing me of dishonesty and disloyalty to Booty Edwards. I was shocked. Realizing how it must look to them, I began apologizing profoundly for having made such a mistake, but was abruptly silenced and told to return to my workstation. I was deeply shaken. Who could have tipped off Mr. Loo about the fact that I had considered starting up in private practice? Was this the revenge the Brunei contractor had threatened? I left the office early, unable to concentrate on any work.

Next morning, Mr. Merer had already headed back to Brunei and Mr. Loo's secretary handed me a sealed envelope containing a letter of dismissal signed by her boss. Gathering up my belongings, I walked out without a word of goodbye to anyone.

I felt I owed Mr. Merer an explanation and called him that night. As soon as he picked up the phone, he asked if I could return to Brunei right away, clearly unaware that Mr. Loo had acted quickly to terminate my employment. I told him of the dismissal letter. I also told him of my deep appreciation for his mentorship and support throughout the past four years and apologized sincerely for having let him down. Those were to be my last words to my hero and friend.

The time had come for me to leave Malaysia.

My good friend Tham did what he could to console me and then helped me sell my Austin Mini. I terminated my tenancy of Wong Yoke-meng's flat, thanking him for his generosity. Finally, I went to say goodbye to John and Pearl Eu.

John, ever kind, told me about a job opportunity he knew of in South Vietnam, where an American organization was building orphanages and they were looking for a resident architect. And so it was that en route home to Hong Kong I stopped in Singapore for an interview with John's brother, who was responsible for the hiring. U.S. involvement in the anti-Communist war in Vietnam was escalating in 1966, however I was told that the job site in Saigon was well protected as it was directly across the highway from an American military base, and also I would be put up in a "safe" hotel and need not worry "too much" about Viet Cong attacks. I would be paid extremely well in U.S. dollars, he said, and the money would be deposited into an account set up for me in Switzerland. I was filled with relief. My life appeared to be almost instantaneously rebounding from depressing crisis to unique opportunity – but my instinct told me that I should take time to think about the offer, or at least to consult with Loretta.

I promised to let him know my decision within days and boarded a flight for home.

Fate and Uncertainty | 6

Hong Kong (1966-67)

WORK AND THE FORTUNE TELLER

Reports of deadly attacks on American military bases in Vietnam were in the news frequently in the fall of 1966, so too were stories of South Vietnam's political instability, poor government leadership and systemic corruption. However, the U.S. government was continuing to pour in hundreds of millions of dollars, aiming to win over the South Vietnamese population from the Communist insurgents by providing them with education, social welfare and healthcare. It was obvious to me that there was money to be made there. Loretta, however, persuaded me that there had to be other options, safer options, for my work and our future. Though I had no clue what those options might be, I turned down the Saigon job offer.

With very little money in savings, I lived with Aunt in her flat at Pokfulam, keeping my eyes and ears open for opportunities. When I spotted an advertisement in the *South China Morning Post* for a position as a junior architect with a British firm newly established in Kowloon, I applied for it even though I was over-qualified. I met with the firm's principal who had flown in from London to set up the small office. He too had qualified at the AA School of Architecture and I was quickly offered – and accepted – the job although the salary was much lower than I expected. I started work the very next day, determined to maintain an income stream so that I could fulfill my commitment to my sister's education.

The firm had been commissioned to undertake a major renovation of the exterior of the St. George's Building, a prominent office tower on Ice House Street in Hong Kong Central. The senior architect appeared to be more interested in organizing contractors for renovations to his own home, so a lot of the work fell to me, work that I found rather tedious in comparison to the diversity of projects I had been working on during the past few years. I was desperately in need of finding another option for my future.

Since his return from Winnipeg some five years earlier, my brother had become a founding member of the Canadian University Association of Hong Kong, bringing him into regular contact with people attached to the Canadian Commission (renamed the Canadian Consulate General in 1997). He heard there were good employment opportunities in Canada, particularly now with the planning for Expo 67, the World's Fair scheduled to begin in less than a year's time in Montreal. In addition, he learned that Canada had revised its immigration selection system, seeking professionals and skilled workers by giving preference to such things as education, experience, adaptability and language proficiency. This replaced a system that had heavily favoured European ethnicity over everything else, virtually eliminating most non-white applicants – indeed for some decades Canada's Chinese Immigration Act had largely excluded any Chinese from entering the country. Now, Canada had one of the most liberal immigration policies in the developed world, partly because its expanding industrial base required skilled workers at a time when many Canadians were being lured south to the United States.

And so I decided it would do no harm to submit an application to the Commission, even though I had never considered making a life in Canada. Meanwhile, I reconnected with Peter Pun, a civil engineer with whom I had become good friends in England when he was enrolled in graduate studies at the University of London, and he introduced me to his friend and associate Jon Prescott, a British architect in his forties and a senior partner at the firm that had made its name with the design of the new Hong Kong Ocean Terminal. Jon had earned a reputation as a gifted architect and urban planner and when we met for lunch I was impressed by his openness and cheerful manner. He told me that he was in the process of establishing his own practice and needed someone to handle the projects he had landed, while he himself was subsidizing his income as a visiting lecturer at the University of Hong Kong. Our meeting went very well and his tentative offer of employment was generous. We parted with him promising to get back to me with a final decision within forty-eight hours.

Now I had two potential options for my future – working in Hong Kong for Jon Prescott or possibly emigrating to Canada – and the uncertainty was nerve-wracking. And not just for me. Loretta decided to ask a friend to set up an appointment for us with a palm reader of good reputation.

When we entered his small chamber on the upper floor of a low-rise building in a residential neighbourhood of Kowloon, the fortuneteller greeted us as though he could see us, although his eyes were completely sightless. He got down to business right away, explaining that his method of *suan ming* ("life prediction") was to feel the palm with his fingers. First, he asked me to give him a word and instinctively I said "*Kung*" ("Work"), then he asked for my right hand and began to go over its palm meticulously with his right thumb, sometimes in forward and backward directions, other times with side and circular movements. Then came his predictions.

"At present you are holding onto a job that you don't like," he stated firmly. "There will be a new job that you do like in a place with its back against a hill and its front facing water to the north. This will happen after five days but not later than one week from now. If it does not come true, you can come back and tear down my signboard."

I was astounded. He was certainly accurate about my dissatisfaction with my current work, and I knew that Jon Prescott's home office at mid-level Hong Kong had its back to The Peak while its front over-looked Victoria Harbour to the north. But his time prediction had to be off, as Jon had promised to get back to me within two days, not five.

As I got up to leave, he had some additional words for me, "My friend, you should eventually go to live in a cold place as far away as you can. It will be good for you." I was again amazed, thinking about my application for immigration into Canada.

I called Jon Prescott's home that evening, as it was now two days since our meeting. Jon was not there. His wife informed me that he had left for England because his father was ill, but he would be back in Hong Kong in a few days time. And so it came to pass that I indeed started a job I liked "after five days but not later than one week" from the *suan ming* session, when Jon arrived home and took me on as his assistant architect. As far as I was concerned, the fortuneteller's signboard would remain in place.

I arrived at Jon's home studio every weekday morning just before he escorted his four young children to school and headed off to his duties at the university. His wife Ann, a gentle and kind lady, often welcomed me with coffee. Jon usually returned in the afternoon to go over my work before we retreated to his spacious roof terrace to enjoy the magnificent harbour view and a glass of wine. Sometimes Ann would join in our stimulating discussions covering a wide range of topics and we soon developed a close friendship.

Jon was of the new generation of British professionals who were liked and respected by Hong Kong locals because they were down-to-earth and fair minded. In many cases, the success of expatriate professionals was due to the tendency of *sūng yeúng* ("looking up to foreigners"), he and I conceded over our wine, some locals preferring to engage English architects or lawyers even for a higher fee because they were perceived to be more prestigious or to be more effective in dealing with the government. Our mutual friend Peter Pun, however, maintained that the public perception of strong local Chinese involvement was equally as important to the success of a business. As an English-trained local Chinese, I was someone who appeared to bridge both worlds, and that may be why Peter eventually made it clear that he wanted to hire me himself.

Peter Pun was a good friend of the son-in-law of Sir Run Run Shaw, head of Shaw Brothers, the largest movie production company in Hong Kong, which in 1966 was producing more than forty films a year, a new one starting every nine days. Peter had been engaged to design an expansion to the studios at Clearwater Bay so as to provide a blue-screen projection studio, a warehouse for props, and living quarters for actors. As a civil engineer by training, Peter needed a qualified architect on the job. I turned out to be his choice and Jon agreed to let me go, as he was beginning to find it uneconomical to keep me on.

Just like their film production schedule, the designs and drawings for the Shaw Brothers' new studio facilities had to be executed and completed at lightning speed. The blue-screen projection studio was urgently needed as action movies had become very popular and close-up action scenes were shot in the studio in front of a blank screen, to be superimposed later onto a background scene filmed elsewhere. Parallel to the development of these technical facilities was the need to accommodate an expanding number of new actors, who had to be both trained and housed at the studio.

As the only architect in Peter's office, my workload was heavy and I relished the challenge throughout the first six months of 1967.

BORROWED PLACE – BORROWED TIME

History was unfolding dramatically all around Hong Kong, and Hong Kong could not escape its spillover effects.

To the north, the People's Republic of China was in turmoil. Mao Zedong, Chairman of the Communist Party of China, had launched the Great Proletarian Cultural Revolution in the spring of 1966, with the goal of removing capitalist, traditional and cultural elements from Chinese society and imposing his own brand of socialism. He alleged that liberal bourgeois elements had permeated every aspect of Chinese society and issued a call for the removal of these elements through violent revolution. China's youth, responding to his appeal, formed Red Guard units, a paramilitary social movement that spread throughout the countryside and into every urban centre, resulting in social, political and economic upheaval, widespread persecution, and the destruction of historical sites, antiquities and culture.

To the west of Hong Kong, Macau was also in turmoil. Riots backed by pro-Communist unions erupted in the Portuguese colony in December 1966. Then, following a general strike in January 1967, the Portuguese government agreed to meet many of the pro-Communist demands, placing the colony under the *de facto* control of the People's Republic of China.

In Hong Kong itself, labour unrest was stickhandled into large-scale demonstrations against British colonial rule, beginning in March 1967.

During one particular labour dispute in a Kowloon artificial flower factory in May, picketers clashed with management, riot police were called in, workers were injured and many were arrested. Union representatives protested and they too were arrested, a moment they declared to be the start of Hong Kong's own Cultural Revolution. A series of noisy street protests along with demonstrations and stone throwing outside of Government House ensued, with demonstrators brandishing copies of Mao's quotations, the iconic Little Red Book, shouting slogans condemning "The running dogs", meaning any persons who engaged with capitalist Britain.

Things escalated. Pro-Communist newspapers launched attacks on the colonial authorities. In Central District, loudspeakers broadcast anti-colonial messages from the roof of the Bank of China Building, to which the government responded by setting up even more powerful loudspeakers across the street to transmit Chinese operas and music. Workers in the essential services went on strike. Pro-Communist schools sent students to support the public demonstrations and some movie stars joined in. Bombs were planted and there were casualties on both sides. Curfews were imposed and the police were granted special powers in an attempt to quell the unrest. The high-water mark of this challenge to colonialism was a cross-border raid by Chinese Communist militia on a Hong Kong police post in the New Territories, during which five policemen were killed and eleven wounded.

Governor Sir David Trench dealt with the situation by taking firm but measured action, attempting to achieve a balance between provoking an escalation of the situation and of appearing to be weak. Government intelligence and the reaction in Beijing, which took the form of rhetoric rather than action, told the British that the situation was largely the result of local initiatives, and so they proceeded to work on the premise that Beijing did not intend to force a showdown over the future of Hong Kong at this time, though no one could rule out such an eventuality if the confrontation were to escalate out of control.

Just as the disturbances in Hong Kong had escalated in the heat of the mania of mainland China's Cultural Revolution, so too they began to diminish when that revolution entered a less volatile phase towards the end of 1967. Despite continuing its public rhetoric, the powers in Beijing instructed the leftist organizers in Hong Kong to end the confrontation and it almost instantly died down. During the eight months it had lasted, however, fifty-one people had been killed, more than eight hundred had sustained injuries, and five thousand had been put under arrest.

Daily life on Hong Kong Island never came to a complete standstill throughout the time of upheaval. I still went to the office each day to work on the movie studio projects, simply detouring around roadblocks and marching, banner-waving, Little Red Book-wielding demonstrators. Loretta and her parents moved from Kowloon to the island, believing, as many did, that it was untouchable by China because, unlike the Kowloon or New Territories portions of Hong Kong, it had been ceded in perpetuity to Queen Victoria by the Qing Dynasty in 1842 via the Treaty of Nanking.

Even with the ending of the situation, we all realized that Hong Kong was facing serious social and political problems that were likely to result in more unrest. We also knew that all China had to do to take back Hong Kong, including the island, was to cut off the water supply or to open a floodgate of 'refugees' from bordering Guangdong province. One thing was certain: the future of Hong Kong lay not in the hands of anyone in the colony itself but in the hands of the powerful in Beijing.

The Canadian Commission was flooded with requests for immigration and for tourist visas. Processing of the applications soon became backed up. My own application, however, had been submitted before the start of the troubles and so, after interviews and medical checks, I was fairly quickly accepted.

Once again, I had a life-changing decision to make: continue working at Peter Pun's office in Hong Kong or make a fresh start in Canada. And once again, as in Kuala Lumpur, it was the upheaval created by civil unrest that turned the decision into one that became relatively easy. I could no longer see a bright future in my homeland.

Montreal topped the list as my preferred destination, a cosmopolitan city likely to be similar to those I had enjoyed in Europe, I thought. Loretta's parents decided to visit Expo 67 and to take Loretta, in the throes of learning to be single again, with them. That cinched my decision. Montreal it was.

I said goodbye to my family with sadness. My grandmother was now ninety-six years old and I had no way of knowing if I would ever see her again. Aunt was on her own at seventy-six and I knew she wanted to be independent but was going to miss me. My mother was still working hard, perhaps too hard for a fifty-six year old, and it was my fervent hope that she and my father would be able to join me in Canada in the not too distant future so I could take care of them in their retirement years.

Saying goodbye to Loretta was easier. We knew it would not be long before we would meet again, this time in Montreal – the "cold place, far away" of the fortuneteller's prediction.

Adjustments and Opportunities | 7

Canada (1967-1970)

CAREER AND FAMILY – JOY AND SORROW

My port of entry into Canada was Vancouver, British Columbia, and my first impression left much to be desired. Vancouver's international airport in 1967 was a rather small and aging building, suggesting a rather insignificant city, not at all in keeping with my expectations, and the weather was wet and gloomy in spite of it being summer. These feelings of anticlimax, however, were soon eclipsed by the huge sense of positive momentousness that swept over me when I read the words on the small stamped document that was ceremoniously stapled inside my British passport: "This card, when stamped by a Canadian immigration officer, is evidence that the rightful holder is a landed immigrant. This card is required for customs clearance and when making application for citizenship. It will also prove useful for many other purposes."

It was August 31, 1967. Canada was just two months into its second century as a nation and I was suddenly filled with a sense of enormous potential for the future. I was eager to continue on with the second leg of my journey that day. I was heading to Toronto, where a cousin of my mother, a retired businessman in his seventies, was expecting me. After researching employment prospects in Canada, I had recognized that

Ontario was the province offering the most job opportunities and so, though I was drawn to Montreal, Toronto had to be my first destination.

The flight across the continent filled me with amazement. How long it took to cross the country, the vastness of the mountain ranges and the unending prairies so sparsely dotted with signs of human habitation. The elderly gentleman sitting next to me must have noticed my astonishment and said, "Young man, this is the place of the future." I did not understand what he was getting at until years later, when I wished I'd had the foresight to somehow accumulate property in the western provinces back then, as all of them were to experience impressive economic growth in the years to come. At the time, however, the focus for this twenty-nine-year-old was on finding a job and putting a roof over my head.

While I was waiting for a taxi at the Toronto International Airport, a young man struck up a conversation, introducing himself as Jim. When I told him that I was a new immigrant, he responded with a hearty, "Welcome to Canada!" and shortly after, when his equally friendly mother came along in a car, they offered to drive me into the city. My encounter with these genial people gave me my first impression of Canadians, one that continues to this day: kind hearted and sincere, caring, unassuming and easygoing.

King Lee, my mother's cousin, lived slightly to the north of downtown Toronto. I had once been told that Uncle Lee had not used his real name to enter Canada, just like many other unskilled Chinese workers who emigrated in the 1930s. With limited education, he had endured years of strenuous work under poor conditions in restaurants and laundries, and living conditions had also been difficult, the house that he shared with other Chinese immigrants being poorly insulated and with minimal heating. Hard work and perseverance paid off and when the business and properties that Uncle Lee eventually owned in downtown Toronto were expropriated for a good price by the municipal government to accommodate the construction of a new city hall, he could afford to retire comfortably to a leafy residential neighbourhood, driving back to his old neighbourhood, Toronto's Chinatown, every day in his Cadillac to socialize with friends.

Encouraged by his success, I eagerly anticipated the opportunities that might lie ahead for me too in Canada.

Jon Prescott had put me in contact with an urban planner friend of his in Toronto who might be able to give advice or assistance on employment in the area. I visited Max Bacon at his home near the Don Valley, then considered to be on the outskirts of the city, and he liked what he saw in my portfolio. However he also advised me that job openings were limited for people with no Canadian work experience.

I found Toronto in 1967 to be surprisingly Anglo and lacking in the kind of cosmopolitan spirit I had enjoyed in European and Asian cities. My heart continued to pull me towards Montreal, however shortly before I was to leave Toronto to rendezvous there with Loretta and her family, Max Bacon arranged for me to meet his brother-in-law, Tony Griffiths, an English architect who was an associate with Murray & Murray Architects, an established firm based in Ottawa, Canada's capital city. Tony and a colleague were in Toronto on a recruiting assignment for the firm.

Tony was not too much older than me and we hit it off right away. By the time our meeting ended, I had gratefully accepted a tentative offer of a position as a project architect with Murray & Murray at a salary of seventy-five hundred dollars (Canadian, of course) a year. Though my research had indicated that the going rate for an architect with my qualifications and experience was closer to nine thousand dollars, I was anxious to begin gaining Canadian work experience. I agreed to meet with the firm's senior partners in Ottawa in two weeks time for a final interview, following my visit to Montreal during which I hoped to be able to explore that city's employment opportunities too.

Expo 67 and the vibrant city of Montreal offered the most exciting introduction to my new country. Expo is considered to have been the most successful World's Fair of the twentieth century with sixty-two nations exhibiting and more than fifty million visitors. The most popular pavilion was that of the Soviet Union which featured a replica of the Vostok 1 spacecraft in which Yuri Gagarin had made the first human flight into outer space just six years earlier. I was particularly impressed by the American pavilion, a huge geodesic dome designed by Buckminster Fuller, and by Habitat, a model housing complex designed by Israeli-Canadian architect Moshe Safdie. The fair and its host city were alive and buzzing.

It appeared to be a good time to be living in Canada, not least due to the recent introduction of major social programs including universal health care, the Canada Pension Plan, and post-secondary student loans. A forty-hour workweek had been instituted with a minimum two weeks of vacation time and an increased minimum wage. I began to feel that I had come to the right country. All I needed to kick-start my new life was a job that I could enjoy.

To my disappointment, I soon found out that work as an architect in Montreal was hard to come by. With the completion of the Expo site and its offshoot developments, many architectural and engineering firms were actually downsizing and their employees were moving west to seek other employment. I also detected an undercurrent of political discontent in the city, most evident in threats by the Front de libération du Québec, a paramilitary organization, to disrupt the World's Fair, though that never actually occurred. Also, just a few weeks prior to my arrival in Canada, French President Charles De Gaulle had caused an international incident when he ended a speech to thousands gathered at Montreal City Hall with an exhortation for a Quebec independent of Canada, , shouting out, "Vive Montréal! Vive le Québec! Vive le Québec libre!" It thus became obvious to me, especially with the standing offer from Murray & Murray, that Ottawa was a good compromise. Though technically in Ontario, the capital city sits right on the border of the Province of Quebec and Montreal is less than a two-hour drive away.

At the end of their visit to Canada, Loretta's family departed for Hong Kong, the riots there having died down sufficiently for their lives to begin to get back to normal. Standing next to Loretta, her mother looked at me steadily and said with a warm smile, "She's all yours." The stars were surely aligned. I was about to turn thirty and was embarking on a brand new life with the woman I loved.

Murray & Murray Architects had been founded six years earlier by two brothers from Ireland, Tim and Patrick Murray. As well as being architects, they had trained in town planning at the University of Liverpool, from which school both Jon Prescott and Max Bacon had also graduated. The Murray brothers had made a name for themselves in the profession and in the Ottawa community. When I arrived at their offices in mid-October 1967, I was greeted warmly by Tony Griffiths and introduced to the brothers. Tim was in the middle of putting his professional touch on a building perspective in his office and quickly handed me over to his younger brother, Pat, who reviewed my curriculum vitae and work portfolio, offering words of praise and then saying, "Welcome to our firm. Your salary will be seven thousand dollars a year." I was taken by surprise at this figure as it was lower than the offer made in Toronto, however I quickly recovered my composure, knowing that it was not worth risking losing my first job offer in Canada for the sake of five hundred dollars. I started work the following day.

Loretta and I were married quietly in a private ceremony in Ottawa, our three-year mostly-long-distance courtship having sealed our devotion to one another. We happily set up house in a very humble motel room equipped with an electric cooking ring so that we could prepare our own food. As I settled into my job and the anticipated drama of a Canadian winter fast approached, we decided we should purchase a car for ease of getting around. The brand new 1967 Plymouth Valiant cost us thirty-five hundred dollars, and on Loretta's advice I made a down payment of fifteen hundred and financed the balance over two years – I was quickly learning that a steady job in North America provided the collateral for borrowing money to buy things that otherwise one could not afford.

We each needed to pass a driving test in order to obtain our Ontario driver's licences to replace our international ones. We could not afford professional lessons and took turns practicing driving on the unfamiliar right-hand side of the road. Loretta took the official test first and passed with flying colours. My test, with the same examiner, followed immediately afterwards. At the end of it, he turned to me and said, "You made one serious mistake: You did not turn your head to look at the blind spot before changing lanes. I would fail you, if it was not for your wife who is a better driver than you." Thanks to Loretta, we each obtained a driver's licence that day and I would never again forget about the blind spot.

With the security of a regular income and the freedom of personal transportation, there was only one essential element missing from our life: a more comfortable home. Tony Griffiths and his wife Nan came to the rescue. Their house in the Golden Triangle area of Ottawa, a pleasant residential neighbourhood adjacent to the core of the city, had a one-bedroom apartment in the attic with its own separate entrance, and they generously offered it to us on a month-to-month basis at a rent we could afford. We also could park our car in their side driveway, close to an electrical outlet for the block heater that would keep the engine just warm enough to start without too much resistance in the fast-approaching winter.

Our first winter in this "cold place, far away" was truly unforgettable. We had to learn to dress in layers, after time and again finding ourselves sweating after moving from the frigid outdoors into a centrally-heated store or home, and I learned to expect a few moments of blindness as my frozen glasses fogged up in the sudden indoor warmth. We learned to adjust our driving practices too, going slower than normal and applying the brakes sufficiently gently to avoid skidding. When the car became stuck in the snow, we mastered the skill of rocking it from side to side while pushing it out of the obstruction, all the while trying not to hurt any back muscles in the process. We perfected the art of snow shovelling, without which there was no getting our car out of the driveway in the first place, and we learned not to be surprised when its keyhole froze up, keeping us locked out of the vehicle until the bright winter sun could warm things up a degree or so. Fortunately, our new abode was not far from the Murray & Murray offices and I could easily walk there. I could even slip home for lunch with Loretta, which I did as often as I could.

There was another advantage to our new accommodation arrangement. I was working directly under Tony, the firm's chief designer, and living upstairs in his house allowed me to sometimes bring work home to discuss with him in the evening. Tony had entrusted me with the development and production of a master plan for the campus of one of the province's two newly created colleges of applied arts and technology, Algonquin College. After completing the master plan, I was given the task of designing the first building on the Woodroffe Avenue campus, an expansive boiler house, essential for the heating and cooling of all the buildings that would follow. I expressed these essential technological functions architecturally by featuring exposed steel structures and impressive chimneys. Next, I designed the archetype for the covered pedestrian walkways that would link campus buildings, again applying modern steel configuration. I took pride in this work.

There is a Chinese saying, "Human beings should aim high; only water aims low." A good way for me to aim high in my career in my new homeland was to become licensed by the Ontario Association of Architects, the regulating body for the practice of architecture in the province. The fact that I was registered as an Associate of the Royal Institute of British Architects and had five years of professional experience already under my belt did not enable me to automatically attain an Ontario license. For that, I needed to accumulate two years of practice experience under the supervision of a person already licensed by the OAA and also complete a series of courses in Toronto over a period of no less than two years. At the end of all of that, I would become eligible to sit the Ontario licensing exam. I was buoyed by the fact that my job with Murray & Murray, though paying less than I'd hoped, was at least helping me fulfill the first requirement.

Then came the bombshell that shook me to my core.

My mother had once advised me that I should focus on building a solid foundation for my career before getting married. While the foundation-building had not always gone as smoothly as I had hoped, I was now in a promising phase of my professional life, was happily married, and finally in a position where I was confidently anticipating the day when my mother would retire and live comfortably with Loretta and me in Canada. But life for her did not turn out the way I wanted it to.

On February 16, 1968, not quite six months after I'd arrived in Canada, I received a telegram from Hong Kong. My mother had passed away on the operating table while undergoing emergency surgery. There had been no warning. I was devastated. She was still only fifty-six years old.

I subsequently learned that she had experienced severe stomach pain before being rushed to the hospital. Her symptoms indicated the possibility of pancreatic cancer and surgery had revealed that it was too late and the problem was incurable. I was filled with deep sadness that she had been unable to afford the regular health check-ups that might have provided early detection of her condition, and by the fact that none of her children were with her in her final hours, my brother and his family having recently returned to Winnipeg and my sister now studying in London.

I needed to be in Hong Kong right away, to be with her for one last time, to organize her funeral, and to bury her. I caught the first available flight.

I arrived in Hong Kong early in the morning and went straight to the funeral home. Sitting with my mother, I reflected deeply on her lifetime of loving care, her endurance as a working wife and attentive parent, her determination to make my studies in London a reality, and her unfailing faith in me and in my ability to build a good life. Beneath my grief, I experienced a profound sense of gratitude for having had her innate wisdom and gently portrayed high moral standards as a constant beacon in my life. That beacon would never dim.

Reverend Lew, the husband of my mother's goddaughter Milly, was in charge of the Chinese Christian Cemetery in Hong Kong, not very far from Aunt's house at Pokfulam and where my mother too had once lived. As she had been a highly respected and active church elder, Reverend Lew chose for her a burial plot on a slope with a commanding view of the waters of Victoria Harbour and close to the entrance to the cemetery, a spot usually attainable only by those of greater wealth. It was an enormous consolation to know that she would rest forever in a place with such good *feng shui* ("wind water", meaning auspicious orientation believed to help improve one's life, both before and after death). I applied my design skills – skills that my mother had helped make sure I gained – to the creation of her gravestone, choosing the form of the cross that she so loved and engraving it with the names of her children and grandchildren in Chinese to keep her company.

After settling the hospital and funeral accounts and making a donation in my mother's name to the Ying Wa Girls' School where she had been a teacher for so long, I once again bid goodbye to my grandmother, to Aunt, and to my father who, at the age of fifty-eight, would now have to take over the role of steady provider for his family for the first time in his life. En route back to Canada, I stopped over in London to reassure my grieving sister that at least the financial support for her education would continue.

I would now have to work harder in order to ensure this was indeed so.

THE STEPPING STONES

The success of Canada's new immigration selection system favouring professionals and skilled workers enabled employers to pick and choose among the growing number of qualified job applicants, making it possible for them to pay relatively low salaries. Educated immigrants were flooding in from Hong Kong (people seeking a more secure future away from the effects of China's Cultural Revolution), from the United States (tens of thousands of 'draft dodgers', young people wanting to avoid conscription into the Vietnam War), and from Czechoslovakia (refugees fleeing the Soviet-led invasion of August 1968). I realized it was not the most favourable time to be asking for a raise but I needed to increase my earnings so as to continue honouring my family commitments.

After almost a year with Murray & Murray, I sought Tony Griffiths' help in asking the brothers to increase my salary to nine thousand dollars, reflecting my professional performance and market inflation over the past year. He came back with their offer of eight thousand. I was disappointed, especially knowing that the norm for someone with my experience was nine. I realized then that the only way I could "aim higher" was by selling my newly-gained Canadian work experience to another employer – that way, if I chose to do so, I would be in a position to negotiate with Murray & Murray from a place of greater strength.

Massey and Flanders, Architects were advertising for an assistant architect. They were a small firm in Ottawa established by Hart Massey, son of Vincent Massey, Canada's first native-born Governor General, and by John Flanders, an architect from England. I was granted an interview at their offices not far from where I lived and was deeply impressed by a photo display in their lobby showing one of the firm's projects, a stunning home overlooking a small lake in Rockcliffe Park, a toney residential community adjacent to central Ottawa. The home design had received the Massey Medal for Architecture, the precursor of a Governor General's Medal. I had the distinct impression of a business established by a family of eminent stature.

Hart Massey was a quiet-spoken person of serious demeanour, quite short in height. The firm had recently been commissioned to design Innes College for the University of Toronto, he said. Two assistant architects, two technologists and a secretary had already been employed. Mr.

Massey liked what he saw in my portfolio, which now included samples of my Canadian work experience, and offered me a salary of ten thousand dollars a year. Without hesitation, I accepted.

When I handed in my notice at Murray & Murray, they appeared surprised at the amount of my new stipend, saying they regretted that they could not match it. We parted on good terms. I was immensely grateful for the experience I had gained with the firm and in particular for the support, encouragement and friendship of Tony Griffiths.

With Loretta's unceasing support, I was enjoying my responsibilities and my creativity as an architect – and also as a father. Our little son, Theodore-Ching – "Gift of God" (in Greek) plus "Upright" (in Chinese) – added to our joy and contentment. We spent weekends visiting with friends in Ottawa and in Montreal or heading up into the peace of the Gatineau Hills, a mere fifteen minutes by car from our downtown Ottawa home. There we hiked the wooded trails year round and in winter took downhill skiing lessons at Camp Fortune.

Pierre Elliott Trudeau became leader of the Liberal Party of Canada in April 1968. Two weeks later, he was sworn in as Prime Minister, soon thereafter calling a countrywide election and winning handily. His overt intellect and political acumen aroused passionate reactions among the people of Canada. Though forty-eight years old, he had become a symbol of generational change, not least because of his famous declaration as Minister of Justice: "There's no place for the state in the bedrooms of the nation."

The country was swept by an unprecedented wave of what the media dubbed Trudeaumania, reminding me of the excitement around the late John F. Kennedy. Trudeau dated movie stars and international celebrities, he drove sports cars and went white water canoeing, he was seen sliding down the banister in Ottawa's most elegant hotel, the Chateau Laurier. Almost overnight, my perception of Canada as a somewhat dull and rather conservative place disappeared and I was inspired to seize all the opportunities that surely lay ahead in such a youthful country.

Loretta and I had discovered that in Canada people with very little capital could borrow money to purchase an income property, anticipating that the profit to be made would be greater than the interest that had to be paid on the loan. There was a triplex (a building divided into three apartments) listed for sale for forty-eight thousand dollars on McLeod Street in the Golden Triangle neighbourhood where we were living, also within walking distance of the Massey and Flanders offices. The vendor was Commodore Frank Freeborn, a retired naval officer, who appeared to be quite eager to sell. He was also willing to assume a first mortgage of twenty-eight thousand dollars, repayable over thirty-five years at seven percent annual interest. We, however, needed to come up with the remaining twenty thousand as a down payment. After pooling together everything we had, including what was left of the forty-five hundred dollars in savings that I had brought with me from Hong Kong, we were able to raise fifteen thousand. We were still short by five thousand dollars.

I was prepared to upgrade the condition and value of the property myself by painting, fixing up the common area in the basement, providing laundry facilities, resurfacing the driveway with gravel, and installing outdoor electrical receptacles for vehicle plug-ins in winter. We figured we could live in one of the three apartments ourselves while the rent from the other two units, increased just slightly from their current amounts, would be sufficient to cover our interest, principal, property taxes and insurance obligations. I made some further calculations and recognized that if the purchase price were to be reduced by five thousand dollars, then the down payment we had managed to put together would be sufficient. So I made a counteroffer of thirty-eight thousand dollars, anticipating that Commodore Freeborn would settle halfway at forty-three thousand. Happily for us, that's exactly what happened.

An unanticipated bonus came with our new home. There was a large chesterfield (sofa) in the living room of the second floor apartment where Loretta and I planned to live. The commodore offered it to us at a reasonable price, but as an architect used to eye-balling measurements, I knew that the chesterfield could not be removed from the apartment without going to a lot of trouble such as taking down a door or dismantling a window, so I turned down the offer. When the Commodore handed over the premises, however, we discovered we'd acquired the chesterfield anyway.

It was 1969 and Loretta and I were now property owners in Canada. We fully resonated with the words of Ontario's unofficial anthem, *A Place to Stand, A Place to Grow*, a song of affirmation we had first heard at Expo 67, a mere eighteen months before.

As property owners, we were soon exposed to grassroots community politics. There was a proposal to construct an arterial road to facilitate traffic flow in and out of the downtown core and this major roadway would cut right through our community, requiring the demolition of houses and devaluing properties in the quiet neighbourhood of single family homes and small apartment buildings. A community meeting was organized, chaired by our friend Tony Griffiths whose home was also affected, and I was among the residents mobilized to protest the proposal to the representatives from City Hall and their traffic consultants who had been invited to address the meeting. The Centretown Citizens Community Association was born that evening, an association that would go from strength to strength in the following decades, playing a large role in area politics at every jurisdictional level.

Some of the speakers from the community that evening in 1969 would go on to assume important political responsibilities. Lorry Greenberg would be elected to City Council one year later and become Mayor of Ottawa in 1975. Michael Cassidy would also be elected to City Council in 1970, then become a Member of the Ontario Provincial Parliament in 1971, leader of the provincial New Democratic Party in 1978, and a federal Member of Parliament in 1984. Then there was Joe Cassey, who would be elected to City Council in 1979 and subsequently be re-elected to three additional terms.

Our protest culminated a few months later at the meeting of City Council where the vote on the arterial roadway, yeah or nay, was to be taken. To our immense relief, after minimal debate it was overturned in a majority decision. The integrity of the Golden Triangle neighbourhood, ideally situated between the small restaurants and retail stores of Elgin Street that formed the base of the triangle and the parklands bordering a curve in the Rideau Canal on the other two sides, had been saved.

Taking part in this community action made me feel that I had graduated from immigrant-hood into being a full participant in the Canadian way of life. It felt good.

As the population of Canada grew, so too did the bureaucracy of the federal government and its supporting services and industries in the nation's capital. The demand for housing in Ottawa was increasing steadily. I anticipated a healthy market for rental apartments and a gradual increase in their value, especially within the area where we lived, so close to Parliament Hill (home of the Parliament of Canada) and a great many government offices. By applying the same investment principles of leveraging on borrowed money, Loretta and I were able to purchase the triplex building right next door to our first one.

Many downtown rental units did not accept tenants with children. This had become a challenge for young parents, particularly those without cars, who worked downtown and needed to be able to get home in a hurry if there was a family emergency. I had a visit from one such person, a single mother, who was anxious to rent one of our newly acquired units, having been turned down by other landlords. Remembering what it had been like to experience bias from potential landlords during my student days in London, I unhesitatingly gave her a two-year lease. A short handful of years later, that young mother, Evelyn Gigantes, was to be elected to the Ontario provincial legislature and went on to win a seat there a total of five times. She even served as the province's Minister of Housing, in which capacity she, not surprisingly, facilitated the construction of affordable housing units and also voted to maintain a ceiling on rent increases.

My work on the Innes College project for Massey and Flanders was not stressful, as Hart Massey liked to keep a tight grip on every detail. The project reached its final design stage and was submitted to the University of Toronto along with preliminary construction cost estimates, and then, out of the blue, we were blindsided: there had been a change of mind and the client no longer wanted to proceed with the project. One by one, we were called into Mr. Massey's office. Termination was immediate, with compensation in the amount of one week's pay.

When I gave the bad news to Loretta, she showed very little concern. Instead, she suggested that this might be the opportunity for me to once again "aim higher" in my profession by going ahead and sitting the OAA provincial licensing exam, having now accumulated enough Ontario experience and having completed the requisite courses in Toronto. I could also seek the best North American qualifications possible, she added, and to enable that to happen she was willing to borrow money from her parents to supplement what we had managed to save. How beautifully she brought to my mind the Chinese philosophy of "In crisis lies opportunity."

I decided to study for a master's degree in urban planning, following the example of Jon Prescott and others I knew. This would expand my architectural training and professional profile by enabling me to look at design and construction in a wider context. As a mature student – I was now almost thirty-three – and with eight years of architectural practice behind me in England, in Asia and in Canada, I felt that I had a fair chance of competing for a place in a good school, the best school in North America that I could find. I narrowed the list down to four possibilities: the University of Toronto, the University of Pennsylvania, the Massachusetts Institute of Technology (MIT) and Harvard University.

To help in my decision, I wanted to visit each of the schools before formally applying. Being somewhat familiar with Toronto already, Loretta and I headed for the three U.S. campuses, making the University of Pennsylvania our first stop. Penn was offering an attractive two-and-a-half-year graduate program combining twin degrees in architecture and urban planning, however we were really put off by a traffic policeman who approached our car very brusquely while we were hesitating at an intersection in Philadelphia, his menacing black uniform and dark sunglasses giving us a very discomfiting feeling and his dismissive manner implying that it was insufferable for us to hold up traffic for even a few seconds, strangers in town or not.

Our next destination was Cambridge, Massachusetts, home to both MIT and Harvard. The unique environment of that city – a pleasant mixture of university campus facilities and supporting commercial development in very close proximity to Boston, a metropolis with a rich history and a vibrant Chinatown – immediately impressed us. Both MIT and Harvard offered two-year graduate programs in urban design with a wide range of course selections and the faculty members I met with were very accommodating. Loretta and I returned to Ottawa with a sense of eager excitement about the future.

I applied to Toronto, to MIT and to Harvard. Toronto responded first, even offering me a scholarship, but our delightful visit to Cambridge had made Loretta and me hopeful that we might have the opportunity to experience living there. When both MIT and Harvard also offered me placements, I found myself once again having to make a difficult major decision, torn between two schools, both of them ranked amongst the best universities in the world. Then I remembered Father Chan, Albert Chan, my Upper 6 Form Master and high school hero whose teachings had stirred in me a deep sense of my own identity and potential. I decided to follow in his footsteps and chose his alma mater, Harvard.

A few weeks later, I received a telephone call from Pat Murray seeking my help for his friend Basil Miska, a partner in the firm Miska and Gale, Architects. Miska and Gale had been engaged by the Tridel Group of Companies to participate in a design-build competition sponsored by the Ontario Housing Corporation (a provincial government agency charged with providing affordable housing) for a sizable development of medium-density housing in the Lowertown area of central Ottawa. They were desperately in need of an architect with experience in townhouse design and site planning, to be hired on a contract basis for the short duration of the competition. Having won the Ideal Home Competition in London and having gained experience in site planning on various projects in Brunei, I had the skills to fit the bill. I also was available and there was sufficient time for me to help out before leaving town for Harvard. The contract paid very little but I got down to work right away.

Basil Miska, in his forties, had been socially and politically active ever since arriving in Ottawa from Winnipeg many years earlier and was now well connected to people in the federal government. His partner Alastair Gale, an immigrant from England, was a more reserved individual. In his thirties, he was the 'behind the scenes' partner of the firm, overseeing day-to-day production and administration while leaving much of the business networking and marketing to Basil. Their staff of three technologists and a secretary-receptionist operated out of a three-storey brick house within short walking distance of my home, enabling me to get home quickly so I could spend the evenings studying for my upcoming OAA provincial professional practice exam.

I was given free rein in the design of the housing project and enjoyed the casual working atmosphere in the office. Basil had an easygoing manner and dry sense of humour: instead of promising me a cash bonus if my work won the competition for his firm, he pledged me his old skis and "maybe" also his drafting table.

In late August 1970, exactly three years after my arrival in Canada, I received two pieces of good news. I had passed the provincial exam and was now a Member of the Ontario Association of Architects (OAA) and automatically also a member of the Royal Architectural Institute of Canada (MRAIC) – I finally had a licence to practice independently, if I so chose. As well, my submission had won the competition, and Miska and Gale had been commissioned to proceed with the detailed design and construction of the Lowertown housing project.

These were indeed nice good-bye presents as I departed for Harvard. Returning to school eight years after graduating from the AA School of Architecture in London, and now with a wife and two small children – Theo had been joined by a little sister, Kim-Pui ("Charmingly beautiful" plus "Admirable") – I felt a great sense of responsibility. But this emotion was outweighed by an even stronger sense of positive anticipation for all the possibilities that lay ahead.

Basil Miska's parting words rang in my ears, "We work well together. Come back to see us when you finish."

The American Dream | 8

Harvard and Beyond (1970-1972)

A NEW PERSPECTIVE

L oretta and I headed south for Cambridge, Massachusetts, with our two little ones and all our basic household belongings loaded into a brand new Chevrolet station wagon that we were able to purchase tax-free for export because we would be living outside of Canada for more than six months. We were filled with excitement, though we knew our new life would also bring challenges.

As a university town, Cambridge was full of transient students and faculty members and rental apartments suitable for families with young children were rare. We were added to a waiting list for graduate student housing and in the meantime were fortunate to find a two-bedroom apartment on Harvard Street within walking distance of Gund Hall, the location of most of my classes. Harvard Street, in spite of the prestige that name implied, was in a rather unsafe neighbourhood – quite a change from peaceful Ottawa – with buildings in various stages of deterioration. There were definite compensations to our new lifestyle, however. We were amazed at the variety of consumer products available and at their prices. We bought our first colour television – a thirteen-inch RCA on a swivel base – for three hundred U.S. dollars, a much lower price than we would have had to pay in Canada.

My first day of classes in the Master of Architecture in Urban Design program at Harvard's Graduate School of Design was a refreshing experience. I relished the liberal learning environment and invigorating atmosphere – quite a contrast to the buttoned-down British-style education I had experienced throughout my life to date. The Harvard faculty discouraged passive learning, with lecturers acting more like orchestra conductors, drawing feedback from students and facilitating debate, discussion and the cross-fertilization of opinions and ideas.

Professor Wilhelm Viggo von Moltke, who had trained in Berlin and received his master's degree in architecture from Harvard in 1942, headed the urban design program. Most of the other faculty were much younger and they favoured long hair, beards and denim jeans, making it difficult to distinguish them from the student body, especially on a campus that was decidedly anti-establishment at a time when America was in the throes of the war in Vietnam.

With the exception of two of us from Canada and a few from Europe, the students in my urban design class were mostly young Americans, many of them fresh from undergraduate studies. Peter Turner was my fellow Ontarian, a graduate of the University of Toronto and, like me, with professional working experience under his belt. Then there was Mark Hall, an American close to my age who was married and had a son – he also had the luxury of a full scholarship from the U.S. National Science Foundation that included a generous allowance for living expenses. Peter, Mark and I quickly became good friends.

Apart from the mandatory urban design studios and workshops, I was able to set my own curriculum from an extensive range of courses. After a few months, however, I came to realize that none of them went deeply enough for my liking into the fields of economics, sociology and political science – the areas beyond the sphere of design that I wanted to develop in order to broaden and inform my practice of architecture. Mark Hall and Peter Turner felt the same way. We discovered that within the urban design program there were two other study streams, one of which – City Planning in Urban Design – included courses that could take us into these areas. In order to switch over to the new stream, however, besides passing a compulsory course in statistics, our request would have to be approved by a senior City Planning faculty member. Fortunately for us, Professor Francois Vigier enthusiastically agreed to do this for us, and Mark, Peter and I suddenly found ourselves in the Master of City Planning in Urban Design (MCU) program.

With this strategic change of focus, course selections became very appealing indeed. Professor Jim Brown, director of the Harvard-MIT Joint Center for Urban Studies, taught an engaging course on decision analysis, and happily for us he was also assigned as our mentor. MIT courses on social behaviour and the technology of change were now added to my curriculum and I was able to take advantage of the Harvard Law School library to support concurrent studies in the legal aspects of development planning.

If I were to choose my most inspiring teacher that first year at Harvard, it would have to be Mortimer Zuckerman, who was born in Montreal, entered McGill University at the age of sixteen and received a Master of Laws from Harvard at twenty-five. He taught a course on urban land economics, which included development strategies on how to increase the value of real estate – he would later validate his own teachings by becoming a real estate billionaire – and he provided access to supplementary lectures and case studies at Harvard Business School due to being an associate professor at that respected institution. His lectures were compelling and his presentation style entertaining – there was always an overflow of students in the theatre. It was his influence in particular that helped me build a solid foundation for my own professional and business development.

A HAIR-RAISING EXPERIENCE AND NIXON

Switching study streams required me to take more courses, each of which had a long reading list leading to more time spent in libraries. I was also taking more than the requisite number of courses so that I could graduate in eighteen months rather than the two-year standard, as being a student with a dependent family was an expensive undertaking. Getting to lectures at MIT and the Harvard Business School, both of which were further away from home than Gund Hall, also required extra time. As well, I usually took Theo to school each morning and picked him up in the afternoon, sometimes between lectures, as it was not safe for Loretta to travel alone through our neighbourhood. My schedule was jam-packed.

I began to notice my hair was falling out, not just a few at a time but in alarming clumps. This continued for several weeks to the point where I was almost becoming bald, so Loretta insisted I seek medical attention. A doctor at the Harvard University Health Services assured me that my condition was no cause for alarm and that baldness was common within the university community where people can be under a great deal of pressure. He agreed, however, to my request for a referral to a dermatologist, though I would have to wait almost a month for the appointment. Loretta decided to take matters into her own hands in the meantime.

She had heard that doctors of traditional Chinese medicine often use alcohol as an external stimulant for the body's internal system, so she purchased a small bottle of brandy and rubbed it gently into my scalp each evening until the day of my scheduled appointment. "Your hair is beginning to grow again," announced the dermatologist, examining my scalp with a magnifying glass and assuring me that there was nothing for me to worry about. I never did tell this Harvard medical specialist about our traditional Chinese treatment, which we continued for several more weeks until I once again had a full head of black hair.

To gain course credits, Mark Hall and I applied to the Harvard-MIT Urban Field Service in the summer of 1971. This was an on-going program established jointly by the two universities to facilitate urban renewal in Boston. Mark and I submitted a proposal for a development plan within the city's historic Chinatown, the hub of Asian-American life in the north-eastern states. We had consulted with the leaders of the local community association, had been offered the use of office space above the community administration office, and been promised local Chinese high school students as field assistants and also some funding from the state government. Our proposal was well received by the Urban Field Service. Tunney Lee, Professor of Architecture and Urban Studies and Planning at MIT, was assigned as our project advisor, the ideal person for the role because he had been born in Chinatown and had lived most of his life there.

The main goal of our project was to identify the neighbourhood's potential areas of renewal and then to formulate development strategies, all in consultation with local businesses and residents along with other key players such as Mayor Kevin White, city officials, government funding agencies, financial institutions, social program providers and developers. With the help of our team of summer students, Mark and I set up a field office with rudimentary furnishings and supplies. After extensive research and interviews with the stakeholders, we produced graphic displays and three-dimensional models of the various development options. We then invited all the stakeholders to join us in playing The Development Game, in which everyone gathered around the large master model and 'acted' their own community roles in the simulated development process. Through their ensuing discussions, arguments and exchange of ideas, development conflicts and potentials were identified, resolved and recorded, all of them contributing towards our final development concept plan. The seeds the community planted together that summer were to flower most conspicuously three decades later in the development of the long-awaited and much-heralded Boston Chinatown Master Plan 2010, created under the guidance of none other than Professor Lee.

My experience working in Chinatown that summer was fulfilling and invaluable. It also had its own unique hair-raising moment.

Working in the field office one afternoon, I had an unexpected visit from two well-dressed American men who quickly identified themselves as agents of the Federal Bureau of Investigation, the FBI, the U.S. agency that serves as both a criminal investigative body and an intelligence and counterintelligence service. They 'invited' me to accompany them to their car which was parked right outside and instructed me to get in the front passenger seat. One of the agents then took the driver's seat and the other the back seat directly behind me, instantly causing me to recall all kinds of threatening movie scenes: federal agents intimidating suspects and innocent people being strangled from behind by mobsters. None of that happened, of course. The agents handed me some photographs and asked if I recognized the man in them. When I said no, they told me that it was Neil Sheehan, a *New York Times* journalist who had given copies of top-secret federal documents to his newspaper for publication – and he also happened to have an apartment in the building where Loretta and I lived, and indeed some of the classified documents had been found there.

They were talking about the Pentagon Papers, whose recent publication had exposed the fact that successive presidential administrations had misled the American public regarding the chances for success in the Vietnam War. The journalist, Sheehan, had received the documents from Daniel Ellsberg, a military analyst who had leaked them in an effort to bring an end U.S. involvement in the conflict. Ellsberg would later be indicted on charges of stealing and holding secret documents, until the charges were dismissed after irregularities appeared in the government's case, including illegal wiretapping conducted by the covert special investigations unit that would, one year after my own FBI encounter, lead to the downfall of President Richard Nixon in the notorious Watergate scandal.

In the car that day, my mind was racing. Presumably the FBI had set up surveillance cameras and possibly telephone wiretaps on all the apartments in our building, and with my Asian profile and the amount of time I spent in Chinatown I had become a suspect by presumed association. Anything could happen now. The agent in the back seat muttered something to his colleague about me being a British subject and that I was "clean" and the next thing I knew I was politely released and they sped away. The startling experience had ended as suddenly and unexpectedly as it had begun.

I was later amazed at the realization that my own life had become linked, in a small way, to the Pentagon Papers and Watergate, two significant events in U.S. history.

After a year on the waiting list, Loretta and I finally got word that an apartment was available in the Peabody Terrace student housing complex. We were delighted. This grouping of high- and low-rise buildings adjacent to the Charles River had been designed by an icon of the modernist era, Josep Lluis Sert, who had served as Dean of the Harvard Graduate School of Design and had initiated the world's first degree program in urban design. Our three-bedroom apartment was on the second floor of a three-storey building, with a convenience store and laundry facilities on the ground floor and a parking garage and children's play area close by. The surroundings were much more pleasant than Harvard Street and, as if all of that was not enough, the rent was lower.

Mark Hall and his family also moved into the complex, enabling more spontaneity in our all-too-rare opportunities for socializing. Other neighbours included newly-weds Tricia Nixon, elder daughter of the U.S. president, and her husband Edward Cox, who was studying at Harvard Law School. But the presence of Secret Service agents there to protect the young couple did little to deter crime in the area. The bicycle I purchased for commuting to classes was stolen within a week, even though it had been chained to steel balustrades inside the enclosed entrance to our building. Much worse, Loretta witnessed a violent mugging in broad daylight in the parking lot visible from our kitchen window.

In spite of this, we were well contented with our new living conditions and continued to make the most of the bonuses of living in Cambridge. The pleasures were many. Proximity to fine museums and art galleries, Boston Pops concerts, MIT day camps for the children, feeding the swans in Boston Common, drive-in movie theatres, discount retail outlets, roadside stalls serving piping-hot baked clams, and beautiful New England scenery. All of it in combination created a uniquely enjoyable period in our family life.

However, we began to miss the enduring peace of our lives in Canada. I became eager to complete my studies even sooner than was possible on the fast track I had adopted and Loretta supported me in this, in spite of the additional work that cut dramatically into our scarce family time. And so it was that by the end of February 1972 I had earned enough credits to fulfill the requirements of the Master of City Planning in Urban Design program. I graduated with an MCU (Harvard) degree one full semester ahead of my class.

We were ready to return to Canada.

THE CROSS ROADS

Once again Loretta and I loaded our little ones into the station wagon and stowed our belongings in the back. This time, however, we also had overflow – household items we had accrued over the past sixteen months – and had to rent a small trailer to pull behind. First stop would be Montreal, but our final destination was still unknown.

Loretta and I had defined the markers we were looking for in our next home location. They included job security and advancement opportunities, good education for our children, accessible health care, personal safety, and social contacts. Now that I had obtained qualifications from a university of worldwide repute, the choices of location for my professional future had been opened wide but we knew that the U.S. was not for us at this time due to the lack of universal health care, challenges in its public school systems, personal safety issues, and the Vietnam War.

Having earned my licence to practice independently in Ontario, we looked closely at the possibilities within Canada. We had already established a base in Ottawa, of course, however that was more by happenstance than by choice. I still had a longing to live in a more cosmopolitan city.

Then there was Hong Kong. The economy there was improving and so too was stability, thanks to the winding down of the Cultural Revolution in China. As well, the Canadian government had recently established diplomatic relations with Beijing, one of the first Western countries to do so, making it less risky for Canadian citizens like Loretta and me – we were shortly to take our oaths of citizenship – to be living there in the event of conflict erupting between China and Hong Kong.

Once again, a major life decision had to be made.

Our immediate destination on the day we left Cambridge was Montreal and the home of our close friends Joe and Irene Yau. Loretta had known

Irene since her student days in London and our children and their little girl played well together. The five-hundred-kilometre journey north (three-hundred-plus miles) from Massachusetts took ten hours because of a heavy snowstorm, double the time it usually took, but our eagerness to be in Canada again surpassed any frustration at the difficult driving conditions. It felt good to be greeted with "Bonjour!" as we crossed the international border into Quebec. For the first time in my life, I knew what it was to 'feel' Canadian.

Joe and Irene welcomed us with a delicious Chinese hot pot dinner and kindly agreed to store many of our household belongings, all packed into parcels of various sizes, until we knew where we would be settling. We were leaving for Hong Kong in about a week. If we decided to stay there, Joe and Irene would forward the parcels to us, keeping for themselves, at our insistence, the colour TV and station wagon.

In Ottawa for a few days, we took care of some essential business and proudly took our oaths of Canadian citizenship. Before we left for Hong Kong I paid a courtesy visit to Basil Miska and Alastair Gale, who thanked me again for winning them the Lowertown housing project now under construction. Basil laughingly reminded me of my overdue "bonus" – his skis – though this time there was no mention of including his old drafting table to sweeten the pot; then, wishing me luck in Hong Kong, the partners promised to stay in touch in case I decided to return to Ottawa.

Our homecoming to Hong Kong in March 1972 was a joyous event for Loretta and me and for our families. My grandmother was almost one hundred and one and in amazingly good health under the care of her son, my father, who had turned sixty-three. Aunt was now eighty-one, still with lots of energy and still living at Pokfulam. Loretta's father and mother, in their late sixties and fifties, were still active in their business.

Both families were clearly overjoyed to be able to spend extended time with our two children.

Loretta's parents made us welcome in their home. We enrolled Theo in the Hong Kong International School, as English was his first language, and Loretta and I greatly appreciated the luxury of having babysitting readily available for toddler Kim, thanks to the household domestic helpers. It all seemed perfect and I was eager to investigate professional prospects in the city.

Jon Prescott was still teaching at the University of Hong Kong and practising architecture on his own, but he was thinking of moving his family to Australia. Peter Pun no longer handled architectural projects like the Shaw Brothers Studio, focussing instead on civil engineering contracts. The chances of my professional collaboration with either one of them appeared to be out of the question. Someone suggested I apply to the Architectural Division of the Department of Public Works, however I was convinced that my graduate degree from Harvard would most likely be considered overkill by the colonial civil service. And so, after a couple of months of dead ends, I felt myself becoming discouraged. The words of the fortune teller kept repeating in my mind and I began to wonder if I had given up on Canada – the faraway cold place – too soon.

Then, true to the Chinese proverb, "With time and patience the mulberry leaf becomes a silk gown," I received the phone call that was to set my life on its future path.

Basil Miska sounded excited. His friend Maurice Major, an Ottawa real estate agent, had told him that the People's Republic of China had just purchased a property in the Canadian capital for their permanent embassy and the grand old building would need to be renovated. Basil thought that I, "being Chinese", he said, was the "natural person" to approach the embassy about the provision of architectural services. He could not know how far-fetched that proposition sounded to someone born and raised in a British colony, who could barely speak one word of Mandarin, and who was currently living on the opposite side of the globe. Nevertheless, I appreciated his confidence in my abilities and recognized the potential benefit of a professional collaboration, if I could succeed in delivering what he wanted.

I promised to see what I could do. Then I made a plan.

With Aunt's help, I contacted Mr. Tsang, a legal assistant and Chinese translator in a Hong Kong law firm whom I had known in my younger days and who was a member of the congregation at Aunt's Chinese Lutheran Church. He kindly agreed to help me prepare a letter to the embassy on behalf of Miska and Gale. I composed the English draft introducing the firm, myself as its senior associate and liaison person, and offering our professional services. I also made reference to my Harvard qualification, as I knew that Ivy League universities are held in high esteem throughout Asia. The letter emphasized Miska and Gale as being a fully Canadian practice, implying an opportunity for Beijing to deepen relations with the first country in North America to officially recognize their government. I designed a new letterhead for the firm, featuring its name in Chinese printed in 'Communist' red, and then Mr. Tsang transcribed the letter by hand into simplified Chinese characters, the official written language of Beijing. The letter was sent to the embassy from the Miska and Gale office in Ottawa.

It was a long shot, I thought, but there was no harm in trying.

Architecture is the art of anticipation, I'd been told at the AA, because it creates structures that will be useful into the future. I decided to apply that same art to my life and began taking lessons in Mandarin, just in case the unlikely did happen, all the while continuing to investigate avenues of opportunity for work in Hong Kong. Aunt joined me for the Mandarin lessons and in between our weekly sessions I practiced conversing with the sales staff at the China Emporium, a large department store on Queens Road Central. The real test of my new language skills came out of the blue, however, after two months of silence from Ottawa during which I had all but given up on the embassy project. I was to contact Mr. Yuan, Fourth Secretary at the Chinese embassy, as soon as possible, said Basil Miska.

I called Secretary Yuan that evening, knowing that Ottawa was twelve hours behind Hong Kong time. Loretta was by my side, lending me courage as I struggled to express myself in Mandarin and to understand what was being said back to me. I got the impression that Secretary Yuan knew a lot about me, presumably from security checks into my background. In my nervousness with the language, I was conscious of my voice becoming louder and louder, but somehow I managed to get across what I needed to say and also to understand Secretary Yuan's "urgent" request for me to meet with him face-to-face in Ottawa. It appeared I had indeed managed to chart a potential new course for Miska and Gale, and hopefully also for myself.

After four months in Hong Kong, my family and I were returning to Ottawa.

As it turned out, we were, in point of fact, going home.

Little Theo loved to ski with his mom and me. Loretta and I introduced both our children to the pleasures of winter sports at an early age, starting with skiing because of the inviting trails and groomed slopes within easy distance of our Ottawa home.

(TOP): Clearing the snow from our 1967 Plymouth Valiant, de-icing its frozen locks, and driving safely through snow-packed streets was a new "sport" that Loretta and I had to master in our new country.

(BOTTOM): Our young family – Theo, the thoughtful older brother, and little Kim, the free-spirit – brought great joy to our home.

Proud papa with newborn daughter.

The Harvard graduate – with hair, thanks to ancient Chinese remedy (1972).

Architect and 9
Chinese-Canadian

(1972-1987)

It felt good to be back in Canada. Though our roots and formative years were deeply and forever planted in Hong Kong, Loretta and I experienced an emotional resonance with our adopted homeland – and with Ottawa in particular – that made it feel so much like our natural element in adulthood. It was where we had set up our first home as a couple, grown our young family, become property owners, and contributed to the well-being of the community. It was where we had created a space, both literal and figurative, that was uniquely, indisputably and comfortably our own. There was no doubt about it, Ottawa felt like home, and its fresh air and safe environment were simply the icing on the cake.

I was provided with a modest retainer for my services as an associate of Miska and Gale and I was counting on the Chinese embassy project to be firmed up so as to cement my future prospects with the firm. Within a month of our phone conversation, I met with Fourth Secretary Yuan at the embassy's temporary quarters, which had been set up in the penthouse of an apartment building not far from Parliament

Hill soon after formal relations between Canada and China had been established two years earlier.

A serious-looking man in his late fifties clad in a dark grey version of the obligatory Mao suit (a Chinese tunic suit), Fourth Secretary Yuan seemed pleased that I had kept my word in coming to see him so promptly. Canada was China's important new friend, he said, referring to the fact that the Canadian government had been the first in North America to recognize the government of the People's Republic. He was also clearly pleased to be dealing with someone of Chinese origin and appreciative of my efforts to communicate in elementary Mandarin. After some preliminary discussion, he announced that Miska and Gale were indeed to be entrusted with the design of the renovations to the embassy's new facilities. A site visit was scheduled for the following week.

The expansive four-storey stone edifice on St. Patrick Street in the Lowertown area of central Ottawa was appropriately imposing for the diplomatic quarters of an emerging major player on the world stage. It had been built in the 1860s on the banks of the Rideau River just a few hundred metres upstream of where it empties into the mighty Ottawa River and had served as the convent of the Good Shepherd Sisters for more than a century until they sold it to the Chinese government. It would be a major undertaking to transform the aged building into one that could fittingly accommodate an official residence for the Chinese Ambassador – it would be some years before the ambassadorial quarters would be moved out of the embassy into a residential community, as most countries preferred – plus living quarters for diplomatic and support staff along with the working offices for everyone in the consular, trade and various other governmental sections. The most pressing need, however, was for a garage large enough to house the embassy's fleet of cars.

Alastair Gale accompanied me on the first site visit. Fourth Secretary Yuan and several of his colleagues, all dressed in Mao suits, escorted us to an ancient elevator on the main floor and, to my surprise, it headed downwards rather than up. Instantly, images of the first James Bond movie flashed through my mind: Dr. No, of Chinese-European extraction and always shown in a Mao suit, had a secret facility full of weapons of mass destruction hidden under the ocean and accessed by elevators ominously "Going down". As it turned out, however, we were not even going underground as the building's main floor was almost a full storey above street level. When the elevator doors opened we found ourselves in what had been the nuns' laundry, an oversized room which, said Secretary Yuan, they hoped could be further enlarged by the addition of an extension out into the rear yard. This enlarged space would serve as the garage and he wanted it completed before the onset of winter.

Over the course of the next three months as I worked on this project, embassy staff members began to approach me with increasing trust – indeed a mutual trust was developing. New to Canada and Western culture, they were initially very cautious in their dealings with outside contacts and I felt honoured when they started looking to me for guidance about some of the many things that confused them, little things like the Western custom of standing throughout a social gathering, drink in hand, when the Chinese custom is to sit comfortably while networking. Some even approached me about personal matters, and so when it came time to launch into the second embassy project, with the garage successfully completed and operational, I did so with a great deal of personal commitment and enthusiasm.

The second assignment was the design and construction of a formal main entrance, creating the 'face' with which China would greet all who approached her embassy. In consultation with designers from Beijing, I conceived a dramatic yet understated canopy to shelter the wide flight of steps leading up to the expansive double-doorway in which would hang an imposing pair of tall, heavy, carved doors crafted in solid oak. It was during the final stage of executing this doorway that I received an urgent phone call at home very late on a Friday afternoon in mid-February. It was the embassy's First Secretary and he seemed to be in a panic: there was a wide open hole where the new doors were supposed to have been hung that day. Besides being left exposed to frigid temperatures and whatever winter storms might come over the course of the coming weekend, the embassy would also be far from secure until the doors would arrive on the Monday. Could I do anything?

By sheer good luck given the lateness in the day, the supplier answered when I phoned his workshop. The doors were indeed ready, he said, but all his men had left for the weekend and there was nothing he could do without them. I was shocked by this lack of concern but knew instinctively that it would be useless to protest so I simply told him that I would pick up the doors myself within the hour.

The early darkness of midwinter had descended and I was not a good night-time driver, however once again I was blessed by having the help of my dear wife who, as the driving examiner had so rightly declared, was superior behind the wheel and always a strong supporter of my work. We set off together on our mission of mercy. The newly crafted doors were extremely heavy – tough on the suspension system of our station wagon – and we were forced to make the fifty kilometre-journey (thirty miles) back to Ottawa at a snail's pace with the precious cargo protruding far out from the open tailgate. It was a cold and precarious ride indeed. I had alerted the embassy that we were on our way and so we were met at the front entrance by the resident carpenters who quickly had the doors installed under the watchful eye of a greatly relieved First Secretary. We were *all* greatly relieved. They were very appreciative of

Loretta's and my efforts and I also like to think that we helped them realize that "Comrades of the working class" and "Bourgeois architect and his wife" were not such disparate entities after all.

This diverted catastrophe led to many marvellous experiences. Loretta and I became frequent guests at the embassy, enjoying sumptuous dinners prepared by chefs from mainland China and deepening our friendships with those around the table. As is traditional, *jingjiŭ* ("toasting") was an important part of these occasions, usually committing to ongoing friendship, success and good health. To participate in these toasts, everyone stood up, glass raised in the right hand while supported on the bottom by the left, each person endeavouring to hold their glass lower than those of others in order to indicate respect. Many people could toast to one person but it was not appropriate for one person to toast a group unless the toast presenter was the leader of the group. Serious toasting required participants to *gānbēi* ("dry glass", meaning to drink the whole glass in one gulp) and I quickly learned that it was considered impolite not to reciprocate when others *gānbēi*. I was beginning to master mainland Chinese social etiquette. I could not have imagined that this knowledge would be of benefit a few years down the road when I would find myself embarked on a new career.

The embassy continued to seek my professional input on various projects over the course of the next several years, including the renovation and expansion of a nearby property on Cobourg Street for their Educational Affairs section and the assessment of another off-site facility on Stewart Street for housing China's official press agency, the Xinhua News Agency. Friendships with staff members deepened over spontaneous lunches in their cafeteria and Secretary Yuan sometimes sent home with me a container of special yeast so that Loretta could bake traditional Chinese buns for our family on the weekend.

I gradually gained a clearer perspective on the new China and its challenges and changes over time. I was there in January 1976 when the news came that Premier Zhou Enlai had passed away and had the honour of signing the official book of condolences. Some ten months later, following the death of Chairman Mao Zedong, I felt the changes resulting from the re-emergence of Deng Xiaoping, who had previously been targeted and branded as a reactionary during the Cultural Revolution. Once he took over at the helm, China took off and never looked back.

PROFESSIONAL CHALLENGES AND A TURNING POINT

The pleasure of our first summer back in Ottawa from Harvard and Hong Kong was eclipsed by sadness. Not long after our return, we received word that my grandmother had passed away on July 7. Born in 1871 and brought up in the ancient Chinese tradition, somehow the older my grandmother had become – she died at the age of one hundred and one – the more ahead of her time she had shown herself to be, constantly amazing me. I mourned her loss deeply. I would always be grateful for her frequent words of encouragement, saying time and again that our family would one day be proud of my achievements.

I was determined to live up to her expectations. It was time to pursue a more formal status for myself within Miska and Gale, a status that would reflect the benefits I had brought to the firm by capturing the Lowertown housing project and the Chinese embassy contracts.

Basil Miska, ever a pragmatic businessman, came up with an idea. Instead of making me a profit-sharing partner of Miska and Gale, Architects, a separate firm was established under the name Miska, Gale and Ling, Architects and Planning Consultants. Quite soon, thanks to my Harvard qualification in urban planning, this new firm won a contract with the Department of National Defence and I began working fulltime as a consultant on the planning of military bases in Canada.

The contract was for one year, renewable on an annual basis. The fee we charged was fairly modest and I received the full amount, however I was willing to be patient and to trust that my prospects would soon improve, especially as the nature of my work provided the firm with an inside track on upcoming military base design and construction contracts.

The pace of work as an in-house consultant at the National Defence headquarters in downtown Ottawa was slow and leisurely compared to what I was used to. Other than occasional visits to military bases in Canada, much of my time was spent in the headquarters writing reports or in discussions with departmental colleagues, and a full hour for lunch plus two coffee breaks were considered obligatory each day. In the summer, so that staff could enjoy the outdoors during the warm season, office hours began an hour early and ended at three in the afternoon and this enabled me to spend the remainder of the workday back at the Miska and Gale office taking care of other assignments. Because of this, I gained insight into how to succeed as a private-sector business in a town that is substantially government-sector.

Basil Miska was working hard to develop business opportunities for the firm. His enthusiasm and efforts were not diminished by the sudden and unexpected diagnosis of prostate cancer, which was fairly soon deemed to be in remission and Basil's energy seemed boundless in spite of it. He began inviting me to accompany him to dinner with clients or to federal government events – at that time, there was a majority Liberal Party government in Ottawa under Prime Minister Pierre Trudeau. After a while Loretta also became involved. As a Home Economics graduate trained in London, she was an accomplished chef in both Western and Chinese cuisines and to Basil's delight she prepared elaborate multi-course dinners for clients and political contacts at our home, often serving Peking Duck, the traditional highlight of a Chinese menu, which took her three days to prepare. These social evenings were a big hit, often continuing until the wee hours of the morning.

I also became part of a group of Basil's friends, all members of the governing Liberal Party, who met for dinner and a casual game of poker once a month. The purpose of these gatherings in one another's homes was simply to relax in good company, enjoying home cooking and good wine far removed from stressful work schedules. No serious gambling took place and it tickled my funny bone to see a former finance minister of Canada compete for a small pool of quarters (twenty-five-cent coins). These evenings regularly included Ben Benson, the former finance minister and current Minister of Defence, along with Gus Cloutier, his executive assistant, and Len Hopkins, his Parliamentary Secretary as well as a Member of Parliament in his own right. These gatherings, however, led to a rather startling episode of déjà vu for me, one that provided a little glimpse into Canada-China relations during that era of the Cold War.

The two men who approached me in the Miska and Gale office one late afternoon identified themselves as officers of the Royal Canadian Mounted Police Security Service, the precursor of the Canadian Security Intelligence Service. I was totally surprised and shocked, instantly remembering my encounter with the FBI in Boston some eighteen months earlier. They told me that they were aware of my work at the Department of National Defence, of my "association" with the Minister of Defence, his executive assistant and his Parliamentary Secretary, and of my many visits to the Chinese embassy. My pulse began to race. They then assured me that I was not suspected of espionage, having earned high level security clearance before being approved for the National Defence contract. I silently willed myself to breath more normally again. What they were looking for, they explained, was information about the interior layout of the Chinese embassy – could I help them there? I politely informed them that my professional code of ethics prevented me from violating a client's right to confidentiality and the encounter came to an abrupt end. They simply said goodbye and left the office.

In the summer of 1974, Loretta and I took our children to London to visit the three of her sisters who still lived in Britain – two were still at their university studies and the other was married to my old friend Freddy To, my musical soul mate and the person who had introduced Loretta and me a decade earlier. Less than a week into our vacation, we received the difficult news that Basil Miska had passed away, particularly shocking as he was so young – just in his forties – and his cancer was supposed to have been in remission. Basil had been generous in his political and social mentoring of my career and I was left with a keen sense of sadness. I also became concerned about my future. I still had no formal position within Miska and Gale 'proper' and did not want to continue with the uncertainty of a year-by-year contract with National Defence, especially one that I did not find sufficiently challenging.

Alastair Gale asked to meet with me immediately upon my return to Ottawa. I arrived at the office not knowing what to expect.

Alastair began by saying that our professional backgrounds were compatible, both of us having trained in Britain, and each of us had skills that complemented the other's – my urban planning qualification and the social and business contacts I had inherited from Basil perfectly augmenting his own skills in project management and company administration. He went on to say that Miska and Gale had recently been commissioned by the federal Department of Public Works as the architects for the renovation of the Langevin Block, the working headquarters of the Prime Minister's Office and the Privy Council Office. The design stage of this significant project had already begun, but in order to remain in compliance with the conditions of the commission, Miska and Gale was required to have two partners. Furthermore, he said, the practice had recently gained a diverse portfolio of work from the private sector and he needed strong support. He then invited me to become an equal partner with him and our practice would henceforth be under the name of Miska, Gale and Ling, Architects and Planning Consultants.

It seemed my long-awaited proverbial ship had come in.

BUSINESS DEVELOPMENT – BLESSING THE POPE

Our new company continued to occupy the ground floor and part of the next floor of the three-storey house at 157 Gilmour Street, a ten-minute walk from Parliament Hill. We rented out the remainder of its rooms to a structural engineering firm and an interior design firm. By Ottawa standards, Miska, Gale and Ling was a small practice, even when the number of our employees practically doubled to become seven, including two graduate architects, at which point we built an addition to the house which provided me a spacious, sunny office overlooking the peaceful greenery of Minto Park.

Alastair Gale was respected by clients for his thorough knowledge of construction practices and his excellent working relationship with public agencies like the folks at City Hall, whose approval was required for most development and renovation projects. Meanwhile, I enjoyed the challenge of incorporating clients' economic and social needs into creative design and urban planning concepts that they would find engaging. As a principal of the firm, however, my role was to continue Basil's legacy of political, social and business networking. To this end, Loretta and I continued to host dinners and receptions at our home, our new home, in the village of Rockcliffe Park, a leafy enclave of large residential properties close to downtown Ottawa and a neighbourhood favoured by business leaders and dignitaries, counting among its residents foreign ambassadors and Canada's parliamentary Leader of the Opposition.

Computer drafting and electronic graphic reproduction had not yet been heard of and desktop computers were still far from being user-friendly, so it was little wonder that our office secretary insisted on continuing to use an electric typewriter instead, even when a friend of Alastair's set us up with an IBM computer. Around that same time, an engineering firm introduced us to the fax machine, amazing us with the speed at which documents could be transmitted to a recipient across town or across the globe, however it would be more than a year before we purchased such a machine ourselves, given Alastair's somewhat conservative nature as a managing partner. Our drafting tools remained 'traditional' too, continuing to be labour intensive, especially when having to make every drawing for all federal government projects bilingual (English and French).

To my surprise, though far removed from my youthful dream of becoming a free-spirited designer, I found myself deeply content as an architect in a steady, business-oriented practice built on the trust and confidence of clients. Our jobs came in three categories: government projects that paid well, self-generated projects that were taken on as business investments, and bread-and-butter projects for developers who drove a hard bargain when it came to the fees. Each category demanded a different set of business and marketing skills and all of them required a clear understanding of user needs, development objectives and socio-economic criteria along with the ability to ensure every project could remain useful into the future.

One of my favourite government projects was the renovation of the Langevin Block immediately opposite Parliament Hill. Built in the Renaissance-Second Empire style during the 1880s, the block-long edifice boasted three main floors, a two-storey attic, plus a basement and sub-basement, and the sweeping staircase that rose from the grand central entrance hall impressed all who set foot inside. In 1974, the Government of Canada decided that the building needed to be upgraded in order to accommodate the working headquarters of the Prime Minister's Office and the staff of the Privy Council Office which provided non-partisan advice and support services to the Prime Minister and to Cabinet. Miska and Gale (and subsequently Miska, Gale and Ling) was hired as the architects. It was the firm's first commission of national stature.

The project required the restoration of the building's historical features including its facade of olive-coloured sandstone, round-headed windows flanked with pink granite columns, elaborately-decorated gabled dormers, prominent cornices, carved chimneys and copper-clad mansard roof. It was also essential to completely overhaul the interior to meet modern-day standards, including the installation of new electrical, heating and cooling systems, contemporary lighting, efficient elevators and space-saving spiral staircases, all in harmony with the building's interior of classical arches and decorative mouldings so as to ensure that the new upgrades respected the old forms.

Alastair and I welcomed the enormous challenges of this unique project. We had to coordinate with representatives of the Prime Minister's Office, the Privy Council Office and Public Works Canada (the government department responsible for federal properties) while at the same time leading a team of engineering and cost consultants and ensuring that the work of the general contractor, supported by numerous sub-contractors and suppliers, met the required design, operation, and health and safety standards. Alastair's skill and experience in construction and project management were inestimably useful. They complemented my own ability to translate the clients' twentieth century needs into contemporary interior designs that harmonized with the building's nineteenth century features. We were indeed a symbiotic duo, just as Alastair had said.

The Langevin Block occupied my attention day and night for an entire year. Often in the middle of eating dinner at home, a design idea would come into my mind and I would rush back to the drafting board at the office, burning the midnight oil as I maximized the moment of inspiration. It was worth it, however. The project was completed within budget and on schedule, enabling the distinguished tenants to move into their new quarters in the late summer of 1975. Shortly thereafter, the renovated building was designated as a National Historic Site.

Just eight years after my arrival as an immigrant, I'd had the privilege of contributing to a project that would support the political engine of Canada for a long time into the future. That felt enormously gratifying. So too did meeting face-to-face with the principal tenant of the building, Prime Minister Trudeau.

Not too long before the completion of the project, Loretta and I were introduced to Mr. Trudeau and his wife Margaret at a reception in a neighbour's home. Knowing what I was working on, he began our conversation with a number of questions on security, a serious look shadowing his face. I was prepared to brief him on the entire renovation but quickly realized that he was already quite familiar with it and so I focussed on the topic he had raised: the building's security features. He smiled his approval when he heard that we had installed bullet-proof glass in the windows of his private office – indeed this was something we had considered essential, not least because there was another building a mere ten metres away, right across the street from his quarters in the Langevin Block's western wing. Mr. Trudeau, clearly happy with what he was hearing, went on to say that there was already a need for even more office space than our renovations would be able to provide.

A month or so later, with the Langevin project completed, our firm was commissioned for a second project: the revamping of the Blackburn Building, a multi-storey office complex immediately behind the

Langevin Block. It was ideally situated for the further expansion of the Prime Minister's Office and Privy Council Office, as all that was needed to connect the two buildings was an enclosed bridge constructed at the third floor level above the narrow laneway that separated the two buildings. And so, for much of the following year, my time and energy were committed to the Blackburn project as our firm continued to build a good working relationship with the federal government.

While architectural work for the public sector paid well, it was only rarely available, especially when there was a downturn in the national economy, a change of government, or new government policies favouring the hiring of bilingual (English/French) multi-regional consortiums. All these factors tended to impact negatively on business opportunities for smaller firms like Gale & Ling – we changed the name to Gale & Ling, Architects and Planning Consultants in 1980, six years after the passing of Basil Miska – and it soon became obvious to Alastair and me that we needed to create our own business opportunities. A chance to do so arrived in 1982.

Dow's Lake is a pretty, man-made lake very close to the heart of the capital. It had been created in the 1830s by damming a swamp so that flooding would occur for feeding the Rideau Canal, which had been constructed as a transportation link between Ottawa and the city of Kingston some two hundred kilometres (one hundred and twenty-five miles) to the south on the shores of Lake Ontario. Modern residents of Ottawa benefit from that long-ago decision, as the lake is a pleasant place for boating in summertime when the water is three metres deep (about nine feet) and for skating on in winter when the water is drained to a level of just sixty centimeters (two feet).

The National Capital Commission, a corporation owned by the federal government, is the custodian of the lake and surrounding land along with all the sections of the adjacent canal that lie within the boundary of the capital city. The commission had built a wooden structure in the north-western 'corner' of the lake to house a year-round fast food counter plus, in winter, skate changing and sharpening facilities and, in summer, pedal boat and canoe rental. The operation of this facility had been contracted out to Bill Mason, who also operated a skate sharpening stand located about three kilometres (two miles) downstream on the Rideau Canal at Fifth Avenue. Both were in very poor condition. Bill came to our office one day accompanied by Alderman Terry Denison, a member of City Council and one of Alastair's City Hall friends. They had heard rumours that the National Capital Commission was considering upgrading the facilities, thus putting Bill's future as the concession operator into doubt. The commission might be persuaded to consider having private sector involvement in any redevelopment, they suggested, as this could generate a higher financial return for them at little or no financial risk. They proposed that the four of us form a team and come up with a development plan for preliminary discussion with the commission. Alastair and I were immediately interested. We knew, however, that any such team would benefit from the inclusion of an experienced developer to round out our own architectural and planning skills, and so we approached Jan Kaminski, a mechanical contractor who was also successful in real estate development. Jan gladly accepted our invitation. We now had a strong team of equal partners with diverse talents.

We focussed first on the main facility at Dow's Lake. We all recognized that in order for the development to be economically viable, the National Capital Commission would need to be persuaded to permit more substantial commercial use of the facility than had previously been allowed. Market research told us that restaurants and banquet/meeting spaces would work best, along with upgraded boat rental and skating support services, and so I got down to work on designing a structure that would accommodate these various uses. At the same time, we began negotiations with the commission on the terms for a privately-owned development on their property: The developer would lease the land and water for the construction of a facility (at own cost) for a period of thirty-five years, at the end of which time ownership of the built facility would be handed over to the commission. All revenues generated from the project during those three-and-a-half decades would go to the developer (to recover the cost of leasing the land and water, of financing the project, plus taxes and operating expenses) and after that time revenues and property would revert to the NCC.

As soon as it entered my head, the name 'Dows Lake Pavilion' struck me as the perfect label for the multi-functional, built-over-the-water facility I was designing. Three sit-in restaurants bordered by expansive decks for outdoor dining. Banquet space for public meetings and private functions. A fast-food service counter. A gift shop. Rental facilities for pedal boats, canoes, kayaks and bicycles in summer, and for skates and sleds in winter when people would simply step down from the lowest level of the pavilion onto the surface of the frozen lake. A marina to accommodate boaters summering on the Rideau Canal system, and a boardwalk spanning the northern edge of the lake for strolling along at any time of the year. By necessity, guest parking would have to be accommodated off-site on land just across the street that the National Capital Commission was prepared to lease to us for that purpose.

In compliance with federal government policy, our team's design proposal had to compete with those submitted by other proponents. Happily for us, the Dows Lake Pavilion team won the competition, however there was still another hurdle to cross: our design had to gain the approval of the commission's Design Committee consisting of architects, artists and designers from across Canada. Their standards were rigorous. Although it fulfilled all the desired planning functions, my first rendition was rejected by the committee. "Lack of clarity," they said. I had to return to the drafting board, where inspiration hit me in the form of a mental image of a geometric building I had designed long ago as a student at the AA in London – a central octagon surrounded by a series of rectangles. I also recalled how I had seen open decks used to link buildings at marinas in Vancouver and San Diego. I dove back into the project with excitement. It would be a two-storey building, grown out of an octagonal form, with steeply pitched roofs and white metal cladding. Expansive windows would provide panoramic views of the lake and a semi-octagonal open-air deck at the northern corner of the upper floor would allow people to relax and observe all the activity taking place in the marina, on the boardwalk, and along the adjacent sweep of the scenic water-hugging parkway, Queen Elizabeth Drive.

This time, our design received the seal of approval. We were in business.

We brought in a group of outside investors, with the original five of us remaining as the founding partners. Financing was in place by late winter 1983, enabling construction to begin. A sandbag dyke allowed us to drain the low-level winter water from the site so that we could embed the pavilion's supporting columns into the lake bottom and top them with the facility's base platform before the water level would be raised back up for the boating season – we had to race the clock, as that date was quickly approaching. Fortunately, construction above the high water mark was much less pressured, time-wise.

When Dows Lake Pavilion opened its doors to the public the following summer, it offered an international range of restaurants on the upper level – Mexican, Chinese and German – and any functions taking place in the lower level banquet room, available free of charge to the public, could be catered by one or more of these restaurants. We contracted out the fast-food service operation and also both the summer and winter equipment rental services located on the lower level. Rather unexpectedly, the pavilion became a family affair, with Loretta and a business partner operating the gift shop, and our daughter being one of the first to enjoy the banquet room as we celebrated her sixteenth birthday.

The highlight of that first summer in operation, 1984, had to be the visit of Pope John Paul II. The pavilion had been chosen as the place where His Holiness would board a specially designed watercraft dubbed the Popeboat for an historic eight-kilometre journey (five miles) down the Rideau Canal past tens of thousands of waving and cheering people. That Wednesday – it was September 19 – the Pope was welcomed to the lower deck of the pavilion by a long line of dignitaries including various church officials and the mayors of local municipalities. Loretta and I had been invited to stand slightly apart from the receiving line so that we could enjoy a close-up view of the honoured guest, and finally there he was, only a few feet away. Just as he was about to turn from the receiving line towards the boat, a woman standing next to Loretta called out to him and the Pope immediately paused, looked in our direction, and walked over to shake her hand, then Loretta's hand, and finally – no doubt not wanting to leave out the last person in this small group of onlookers – my hand. Totally taken by surprise, I felt that I should say something spiritual. "Bless you!" is what I heard coming out of my mouth, and ever since then that expression has taken on a life of its own in our family lore.

The papal flotilla that day passed the second small facility that had been operated by Bill Mason, the one located on the Rideau Canal at Fifth Avenue. Our group successfully negotiated with the National Capital Commission for the joint development of a restaurant and skate rental operation on that site too, and today a glass-enclosed eatery – the Canal Ritz – and its spacious outdoor terrace offer unbroken views of the scenic canal from various vantage points and through every season.

The Albion Hotel was one of the oldest surviving hostelries in Ottawa and provided a typical developer-driven project for our firm. Built in 1871 opposite the Carleton County Courthouse in the Sandy Hill area of Ottawa, the Albion's tavern had always been a favourite meeting place for lawyers and for students from the nearby university, but in 1984, when courthouse operations were slated to move to a new location, the city decided it was time to re-examine the whole block on which the Albion sat. Though in a prime downtown location not far from Parliament Hill and the popular Byward Market, the block was underutilised, occupied mainly by structures that had been allowed to run down. City Council expropriated the block and marked it for redevelopment, with the preservation of the nineteenth-century Albion Hotel a requisite condition.

Jarvis Freedman, the owner of the Albion and a successful developer in his own right, came to see Alastair and me. He had sounded out City Hall as to the expectations for the block – the uses and development density they wanted to see there – and he was looking for a conceptual design proposal that would offer socio-economic benefits to the community and also satisfy potential investors. His preliminary ideas included a modern hotel, business offices, residential apartments and a parking structure – no small undertaking – and he intimated that he would pay us very little, however if the project materialized we would then be hired as the development architects.

We heard this often from developers. We took on such projects as speculative work that could, if successful, turn into the bread-and-butter contracts that supported our firm. Indeed, the majority of our projects – residential, commercial and industrial – came from private sector developers like this, many of them becoming repeat clients due to our practical approach in design and sensitivity to their economic needs. This project was no different.

Alastair and I got down to work immediately, he dealing with our client and with City Hall while I applied myself to creating the conceptual design. Then the unexpected happened. Mr. Freedman informed us that he had been diagnosed with a terminal illness and had found a partner who would be taking over the project from him. That partner turned out to be the Thomas C. Assaly Corporation, a major development company in Ottawa. Gone was the assurance that Gale & Ling would be hired as the development architects if our conceptual design was accepted, and even if we were to be hired in that capacity we knew we could expect this new client to drive a very hard bargain on our fee.

Alastair and I quickly met with company head Tom Assaly. To our relief, he informed us that he would indeed honour Mr. Freedman's commitment and we would be the architects if the city approved our design concept. And so, after several more months of work, I produced a conceptual design of a multi-use complex consisting of a twelve-storey office tower above a nine-storey hotel for the western half of the block, with entrance to the office tower from one street, Besserer Street, and to the hotel from another, Nicholas Street. This modern hotel would be linked to the carefully restored Albion Hotel, which would continue its century-old role as a place of refreshment by providing a restaurant for hotel guests and for the public. The eastern half of the block was to house a residential condominium apartment tower, twenty-two storeys tall, and a much needed parking structure. Apartment residents and hotel guests would have joint access to a recreation area featuring an indoor swimming pool, exercise rooms and a sunny rooftop terrace. Albion Place was the name I chose for the complex.

Albion Place won the conceptual design competition – there were two other entries – with Assaly Corporation as the developer and Gale & Ling as the architects. Our speculation had paid off. But it is rarely smooth sailing when dealing with a client who likes to drive a hard bargain.

My design for the new hotel was based on requirements established by the Sheraton chain, which was negotiating with the Assaly Corporation for the right to operate the facility. Those negotiations fell through, however, and our client then entered into an agreement with a French chain of hotels newly arrived in North America. Novotel had a completely different set of requirements regarding room sizes, layout and amenity spaces. I was summoned to an emergency meeting with Mr. Assaly at which I was told that the deadline for submitting the building permit application to City Hall was just two days away and I would have to alter all the design drawings to reflect Novotel's requirements within those forty-eight hours. The pressure was on. I was reminded of how I had felt all those years ago when given a week to produce thirty thousand lines.

And just as back then, what sounded impossible became achievable through creative thinking and sheer stamina, so that forty-eight hours later I was indeed able to hand over the revised drawings. Mr. Assaly looked at them, listened carefully to what I had to say, then simply turned to his lawyer and moved on to another topic of discussion. The following day, I received a call from the lawyer telling me that Mr. Assaly was happy with my work and impressed with my performance – and that he himself had never before heard his client praise anyone to that degree. I immediately felt somewhat compensated for the enforced marathon of the past two days.

Albion Place was completed late in 1987, just as Canada entered a recession. The market for owner-occupied apartments was gone. The apartment tower had to be converted into another hotel, Les Suites, which could honestly boast that its one- and two-bedroom units, each with a balcony, offered guests all the spaciousness of home.

Twenty-five years had flown by since my graduation as an architect in 1962. I had designed a great variety of projects on three continents: private homes, townhouses, apartment buildings, hotels, hospitals, recreation facilities, offices, industrial plants, gas stations, warehouses, restaurants, embassies, colleges and military bases. If I had to single out just one project as a favourite, it would have to be the Dows Lake Pavilion – and not just because that was where I momentarily exchanged roles with His Holiness the Pope, with me giving him a blessing rather than the other way round.

COMMUNITY ACTIVIST

On September 30, 1979, Canada's CTV network's popular current affairs program W5 aired a documentary, *Campus Giveaway*, which claimed, over footage of Asian-looking students attending lectures, that universities in Canada were being inundated by foreign students, Chinese in particular, and that Canadian students were being squeezed out. The implication was a shocking slap in the face: Unless a student looked Caucasian, he or she could not possibly be a Canadian.

That program was to alter the course of my life.

Universities publicly refuted the distorted information contained in the documentary, and ethnic groups and student bodies mounted protests. Chinese community organizations across Canada banded together to form an ad hoc committee with the objective of obtaining a public apology from CTV, a retraction of the false and racist propaganda aired, and a commitment never to produce such discriminatory programming again.

Albert Wu, an Ottawa member of the national ad hoc committee, came to my home one day and invited me to attend a local meeting as it was felt that the Chinese community in Canada's capital city had a distinct role to play in the campaign. As one of the older people there, I sat back and listened to the heated discussions until I noticed that they were going around in circles and getting nowhere. My architectural training kicked in – function (desired outcome) determines form (what is needed to achieve that outcome) – and so I suggested that we focus first on asking ourselves exactly what we wanted to achieve, and the 'how to' would follow. The answer came quickly. There was a specific message that we wanted to get out and it was this: Chinese-Canadians – those of us who had been in Canada for only a few years and those of us who'd been here for many generations contributing to the common good of all Canadians – are equally proud and passionate about Canada, our country, our home. With that agreed, we were able to come up with an appropriate vehicle for delivering this message: we would host an 'I love Canada' gala. By chance, political circumstances provided the perfect timing for ensuring our message was broadcast far and wide.

Quebec's movement to separate from Canada had been dominating the attention of the entire country, and indeed the world, for some time. A referendum on the topic was to be held in Quebec on May 20, 1980 so we planned our Canada love-fest for the eve of the vote, which of course attracted the attention of mainstream media. As the organizing chair of the event, I was gratified when more than four hundred members of Ottawa's Chinese-Canadian community came to the Ottawa Civic Centre to pledge their love to Canada and to express opposition to the offensive W5 documentary. The resulting media coverage was widespread, CTV being the noted exception. I remained involved in the national committee and in due course CTV issued a full public apology and pledged to employ higher journalistic standards and integrity in the future.

This movement gave rise to the Chinese Canadian National Council, the first organization dedicated to the advancement of equal rights for Chinese-Canadians from coast to coast. I was a founding director and served as national vice-president from 1981 to 1984 and as Ottawa Chapter president from 1985 to 1986. I remain involved to this day. What had been a painful experience empowered a community, sensitized a major media network and ultimately helped build better race relations in Canada.

The one and a third million-strong Chinese community in Canada – about four per cent of the population – was far from being a homogeneous entity. Those who arrived between the mid-1940s and early 1970s included university graduates, professionals and business investors from Hong Kong and also from Taiwan and Southeast Asia.[1] Immigrants from mainland China, on the other hand, were mostly unskilled, arriving under Canada's family reunification program to join a family member who had immigrated before 1945. This older generation of Chinese, lacking English language skills, had found it hard to assimilate into Canadian communities and as a result they formed ethnic enclaves – Chinatowns – where they could live among fellow Chinese immigrants.

On top of this diversity of backgrounds, members of many Chinese community associations and family 'clans' were drawn into right- and left-wing political attitudes, those on the right backing the Republic of China (Taiwan) under the Nationalist Government and most of them not particularly open to assimilation into Canadian society, while those on the left were more likely to feel that the People's Republic of China's diplomatic presence in Canada had bolstered their acceptance as Canadians and some professionals among them were eager for increased assimilation. The silent majority, of course, held a neutral position and simply went about the business of taking care of career, family and friends. Ottawa's relatively small Chinese community, numbering less than ten thousand, was no exception.

My participation in the W5 protest campaign brought me to the attention of the Chinese Community Association of Ottawa, an old establishment with an annually-elected board of directors that had long been considered the official voice of the local Chinese community. Traditionally, the board consisted of members who were perceived as being right-leaning, but in 1981 they were encouraging a broader sector of the community to run for election. I was persuaded to put my name forward. I accepted the challenge, was duly elected, and to my surprise found myself one of the association's two vice-presidents.

Hoping to contribute ideas for change, I was quite vocal at board meetings, at times even challenging board decisions. This turned out to be unpopular. When it came time for re-election, rather than being seen as an advocate for positive change as I had intended, it seems I had instead intensified the impression that I was a left-leaning radical and a threat to the local Chinese community. My election defeat, however, took me out of community-level 'politics' and into a broader arena. In 1986, I was appointed by the Ontario Government to a three-year term on the Ontario Advisory Council on Multiculturalism and Citizenship.

It was the first step of my journey towards serving Canada.

HONG KONG-CANADA-CHINA CONNECTIONS

In the summer of 1982, Loretta and I and our children were invited by the Overseas Chinese Affairs Office of the State Council of the People's Republic of China to join several Chinese-Canadian families from Ottawa and Montreal on a visit to China. The invitation was for a two-week tour covering six cities: Guangzhou, Shanghai, Wuxi, Hangzhou, Guilin and, of course, Beijing. The Chinese Government would pay for my travel and hotel expenses within China and for half of the expenses incurred by my family, for whom it would be a first-time visit. It was my second – the first being the trip to Guangzhou (Canton) with my parents and brother in 1946 – and I was greatly interested in seeing the changes and in experiencing firsthand the atmosphere some sixteen years after the start of the Cultural Revolution and six years after the death of Chairman Mao. I also thought it would be good for our children to experience a little of their ancestral country.

We met up with the other Canadian families in Hong Kong and travelled together by train to Guangzhou, where we were welcomed by our hosts, a representative of the Overseas Chinese Affairs Office and an escort assigned to us by the China Travel Agency. To our disappointment, they informed us that Shanghai, remembered by many as the New York of old China, was no longer on the itinerary and had been replaced by Nanjing. The explanation was that Shanghai was "not ready for showing," making me wonder if Red Guard attacks on government buildings in 1966 had been so destructive that it was taking longer than expected to complete repairs. I also found the choice of Nanjing as a replacement destination to be intriguing. That city was renowned as the location of a massacre by Japanese soldiers in 1937 – the Nanking (Nanjing) Massacre – in which some three hundred thousand residents were slaughtered. It would most likely offer visitors an insight into the dark side of Sino-Japanese relations. Indeed, the massacre remains a stumbling block between the two countries.

Shortly after our party's arrival in Guangzhou, we sat down to a lunch of Cantonese dishes and plain rice in our hotel restaurant. The servers' lack of courtesy and attention to our group, as compared to what we would experience in a Canadian restaurant, made me wonder if perhaps they had once been Red Guards, indoctrinated to condemn bourgeoisie like us and finding it hard to adapt to the new China. The friendly hospitality of our hosts, however, more than compensated for our first-day disappointments. They were open and honest about the fact that China was still very much in development and wanted to learn from visitors, particularly from other Chinese like us.

Ours was one of the earliest North American groups to be invited into China and our program featured the best they could offer. Bicycles and buses were the ubiquitous form of transportation for the masses, but we rode in air-conditioned coaches, a tremendous luxury in China at that time. Cars were few and far between, mostly Chinese-made *Hongqi* ("Red flag") limousines or Toyota sedans which were the preserve of senior government officials, and also a number of army trucks. The presence of police officers dressed in green and dark blue uniforms stood out against the sea of pedestrians and cyclists, male and female, all wearing white shirts and dull-coloured pants. Most older people still favoured the unisex Mao suit.

Shopping was organized for us at various Friendship Stores, state-run shops that were off-limits to local people at that time. Like all visitors, we were not allowed to hold or use *renminbi*, the official Chinese currency, and were issued foreign exchange certificates for making purchases. On the black market, these certificates were worth thirty per cent more than the local currency.

Revisiting as an adult some of the places in Guangzhou that I had seen as a child was an intriguing start to our holiday. White Cloud Mountain, the Sun Yat-sen Memorial Hall and Shamian Island, all still impressive in spite of the years of turmoil that had occurred since I'd first seen them, brought back many family memories. I was pleased to find the city much cleaner and in reasonably good shape. Nanjing, the next stop on our highly organized itinerary, turned out to be a most satisfactory replacement for Shanghai, even with the oppressive summer heat that had earned the city a spot on the list of the "Three Furnaces of China" (along with Wuhan and Chongqing). Our visits to the city's Sun Yat-sen Mausoleum and the Nanjing Massacre Memorial Hall left us with a better understanding of modern Chinese history during the time of the Nationalist Government and the Second Sino-Japanese War.

In Hangzhou and Wuxi, two of the most scenic cities in China, we were treated to enjoyable boat rides, the first on Hangzhou's enchanting *Xi Hú* ("West Lake"), whose natural beauty and historical relics have inspired artists and poets throughout the ages, and the second on Lake Taihu ("Grand Lake"), China's third largest body of fresh water, on whose shores lies the ancient city of Wuxi. Beijing, however, was in a category all its own. The four days we were allotted in the capital city left us hungry for more. We were taken to the Great Wall, the Forbidden City, the Summer Palace, the Temple of Heaven and the Ming Dynasty Tombs. We sampled an enormous variety of dumplings and, eaten in the dish's native home, Peking Duck had rarely tasted better. But the historical highlight, for me, was the Chairman Mao Memorial Hall, where the body of the 'Great Helmsman' lies in state in the middle of the vastness of Tiananmen Square.

When we arrived in Beijing, we were told that instead of staying at the air-conditioned hotel listed on the itinerary, we would be put up at the Overseas Chinese Residence which did not offer modern amenities. Some in our group expressed concern about this switch. We should have known better, given the obvious desire to provide us the best treatment possible in spite of the infancy of China's tourism infrastructure. Our ever-obliging hosts were forced to quickly juggle, bumping a group of Chinese-Americans to the Overseas Chinese Residence and taking us to a newly-opened hotel with air-conditioning and serving Western-style breakfasts.

The two-week program was capped off with a trip to Guilin in southern China, renowned for its distinctive scenery on the banks of the Li River. As a child, I had often heard my grandfather quoting the old saying, "Guilin's scenery is best among all under heaven," but until that moment I had only seen it depicted in paintings. It was the perfect ending to our tour of China. On the train ride from Guangzhou back to Hong Kong, I was completely satisfied that my ancestral home was indeed recovering well "under heaven."

In the late 1980s, I finally experienced a sense of clarity as to my identity: I was a British citizen by birth and a Canadian citizen by choice, and after the handover of Hong Kong sovereignty to China in 1997 I would also be Chinese-Canadian, not a third party participant when it came to Canada-China relations. And so when Ottawa Mayor Jim Durrell was invited for an official visit to Beijing in 1987 and asked for my assistance in exploring the potential for a concurrent trade mission to Hong Kong, I was happy to get involved. I was pleased that the mayor was determined not to let Ottawa miss out on the Asia-Pacific business opportunities that other Canadian municipalities were already actively pursuing.

I soon discovered that arranging meetings of real substance between the municipalities of Ottawa and Hong Kong was no easy feat as formal relations had not yet been established between the two and without such a foundation in place there were severe protocol challenges. In addition, the two city governments were not comparable, the mandate of the Legislative Council of Hong Kong reaching far above and beyond that of Ottawa City Council's mandate of providing city services.

There were additional challenges. While the Hong Kong General Chamber of Commerce and the Chinese Manufacturers' Association of Hong Kong both provided strong support to any of their members interested in expanding into overseas markets, there was no comparable support organization for expansion-minded businesses in Ottawa and the scope of the Hong Kong Trade Development Council in Canada was still rather limited. The Canadian Commission in Hong Kong did operate a trade division headed by a trade commissioner but its services were very much underutilized at that time. In spite of these difficulties, I set up the most productive itinerary I could and happily accepted Mayor Durrell's invitation to join his trade mission team.

That team also included Howard Williamson (the mayor's chief of staff), Jamie Fisher and Marc Laviolette (two elected members of City Council), Alcide DeGagné (the city manager), Janet Foo (assistant to the city manager), Vic Whittaker (a successful builder-developer) and Richard Raymond (founder of Raymond Steel, a fabricated structural metal company). For the Hong Kong portion of the mission, we were also accompanied by Bill Marshall (head of the Ottawa-Carleton Economic Development Corporation) and several Ottawa business-men including some from Ottawa's Chinese community.

We arrived in Hong Kong early in May 1987. With only a few days to accomplish our goal of increasing Hong Kong's awareness of Ottawa as a potential seedbed for business, Mayor Durrell kicked the mission into high gear by giving a live interview to Radio Hong Kong that was broadcast throughout the colony. It had been set up for us by Stuart Wilkinson, the Hong Kong government's Director of Communications, who also happened to be Loretta's brother-in-law. Next, taking advantage of a visiting Canadian Broadcasting Corporation (CBC) television crew, I organized a boat trip around Victoria Harbour during which Mayor Durrell was interviewed by CBC and the promotional clip was shown on the Ottawa news the very next day. Then came a meeting with Elsie Elliot Tu, a prominent elected member of Hong Kong's Urban Council, the body responsible for municipal services on Hong Kong Island and in Kowloon, and the remainder of the visit was packed with appointments with private-sector businesspeople. All in all, this first trade mission to Hong Kong laid a foundation on which business connections between the two cities could begin to take root and grow. We were planting the seeds of future trade opportunities at the Gateway to China.

Our official host in Beijing was Chen Xitong, Mayor of Beijing and a member of the Politburo of the Communist Party of China, indeed he was rumoured to be the one who would succeed Deng Xiaoping. On our arrival at the Beijing International Airport, we were received on the tarmac by Vice-Mayor Sun Fuling, one of the eight vice-mayors, and his senior assistants. We were escorted to a richly decorated lounge reserved for dignitaries where we were offered tea and hot towels with which to refresh ourselves. Assisting Vice-Mayor Sun and his officials was a team of interpreters and they politely requested our passports, promising to return them to us at our hotel – we had been exempted from having to individually go through customs and immigration.

We headed into the city in a motorcade led by a police vehicle, siren wailing to clear the way for us. Mayor Durrell rode in the second vehicle, a stretched Mercedes Benz, accompanied by an interpreter and a bodyguard and the rest of us followed in a procession of Toyota Crowns, each with a white-gloved chauffeur. The protocol and atmosphere of this official trip were in sharp contrast to what I had experienced as a tourist five years earlier.

Beijing in 1987 had a population of some thirteen million people. Traffic along the city's wide boulevards was congested, not with motor vehicles but with a sea of cyclists riding shoulder to shoulder as far as the eye could see. At times our motorcade would blast its way through on the wrong side of the road, the police vehicle's siren clearing the way. This was standard procedure, I was told, so that the tight schedules of VIPs could be adhered to.

To my surprise, we were not taken directly to our hotel. Instead we were treated to an evening visit at the magnificent Temple of Heaven, the huge fifth-century Taoist complex which has been declared a masterpiece of architecture and landscape design and designated a World Heritage Site. Over the course of the following days we enjoyed more such guided tours, always by motorcade, to landmarks such as the Great Wall, the Forbidden City and the Summer Palace, and were treated to sumptuous banquets hosted by Vice-Mayor Sun. All the while, we were surrounded by a team of young men, sometimes as many as thirty of them, all sporting military-style crew cuts. They were our bodyguards.

Besides tours of several high-rise residential developments, our business agenda included a formal meeting with Mayor Chen Xitong and his senior staff, ending with the customary exchange of official gifts and group photographs. It being the first official meeting between the two municipalities, discussions focussed on goodwill and the development of future business and cultural partnerships. The essential first step in establishing fruitful relations between the two capital cities had been taken.

The second step was taken a few months later, with Vice-Mayor Sun, his assistants and several Beijing municipal officials paying a reciprocal visit to Ottawa. At the municipal level of government in Ottawa, there were no official vehicles for visiting dignitaries, no motorcades, no bodyguards, and even, for a short while, no luggage – their baggage was temporarily mislaid by Air Canada – however our guests appeared to genuinely appreciate our openness, sincerity and hospitality. I was delighted to give them a tour of the almost-completed Albion Place development designed by my office and it was clear that they were enjoying the serene cityscape, clean air and fresh water that are so much taken for granted in Canada's capital city.

It was gratifying to all of us that shortly after Vice-Mayor Sun's visit, China's 'Crown Prince' also paid a visit to Ottawa. Deng Pufang, the first son of China's paramount leader Deng Xiaoping, came in his capacity as the president of the China Welfare Fund for the Handicapped – he himself was a paraplegic, having suffered spinal cord injuries as a result of a three-storey fall while in the custody of the Red Guards during the Cultural Revolution. When the revolution ended and his family's good name had been restored, he had received medical treatment in Canada at the Ottawa Civic Hospital under Dr. Gordon Armstrong, a respected orthopaedic surgeon, and then returned to China to help establish rehabilitation centres there. His trip to Ottawa this time was to gather support for the China Disabled Persons' Federation, which he had just founded and which he hoped would grow to support and serve the millions of disabled people in his homeland. Indeed, he was later to be awarded the United Nations Human Rights Prize for his work.

Mayor Durrell hosted an intimate lunch for the distinguished visitor in his spacious office at City Hall – a Western lunch catered by Ottawa restaurateur and community philanthropist Dave Smith. There were just four of us at the table and the conversation flowed with a little interpretative help from me. There being no business agenda, it was enlightening to talk with someone who had been prominently a part of such a significant historical event as the Cultural Revolution, and Mr. Deng's comments were frank and his indomitable spirit very evident. Those who had passed through that "testing" had been toughened in their initiative, he said, and they were the ones who would drive the engine of China's reform.

Twenty years after my arrival in the city, I was fully aware of the challenges Ottawa faced in negotiating a place for itself in the stiff competition for business on the international market. Not least among these challenges were its small population (less than one million), its small number of private sector industries (given its government-town nature), its limited financial resources for marketing and promoting itself, and its lack of global business experience in relation to potential Asia-Pacific trading partners. However I also knew that it had a unique and enviable combination of assets to bring to the table: stable political and social systems, quality of life in an unspoilt natural environment, the capacity and eagerness to learn, and a determination to grow, diversify and succeed.

I committed myself to continuing to help my adopted city seize every business opportunity that might come along and in addition to proactively reach across the Pacific Ocean to bring other such opportunities into being.

Bridge Builder | 10
(1987-2012)

In his capacity as mayor of the city, Jim Durrell also served as vice-chair of the Ottawa Board of Commissioners of Police, an independent civilian body with responsibility for such things as setting the overall objectives and priorities for policing in the city and for recruiting and evaluating the police chief. Sitting next to me at a Chinese New Year celebration event early in 1987, Mayor Durrell asked if I would be interested in serving on the board as a community representative. His suggestion took me by complete surprise. At that time, not only did I not even know what the police commission was, but also, as someone brought up in Hong Kong, I was used to regarding police forces as tough and fearful authorities it was best to avoid. On the other hand, the offer was intriguing. I had perceived Canadian police as being dominated by tall, white males and it was interesting that a visible minority person such as myself would be considered by the mayor to be a "good fit" for the organization. I agreed to meet with the current chair of the commission to hear more about the responsibilities that would come with the role.

I met David Hill for lunch at Hy's, a downtown restaurant renowned for power networking. Right from the start of our conversation, it was clear that David, a Queen's Counsel and prominent local lawyer who had made significant contributions to the community as a volunteer, knew quite a bit about my background. Saying that the "system" needed to be opened up and that nepotism within the police force should be nipped in the bud, he suggested that I could bring fresh ideas to the table. There was an immediate board vacancy, he said, and he would like to put my name forward as a candidate for consideration by the Government of Ontario. Thus persuaded, I gave him permission to go ahead.

Word of the provincial government's approval of my appointment to a two-year term effective July 30, 1987 came shortly after I arrived home from the trade mission to Hong Kong and Beijing. Besides being reported in the local media, it made headline news in Chinese communities across Canada: "Ottawa's First Chinese Canadian Police Commissioner". Within days, volumes of background reading material were delivered to my house and I began to realize that my new appointment would soon be consuming a considerable amount of my spare time and energy, as governing a police organization of six hundred officers and over two hundred and twenty civilian members was clearly an enormous and complex responsibility.

One of the documents that particularly drew my attention was entitled *Members of Police Boards of Commissioners – Code of Conduct*. What stood out was the regulation stating that "Board members shall not interfere with the police force's operational decisions and responsibilities or with the day-to-day operation of the police force, including the recruitment and promotion of police officers." This quite appropriately drew a clear line between police governance and police operation, but made me question how effective I could be in opening up the historically white male-dominated system. However, I was more than willing to find out.

A week later, a squad car picked me up from my home and took me to the police headquarters on Elgin Street. Chief Arthur Rice, a World War II veteran who had been running the Ottawa force since 1984, welcomed me with a handshake, asking, "Do you know Alan Kwan of the Shanghai Restaurant? I love Chinese food." After a cordial conversation, I was given a tour of the complex and introduced to the officers who headed up the various divisions. Several received me warmly, saying they looked forward to chatting at the upcoming annual Senior Officers Dinner. Then it was time to get down to business at my first police commission board meeting.

The board room was filled with officers including the chief and his two deputies and also a couple of local news reporters. They all stood to attention when the arrival of the board members was ceremoniously announced, and remained standing until we five commissioners had seated ourselves at the table – that experience brought home to me the seriousness of the official responsibilities I had taken on. My fellow commissioners were Mayor Durrell, City Alderman Rob Quinn, commission chairman David Hill and Mary Hegan, the third community representative. The agenda included both open and in-camera sessions, with the room being cleared of all non-commissioners other than the police chief for the latter. On a steep learning curve, I spoke very little except to ask questions and took particular comfort in noting that there was no ganging up around the table – no 'City versus community' posturing – as the mayor and his alderman often disagreed with one another and so too did my fellow community representatives.

My learning process included a ride-along with an on-duty patrol officer. The Patrol Division is regarded as the backbone of the whole organization, with its officers the first on the scene, running towards trouble as it is occurring. In addition, their frontline experiences provide valuable leads to detectives and narcotics agents, making these other officers' jobs easier. I was picked up from home one Saturday evening by a patrol officer in the familiar blue and white cruiser. I had been looking forward to the experience and had given some thought to my wardrobe, choosing an old beige trench coat à la Columbo – the rumpled fictional detective popular on TV at the time – and equipping myself with a cellular phone, a bulky brick Motorola model of the day.

We headed to Lowertown, a sector of the city with a lot of bars and nightclubs, the area most favoured by sex trade workers and drug dealers. As soon as we arrived we were called to an address where a suspected murder had occurred, however as we approached the scene we were intercepted by the Zone Sergeant and I was hastily escorted to another cruiser and driven away. It was not appropriate, they explained, for a member of the police commission to become a material witness to a crime scene. I was disappointed, but totally understood the operational decision.

The rest of the evening was spent patrolling the less lively area of Centretown and responding to a variety of non-urgent calls. The main excitement of the night came when we were instructed to check out a suspicious vehicle parked outside a house on a street just west of Bronson Avenue. We drove discreetly to the location and were informed by Command Centre that a major drug transaction was in progress inside the residence. Suddenly a man came out of the house and headed towards the parked car, activity that the patrol officer immediately reported to Command Centre using my cellular phone to do so in order to circumvent being overheard by anyone scanning the frequency of the police radio communications system – I was delighted that my personal equipment was proving useful. Then, taking his order from Command Centre, he jumped out of the cruiser and intercepted the suspect just as he was about to get into his car. A confrontational conversation ensued but ended abruptly and the patrol officer simply rejoined me in the cruiser. The suspect, he said, was in fact an Ontario Provincial Police (OPP) undercover agent, a member of a team that was carrying out an OPP-Ottawa Police joint operation – unfortunately, however, the Patrol Division had not been notified.

Those five hours on patrol duty allowed me to experience the real-time working life of a frontline police officer, and also to hear firsthand how the job affects an officer's family and personal life, which was of equal interest to me. I felt I now had a useful foundation on which to base some of the deliberations that lay ahead of me as a member of the commission.

By this period of the 1980s, Canada was becoming an increasingly multicultural nation, a pluralistic mix of ethnocultural communities, and a society that was not only tolerant of its diversity but also more and more proud of it. This transformation resulted in a greater public awareness of issues concerning racial equality, human rights and employment equity. On the practical side, government agencies at all levels of jurisdiction were recognizing that in order to serve their constituencies better, their staffing needed to reflect the pluralism of society. Nationally, Commissioner Norman Inkster, head of the Royal Canadian Mounted Police (RCMP – "The Mounties") began a very public campaign to make Canada's national police service a viable career option for all Canadians no matter their race, gender or ethnic background.

Five months after I had become a police commissioner, I ran into my friend Dr. John Samuel, a retired Ottawa Board of Education trustee who was now chairing the City of Ottawa's Advisory Committee on Visible Minorities. As a social activist of South-Asian origin, he urged me to examine what the commission could do to make the Ottawa police force reflect the racial and ethnic diversity of the population it served, without contravening the provincial code of conduct which prohibited

us from "interfering" with the recruitment or promotion of police officers. I wholeheartedly agreed. Prior to 1986, Ottawa's police personnel included only four members of visible minorities: two Blacks and
two Aboriginals. In 1986, the first Asian officer was hired, but almost
two years later there was no further indication that the ethnic minority
hiring trend had improved. I felt strongly that something needed to be
done to correct this imbalance.

At the next board meeting I took the matter up with my fellow
commissioners. They readily agreed that we should develop guidelines
and policies that could lead to the identification and removal of any
cultural biases in the recruitment process and come up with initiatives
to enhance multicultural communities' relations with the police. To
achieve these goals, the Advisory Committee on Multicultural Police
Recruitment and Selection was created on April 11, 1988 – the first of
its kind in Ontario and indeed in Canada. I became chair of the committee and within a few weeks managed to recruit eight volunteers with
a diverse cross-section of cultural backgrounds to serve along with me.
My friend Dr. John Samuel was of course the first one I asked. The other
distinguished social advocates were Rev. William Wan of the Ottawa
Chinese United Church, Berkeley Harris from the Black community,
Jim Tomkins from the Aboriginal community, Professor Arthur Stinson
from the Anglophone community, Camylle Tremblay-Choquette from
the Francophone community, Bonnie Diamond from the Black community, and Ed Hoosen from the Chinese community. Staff Inspector
Golden Leesen joined us as the representative of Chief Rice.

Over a period of ten months, we reviewed the existing recruitment
statistics and efforts and the selection process that followed. We also
solicited and received input from the Ministry of the Solicitor General
of Ontario, the RCMP, and employment equity experts. Our findings
were sobering.

Among Ottawa's six hundred police officers, only three individuals (half of one percent of the force) were from any visible minority community. This came nowhere close to reflecting the nature of the workforce in the National Capital Region, of which more than eight percent were non-White. To catch up, we would need forty-six additional officers of visible minority ethnicity. When it came to women, there were twenty-three female police officers in Ottawa (less than four percent of sworn members) but women made up almost half of the region's workforce and to reflect this community snapshot we would need a whopping two hundred and forty-seven more female recruits. In addition, the number of Aboriginal police officers, though it had increased from two to four by 1988 (still less than one percent of the force), remained eight short of what was needed to reflect the community – and all these discrepancies were growing with every passing day as the city's population increased.

Our audit of the selection process identified various hurdles that favoured the status quo, including mental ability test questions biased against females and anyone not raised in the culture of North America, a psychological test that was not equitable for candidates of diverse cultural backgrounds, and an initial one-on-one interview that could not ensure an objective assessment of the candidate. As well, the selection board charged with conducting a candidate's final interview did not include anyone with multicultural experience or training.

After close to a year of hard work, our committee presented a report to the police commission on February 20, 1989. We recommended many actions including setting specific five- and ten-year recruitment targets for visible minorities, females and Aboriginals, and the hiring of a minority recruitment officer. We proposed simple new practices such as publishing a multi-lingual booklet on policing as a fulfilling career, and revising all police publications to include images depicting members of our target groups performing in various policing roles. We proposed that the interviewing team henceforth include minority-sensitive members, that fluency in a minority language be deemed a desirable qualification, and that we work with the Ontario Solicitor General's office to improve assessment methods and candidate interview techniques. We also advocated for increased community relations via such things as police participation in career days in schools, and a yearly reception for leaders of local visible minority communities so as to bring them into recurring positive contact with the police service. I ended our presentation by emphasising the importance of making multicultural recruitment an immediate priority and of ensuring that the annual police budget reflect this priority going forward.

Our recommendations were duly endorsed by the commission and received with heartfelt congratulations to my committee. In reality, however, I knew that in order for them to be implemented effectively, they needed the support of the Chief of Police, senior officers and those on the front line. While I was hopeful that a change of culture was on the horizon, the end results remained to be seen.

Four months later, mere weeks before the end of my two-year term of appointment to the commission – I would be appointed to a second term – Chief Rice retired after almost forty years on the force. We selected Deputy Chief Thomas G. Flanagan, a much-decorated "policeman's policeman" to replace him, and as happens with all changes-of-command, a new page was turned for the Ottawa Police Force. Within a year, Germaine Joly was promoted to the senior officer rank of Inspector, making her the highest ranking female police officer in Eastern Ontario.

I continued to serve as chair of the Advisory Committee on Multicultural Police Recruitment and Selection, which remained active with added members from the community. We were starting to make progress in the recruitment of minorities, their numbers increasing from half a percentage point to two-and-a-half percentage points of sworn officers in one year. The city was now served by fifteen visible minority or Aboriginal officers and thirty female officers. Budget restraints, however, meant that it would be an uphill battle to meet the recommended targets.

In July 1991, I was appointed to a third term on the police commission, this time by a New Democratic Party provincial government, the Liberals having lost power in the previous year's election; some pundits mused that my being appointed by two opposing parties was quite unusual. The following year, with the scheduled ending of David Hill's terms of office, I was elected by my colleagues to chair the commission, now called the Ottawa Police Services Board, an experience that was as humbling as it was gratifying and made me keenly aware of the increasing depth of my responsibility – and never more so than when the *Ottawa Citizen* newspaper commented that the police board "can affect the force far more than the chief and his deputies." Later that year, Jim Durrell retired as Mayor of Ottawa and was succeeded in office by Jacquelin Holzman, who automatically became vice-chair of the police board.

Early in my watch, an unexpected incident arose one day when a police chase that had begun in the nearby city of Hull in the Province of Quebec ended in downtown Ottawa with the arrest of a suspect by a police officer from the originating jurisdiction. The new City Council member now serving along with the mayor on the police board happened to be on the scene and intervened in the arrest, supposedly questioning the right of a Quebec officer to make an arrest in the Province of Ontario. The councillor's action contravened the provincial code of conduct regulation stating "Board members shall not interfere with... operational decisions and responsibilities." The story made it into the *Ottawa Citizen* and I had to call an emergency board meeting to deal with the matter.

The police service's in-house legal advisor informed us that it was legitimate for the board meeting to be conducted in-camera instead of being open to the public, however shortly after we began I was informed that an *Ottawa Citizen* reporter was seeking permission to sit in. I immediately sent word denying him access. Minutes later I was told that the newspaper's legal adviser was challenging this decision and was outside waiting to speak with me, so I adjourned the meeting briefly to talk with him and tell him of our decision: we would continue to deliberate the matter behind closed doors. The outcome of our board meeting was made public, however. The councillor was given an official reprimand and City Council later appointed another member to take his place on the police board.

The ensuing news items focussed on the in-camera nature of our meeting, criticizing it. I issued a press release on behalf of the board explaining the rationale for the decision: we would be raising issues of a personal nature pertaining to our colleague in light of his prohibited actions and would also be discussing potentially confidential policing matters. The release went out on the Friday immediately prior to the Christmas holiday break and inadvertently included my home telephone number, which the *Ottawa Citizen* published on the front page of its local section, urging readers to call me to protest. Needless to say, my phone kept ringing. I picked it up each time and took care to speak with every one of the callers, explaining the board's action. About half of the callers continued to disagree with our decision but most of them appreciated that I took the time to talk to them personally. Only one suggested that I should resign.

Councillor Diane Holmes now joined the board as the second representative of City Council, the first being Mayor Holzman. My two fellow community representatives were Kim Meimaroglou, the Greek-

Canadian founder of Bread and Roses Bakery, and Lyallen Hayes, a respected social activist from the Black community. Suddenly, on a board of people with diverse cultural and career backgrounds, I was the only male.

My first experience of leading the review of the proposed annual police budget was quite a challenge. It was 1993 and Ontario was in the midst of the worst economic recession in sixty years, and the provincial New Democrat government under Premier Bob Rae had implemented budget cutbacks in order to limit the province's mounting deficit. In this climate, there were differences of opinion among those of us around the board table, the split being between the two members who represented City Council, which was accountable to local tax payers for the money needed to operate the police service, and the three of us who represented the community. All five of us took seriously our primary responsibility of ensuring the safety and security of citizens, but we found ourselves disagreeing as to the amount of budget increase needed to fulfil this obligation.

The budget proposed by the police included a nine-point-one-nine percent increase. After a great deal of information and data gathering and close scrutiny of the numbers, we three community representatives were satisfied that indeed this was what was needed, however neither of our City Council colleagues had any appetite for such an increment. Predictably, the budget passed our board by three votes to two and was forwarded on to City Council for final approval, as required by provincial legislation. The ensuing debate captured a great deal of public attention. After much tension-filled discussion, City Council failed to ratify the proposed budget and Chief Flanagan and I walked out of that meeting greatly disappointed – however that was democracy in action and did not diminish the respect we five members of the police board continued to have for one another. The provincial police commission eventually arbitrated an increase of two-point-five percent.

I particularly enjoyed the community outreach opportunities that came with my duties as board chairman. Accompanied by the police chief, I visited the families of young people living in underprivileged areas of the city, attended the funerals of crime victims, and participated in events organized by the gay and lesbian community in Ottawa. I executed a contract between the police service and Carleton University to enhance campus safety measures, swearing in the university's on-site security officers as Special Constables.

In 1993, Norman Inkster, the 'top cop' of the RCMP who had initiated and spearheaded the broadening of that organization's eth-nocultural nature, invited me to attend a conference he was hosting in Ottawa, a conference of the international police organization widely known as Interpol, of which he was also 'top cop' at the time. Among the attendees were many heads of police forces from around the world. It was particularly moving for me to meet Commissioner K.H. Li of the Royal Hong Kong Police (the 'Royal' would be dropped following the transfer of sovereignty in 1997). We discovered that we had a lot in common, such as our age, both growing up in Hong Kong, and both being the first Chinese to head up a Westernized police organization. I was impressed by his unassuming manner, though he had well-earned his rise through the ranks from Sub-Inspector to Senior Inspector at the time of the civil unrest in Hong Kong that had been part of my reason for emigrating to Canada, then becoming Superintendent following additional training in England, and subsequently achieving promotion to Deputy Commissioner and then Commissioner. We socialized a few times during his short stay in Ottawa, enjoying each other's company and promising to stay in touch.

Later that same year, the Ottawa Police was to host a national conference on Asian crime in Canada, attracting police members from across the country. I was invited to be on the panel of speakers and decided to do some background research on the topic in Hong Kong, with my new friend's assistance. Commissioner Li's assistants welcomed Loretta and me on the tarmac and took us through a special section of customs clearance before giving us police-escorted transportation to our hotel – shades of Beijing. The next day, we were given an official welcome at a lunch hosted by Commissioner Li at the Police Club and were introduced to his senior staff, including two deputy commissioners who were British. I was impressed to see this indication of the demise of British pre-eminence over Chinese professionals that I had grown up with.

My research included interviewing authorities on Asian organized crime such as the head of the Hong Kong Police Triad Unit and senior officers of other major crime units. I gathered information from local Chinese police officers and from civilian officers of the Independent Commission Against Corruption. I consulted an RCMP officer serving at the Canadian Commission. A picture emerged from these interviews and from the volumes of documents on the topic that I ploughed through – the problem existed, yes, but the North American preoccupation with Asian crime indicated unacknowledged racism and was gravely counterproductive as it enabled organized crime originating in Europe, the Middle East and the Americas to more easily slip beneath the radar.

I was particularly concerned to hear that a Canadian official in Hong Kong had advocated a blanket rejection of any person of Chinese origin applying for immigration into Canada if that person had lived in or frequented Mong Kok (then a notorious district in Kowloon) or travelled to Thailand (known for drug trafficking) or was associated with the Hong Kong movie industry (which was rumoured to be financed by criminal elements), on the mere suspicion of possible ties to organized crime.

On the day of the conference, I was joined on the panel by law enforcement experts and immigration agents and the audience was full of police officers from across Canada, most of them members of an Asian Crime Unit. The other speakers and the questions and comments from the audience painted a picture of a Canada invaded by Asian criminals involved in blackmail, fraud, illegal gaming, drug trafficking and the sex trade. When it was my turn at the microphone, I detailed my findings in Hong Kong and stressed that the designation of a police investigative group as an Asian Crime Unit was inappropriate, as it implied that crime within the Asian community is so prevalent that it requires dedicated policing – there are no European Crime Units. There was dead silence and I could feel the tension in the room. I had spoken what I believed to be the truth but it was clear that the audience was not on my side, though they applauded politely when I finished. So it was a total surprise when, the following year, I was invited back to participate in a second Asian Crime Conference.

This time, I told the audience right at the start that I was prepared to take my gloves off to defend my position, and was greeted with laughter. I tried to be more positive in my presentation, still saying what I needed to say but also recounting a brief history of Chinese Canadians: how they had contributed to nation building and how a Head Tax had been imposed only on Chinese immigrants. I spoke of racial barriers and of discriminatory perceptions that are furthered by things like the W5 documentary on students of Asian origin and the proliferation of the policing label 'Asian Crime Unit'. I praised those Canadian police departments that were actively promoting multicultural policing as being effective policing. This time when I sat down the applause was genuine. I had made peace with the gendarmerie again.

I continued to work closely with Chief Flanagan on a wide range of pro-active police activities, including establishing in-the-community police offices to provide a focal point for problem solving right in a neigh-bourhood. The first Community Police Centre was set up in Ottawa's Chinatown. Constable Kai Liu, a Chinese-born five-year veteran of the force (who would eventually become Chief of Police in Gananoque and then in Cobourg, Ontario) was put in charge of the facility, breaking with traditional policing techniques by working with area residents and businesspeople to prevent as well as solve crimes. It was to be a model for other such centres in the city.

Chief Flanagan retired on March 31, 1993. During a forty-two-year career, his love of working with the community had become legend-ary and he had been awarded the Queen's Commendation for Brave Conduct, the Star of Courage and the Police Exemplary Service Medal. Those of us who served on the Police Services Board were happy to acknowledge his legacy by naming the police headquarters after him and establishing the Thomas G. Flanagan S.C. Scholarship as a means to assist visible minority and Aboriginal women who express an interest in a policing career with the Ottawa force.

Deputy Chief Brian Ford was sworn in as Ottawa's next Chief of Police. Also very much a community-minded person and interested in our multicultural recruitment efforts, he had earned his Master's degree with a thesis on employment equity. I was particularly pleased to work with him on the development of the Ottawa Police Youth Centre which was set up in a decommissioned fire station in the middle of a troubled city neighbourhood. The centre became a place where young people received help with homework and could take part in recreational and personal development programs – a place that offered a proactive, posi-tive approach to preventing youth crime. It continues to do so, indeed the story of the Police Youth Centre and its impact on the community was chronicled in an issue of *Reader's Digest*.

Perhaps the greatest privilege of serving on the police board for seven years was being able to participate in an official capacity in the annual memorial ceremony for officers killed in the line of duty, a tradition that had begun following the death of Ottawa Police Constable David Kirkwood in 1977. At the end of each year's service, Loretta and I had the humbling experience of meeting with and thanking the parents and spouses of some of the fallen officers. I always found myself wishing I could have done more for them. In 1998, our local ceremony was greatly expanded when the Government of Canada officially proclaimed the last Sunday of September to be Police and Peace Officers' National Memorial Day.

HONG KONG-CANADA BUSINESS ASSOCIATION
– THE LAST GOVERNOR OF HONG KONG

Shortly after we returned from the 1987 trade mission to Hong Kong and Beijing, Mayor Jim Durrell asked for my help in forming a local business organization that could build on the base relationships that we had now established between Ottawa and both those overseas markets. This proved harder than expected, as Ottawa businesspeople were more used to focussing on trade within North America, especially with the United States. Fortunately, the Hong Kong-Canada Business Association had been established three years earlier in Vancouver, Toronto and Montreal with the goal of encouraging Canadian companies to utilize Hong Kong as a business "Smart Link" to China. I contacted Robert Brown, the association's national chair, and he agreed to come to Ottawa to see if we could kick-start a local chapter.

I finally managed to entice about two dozen business and professional people to a lunch meeting in a Chinatown restaurant owned by my
friend Peter Lee, many of them agreeing simply in anticipation of the
excellent food. Bob Brown's presentation on his association's mission
and its potential benefits to local businesses, however, soon had them
convinced and so it came to pass that the Ottawa Section of the Hong
Kong-Canada Business Association was formally established just a few
months later. I was delighted to be elected as its first president.

One of the key ingredients in any "Smart Link" with China is *guanxi*
("relationship"), a central idea in Chinese society that, at the personal
level, describes a connection between two people in which either one
is able to prevail upon the other to perform a favour or service. This
same deeper-than-networking relationship plays an important role in
Chinese business as well. It struck me now that the combination of
my own Eastern and Western experience, the relationships I had nur-
tured with people in Hong Kong, Canada and China, and my business
and political networks on both sides of the Pacific – the international
guanxi I had developed – could be of use to both my adopted country
and my country of birth. I came to the conclusion that it was time to
change course in my career.

In 1989, I retired from my architectural practice with Gale & Ling
to become a Canada-Asia Pacific business matchmaker.

From the Chinese perspective, successful business matchmaking requires
both substance and mandate: the companies involved must have acceptable products, sound management, and adequate financial and staffing
resources (the "substance") plus the support of a government, a business
association and/or a financial institution (the "mandate"). I set out to
get this message across to the somewhat hesitant business community
in Ottawa, a community hungry for trading partners during this time

of economic slowdown but uneasy about moving into unfamiliar territory. Gradually, however, the local meetings of the Hong Kong-Canada Business Association provided a regular forum for discussions on the ins and outs of trade with China and the atmosphere within the Ottawa business community began to open up to the possibilities. I became more and more involved in the national organization as well, helping lead trade delegations, organize cultural exchanges and promote government policies on both sides of the Pacific that would increase mutually productive interaction. In 1991, I was elected national chair, inheriting the goodwill and support cultivated by those who had preceded me.

The Government of Canada sponsored Festival Canada in Hong Kong in 1991, a trade show promoting Canadian products including ice wine, salmon and beef. The festival also featured exhibits and cultural events that provided a glimpse into the nation's history, society and tourist attractions. In addition, Canada's *guanxi* was strengthened when the federal government presented a gift to the people of Hong Kong in the form of a ten metres tall (thirty-one feet) Western red cedar totem pole sculpted on-site by Canadian First Nations master carvers Dale and Terry Campbell and erected in Kowloon Park in a traditional pole raising ceremony.

The following year, Festival Hong Kong came to Canada. It was the largest business, sports and cultural promotion ever undertaken by the government of Hong Kong, which was determined to publicize the colony's high ranking on the global Index of Economic Freedom and particularly to promote the fact that this status was expected to continue even after the return of sovereignty to China under "One country, two systems" five years down the road. The festival – motto: Bridge Across the Pacific – would travel to Toronto, Ottawa, Montreal, Calgary and Vancouver. I agreed to chair the Ottawa segment.

As Canada's capital city, Ottawa was the key venue for getting Hong Kong's pro-business message out to Canada's political leaders, with the bonus of the international diplomatic community's presence thrown in for good measure. The Hong Kong government provided a generous budget for the event which took place over the course of a two-week period, and the Hongkong Bank of Canada, which had recently established a branch in Ottawa, provided office space for my organizing committee and team of hired staff and consultants. There were large contingents of visiting athletes and artists to prepare for and we facilitated a wide variety of sporting events such as badminton matches and kungfu demonstrations that were energetically hosted by the University of Ottawa. Exhibitions were mounted at Ottawa City Hall and mini performances were offered in the atrium of the downtown shopping mall, the Rideau Centre.

I quickly discovered that when Canadians thought of Hong Kong in 1992, they focussed on the looming political change and were oblivious to the unique fusion of Eastern and Western culture that epitomized the city. This made my goal of filling all nine hundred seats in the theatre of the National Arts Centre for an evening of Hong Kong culture, music and dance a bigger challenge than I had ever anticipated. Operation Full House was quickly drawn up and activated. Thousands of VIP invitations were delivered to our target audience of federal and provincial parliamentarians, members of both city and regional councils, foreign diplomats, business leaders and institutional kingpins. The day before the performance, public attention was drawn to the festival and the concert by an opening ceremony on the terraced square outside the World Exchange Plaza during the bustling lunch period. The novelty of having policing duties at the ceremony performed by Ottawa's brand new mounted police unit (thanks to Chief Flanagan) attracted extra attention. Operation Full House was a success.

Given my dual roles as chair of the Ottawa Police Services Board and as chair of Festival Hong Kong in the capital, I was particularly pleased by the arrival in Ottawa of a group of high school students who were members of the Hong Kong Junior Police Call, a youth organization with obvious strong police ties. Their visit was made possible by the support of Commissioner Li of the Hong Kong police. The young people were billeted in the homes of Ottawa police officers who made them welcome and initiated joint activities with their local counterparts, the Police Venturers, a Scouts program sponsored by the Ottawa police.

The finale of Festival Hong Kong – a somewhat belated finale as it occurred a month after the festival ended – was the official visit to Ottawa of the new governor of Hong Kong, Christopher Patten, the governor who would hand over the colony to the People's Republic of China in 1997. As chair of the local festival, I had a role to play in welcoming him and found myself in a situation that may be the stuff of everyday life for a diplomat but a challenge for those who are not, like me. Governor Patten had made himself popular in Hong Kong by his habit of taking public strolls among the people and by giving up the wearing of the traditional uniform of his office, the Windsor uniform, long a potent symbol of British authority; however he was decidedly unpopular with the Chinese government in Beijing, where his proposed electoral reforms relating to the election of the Hong Kong Legislative Council had earned him the title of 'Wrongdoer who would be condemned for a thousand generations.' I had a delicate balance to achieve in order to maintain good relations between Canada and Hong Kong and at the same time between Canada and the People's Republic of China.

Governor Patten arrived by chartered plane at Canadian Forces Base Uplands' VIP terminal on the evening of November 12 accompanied by James So, the colony's Secretary for Recreation and Culture, and Stephen Lam, director of the newly established Hong Kong Economic

Trade Office in Toronto and who after 1997 would rise to become the second highest ranking officer of the government of the Hong Kong Special Administrative Region. The official welcoming party consisted of Howard Balloch, Assistant Deputy Minister for Asia-Pacific in Canada's Department of External Affairs (now Foreign Affairs) and International Trade who would soon become Canada's Ambassador to the People's Republic of China, along with a senior representative of the British High Commission in Ottawa and myself. In the absence of an official motorcade, I had made arrangements for two police cruisers to escort us to the Canadian Government's elegant and comfortable guest house for visiting dignitaries at 7 Rideau Gate, close to the official residence of the prime minister. Once there, Governor Patten immediately settled in with a gin and tonic and preoccupied himself with newspaper clippings transmitted from Hong Kong, so I politely excused myself for the night. The major event of his visit was to take place the following day.

More than three hundred invited guests turned out for the speaker luncheon in the Grand Ballroom of Ottawa's most renowned hotel, the historic Chateau Laurier. Among them were members of Canada's Parliament, local politicians of various stripes, many business and community leaders, and foreign diplomats including China's Ambassador to Canada – all of them eager to hear what "The Last Governor of Hong Kong" had to say in his keynote speech, especially as many in the colony, and indeed the world, were still reeling from China's crackdown on protesters in Tiananmen Square just three years earlier. When he spoke of reforming the election process for Hong Kong's Legislative Council and when he posited that the continuing success of Hong Kong depended upon an open administration, public participation in government, a free press and respect for civil liberties, I could just imagine the thoughts in the mind of the Chinese Ambassador. Charged with the duty of thanking the governor for coming to Ottawa and for his keynote address, I had to choose my words very carefully in order to express genuine Canadian hospitality, combined with respect for China as our important trading partner, and confidence in a bright future for the city of my birth.

I saw Governor Patten off at the airport the next day. He left behind a gift to mark the cultural, social and business ties between Hong Kong and Canada – a teak dragon boat (a traditional Chinese watercraft) that was added to the permanent collection of the Canadian Museum of Civilization (later to be renamed the Canadian Museum of History). And when Britain returned sovereignty of Hong Kong to China in July 1997, precipitating the final departure of the colony's last governor, Hong Kong became a "Special Administration Region" of China, remaining a vibrant global business centre but with a renewed Chinese spirit.

After Festival Hong Kong and after serving my year as the national chair of the Hong Kong-Canada Business Association, I became a governor of that organization and later was made an honorary life member of its board of directors. My career as a business and community bridge builder across the Pacific continued to grow.

When I was in Beijing facilitating a joint-venture project between an Ottawa client and the China Patent Office at a time when Ottawa Mayor Jacquelin Holzman also happened to be in the Chinese capital, her presence at our business meeting provided the so-essential governmental "mandate". The following year, 1995, I facilitated a trade and investment mission to Beijing, Hong Kong and Taipei under the auspices of the Regional Municipality of Ottawa-Carleton headed by Peter Clark – another example of governmental "mandate". All such clear official backing and support of trade missions greatly helped to expand opportunities in Asia for Ottawa businesses and led to reciprocal visits to Canada's capital by various private- and government-sector representatives from across the Pacific, a visit by the powerful Mayor of Beijing being particularly auspicious.

Confirmation of Ottawa's growing success in creating a place for itself on the Asian business stage and of its ability to build the indefinable, requisite *guanxi* came in 1999 in the form of the official twinning of Ottawa with Beijing – a coup indeed.

NATIONAL CAPITAL DRAGON BOAT RACE FESTIVAL – THE TEAM SPIRIT

At the 1993 annual fall retreat of the board of the Ottawa Section of the Hong Kong-Canada Business Association, Director Gordon Huston suggested that we introduce dragon boat racing to Ottawa. We had heard stories of the success of Vancouver's eight-year-old Canadian International Dragon Boat Festival and Toronto's somewhat younger International Dragon Boat Race Festival, both these sporting events involving the racing of canoe-like dragon boats – in China, dragons are traditionally believed to be the rulers of rivers, lakes and seas – in friendly competition that dates back in China to the same era as the Olympic Games in ancient Greece. In modern day Canada, these sporting events had proven themselves to be an effective tool for business and community team building and so, after some debate, Gordon had convinced us that such a project indeed fell within our association's business mandate.

Then came a key question: Who should head up the festival in Ottawa? For a long moment we studied one another, after-dinner drinks in hand but forgotten, until Gordon broke the silence and looked directly at me before suggesting to the group that I was "the obvious choice", given my experience in chairing our national association and the recent Festival Hong Kong. When he went on to pledge his bank's support – he was the manager of the Ottawa branch of the Hongkong Bank of Canada – I knew my arm was being well and truly twisted. And so began my journey as the chair of the National Capital Dragon Boat Race Festival.

The immediate challenges were fourfold: the formation of a planning and organizing team, the selection of a venue, the procurement of dragon boats and expert advice, and securing financial support – it was our association's firm intention that the festival would stand on its own feet, particularly in regard to human and financial resources. For the organizing committee, I had to draw on some of the local people with whom I had established *guanxi* over the years – people like lawyer, fundraiser and sportsman Warren Creates, Mike Chambers, another lawyer and an avid competitive canoeist (who was later to preside over the Canadian Olympic Committee) and Lewis Chan, also a lawyer, who headed up the Canadian Ethnocultural Council. Needless to say, I also roped in Gordon Huston, the banker whose idea the whole thing had been in the first place.

For the venue, we selected the Rideau Canoe Club located on the Rideau River at Mooney's Bay, some ten kilometers (six miles) upstream from the Chinese embassy. The club already accommodated canoe and kayak racing along with storage and maintenance facilities and there was lots of open space for spectators and related festival activities. Most importantly, some of its members were experienced racing officials and trainers for dragon boat racing. Happily for us, Mike Scott, a forty-five-year veteran of the club, secured his board's agreement to host the event. We were off to the races, literally – as long as I could find some dragon boats.

Thanks to a contact in the Chinese community, I made a trip to Toronto to meet with Sharifa Khan, a prominent Chinese-Canadian businesswoman who had helped found the Toronto dragon boat festival five years earlier. She generously agreed to provide us with all kinds of support. We could borrow four fully equipped boats from Toronto for our first festival, she said, and they would be shipped by flatbed truck to the Rideau Canoe Club the day prior to the event, with us covering the costs of shipment, damage repairs and insurance. Fortunately, our security arrangements quickly fell into place, thanks to my friends at the Ottawa Police Youth Centre. Volunteers from the centre stepped up and agreed to provide nighttime watch over the boats docked at the clubhouse. The fabled crafts, each of them twelve-plus metres long (forty-foot-ten-inches) and adorned with a spectacular dragon's head at the bow and equally impressive tail at the stern, should be quite safe.

The remaining challenge was to find enough sponsorships to cover expenses: office space for administration, honorariums for staff members, storage for equipment like paddles, drums and life jackets, the rental and set-up of grandstands, signage and other day-of-event necessities, publicity, trophies and onsite entertainment including kungfu demonstrations, Chinese dance troupes, Japanese drum performers, clowns, food stands, gift and souvenir stands, etc. Given our festival's absence of a track record, corporate and media sponsorships were hard to capture. And we were competing for support with another start-up festival, Bluesfest, but whereas blues music was already a known and popular entity among the Ottawa population, dragon boat racing was not yet so.

Rather concerned, I could not help but turn my thoughts to my mother's enduring 'Never give up' attitude and Uncle's belief that opportunities in one form or another always come along. My prayers were answered. First, the Hongkong Bank of Canada offered us free office space, clerical support and storage space. Then the *Ottawa Sun* daily newspaper came on board as our print media sponsor. Next, CJOH, a television station in Ottawa owned by CTV, jumped in with both feet. They committed to providing coverage of the festival and its lead-up; news anchorman Max Keeping – an Ottawa celebrity –

volunteered to be the festival's Master of Ceremonies; and J.J. Clark, the station's popular weatherman, agreed to participate in the opening ceremony. With such pledges of support in our pocket, we gained the credibility needed to attract some financial backing. Canadian Airlines International and the Hongkong Bank of Canada each became a Platinum Sponsor. The recently established Hong Kong Economic and Trade Office in Toronto became a Gold Sponsor, and so too did the Regional Municipality of Ottawa-Carleton and the *Ottawa Sun*. Dave Smith, the philanthropist restaurateur who had catered lunch in the mayor's office for the son of Deng Xiaoping, lent his support by hosting a fundraising dinner in his home.

After months of preparation, the first National Capital Dragon Boat Race Festival was almost ready for launch. To attract racing teams, we set a very modest entry fee, but it was still rather hard going. The businesses in Ottawa that had a lot of Chinese employees familiar with the sport – Bell Northern Research being one – were still in the early stages of active expansion into China and did not yet see the festival as a way to enhance their global corporate profile, however some BNR staffers formed their own teams without corporate support. Local branches of Canada's banks also were reluctant to participate because of the involvement of the Hongkong Bank of Canada, a perceived competitor. And among the mainstream population, the event was seen as being for the Chinese community, while the Chinese community perceived it as being run for the *gweilo* (slang for "Western") community and were hesitant to compete against *gweilo* teams – though the enthusiastic performances of their troupes of colourful dragon and lion dancers at the festival's opening ceremony more than belied this reticence. In the end, we managed to have a respectable inaugural registration of twenty-eight teams, each comprised of ten pairs of paddlers facing a pace-setting drummer in the bow and with a steersperson seated in the stern.

Our media sponsors did a good job of promotion and we provided shuttle bus service between Chinatown and the festival site for anyone who wanted to use it. About five thousand people turned out that summer day, which was very rewarding after so much work. No amount of planning, however, could control the weather. Heavy clouds began to build up shortly after the opening parade of athletes and we watched the skies anxiously, fingers crossed, hoping to make it to the end of the event without rain. It was not to be. A couple of hours into things, a short-lived thunder squall suddenly blew in, causing one of the boats to tip over in front of the grandstand crowd which now had the bonus spectacle of watching the water rescue unit of the Ottawa Police Service spring into action and pluck the doused paddlers from the river. The squall soon passed, however, and the races continued. Now, every challenge thrown our way had been overcome.

Since that first time in July 1994, the festival's popularity has grown in leaps and bounds, eventually moving to larger quarters in Mooney's Bay Park on the opposite bank of the river across from the Rideau Canoe Club. I continued to chair the annual event until 1996 and was succeeded by Warren Creates, who was followed by Mike Chambers and then a long line of dedicated and capable community and business leaders. A pledge challenge component was added to the festival in 1998, enabling race teams and the public to raise funds for local charities. This was so successful that the Ottawa Dragon Boat Foundation was founded in 2004. Under the leadership of, first, Michelle Lavoie and then Sandy Foote, the pledge challenge has succeeded in raising almost two-and-a-half million dollars for charity. And it keeps growing.

From a half-day event with just over two dozen racing teams and a crowd of five thousand, the festival has expanded into a three-day event featuring more than two hundred teams, over five thousand paddlers, and some seventy thousand spectators, all supported by close to five hundred volunteers. Indeed, the Ottawa Dragon Boat Race Festival has become the most popular dragon boat festival in the world, attracting a larger attendance than any other.

POLITICAL INVOLVEMENT – THE LIBERALS

I had grown up in a family that did not involve itself very much in politics, no doubt in part because the British colonial system inhibited the questioning of authority, starting with how children were trained in the regimented education system. Since leaving Hong Kong, however, I had seen for myself that political action – the art of guiding or influencing governmental policy – was key to achieving needed change. My first glimpse of this occurred in London at the British Council's orientation session for Commonwealth students as I listened while young people from Africa and Asia spoke passionately of their countries' anticipated or newly gained independence. As well, I found the culture in the AA School of Architecture to be politically empowering as it not only encouraged us to question what we were being told, but actually expected us to do so. And so I had taken my own baby steps into political activism, helping organize demonstrations against the proliferation of bland buildings in London for the Anti-Ugly League and participating in Ban the Bomb marches. In Canada, the power of community activism really hit home, almost literally, in 1970 when my neighbours and I succeeded in stopping the seven-lane highway scheduled to destroy our residential community, and again a decade later when the CTV television network publicly committed to ensuring higher journalistic standards after the Chinese community had exposed racially biased reporting on one of its programs. There was no doubt that my early life attitude was being significantly altered by my actual life experience.

I arrived as a new immigrant in Canada during the year of its centennial celebrations, a time of great optimism. That optimism went right through the roof eight months later when the charismatic Pierre Trudeau took over the reins as prime minister in the spring of 1968. I was filled with confidence that the possibilities in my new country were endless, a feeling that was further heightened for me when Canada took the bold step of establishing diplomatic relations with the People's Republic of China. Over the next number of years as I focussed on growing my career and on taking care of my family's needs, politics remained a spectator sport I followed with interest on the daily news or on the parliamentary channel on TV. Over time, I felt myself drawn more to the policies and vision of the Liberal Party than those of any other party. They appeared to me to embrace and support the aspirations of the average citizen, rather than of special interest groups or those on the left or right wing of the ideological spectrum. This commitment to balance and the fact that the Liberals encouraged the diverse multicultural nature of Canada appealed greatly to me, and when I found myself involved professionally and socially with quite a few party activists as a result of business networking with Basil Miska, I encountered no reason to become disillusioned.

In 1987, with my architectural career and family life stable, I had an opportunity to become actively involved in politics at the provincial level with the Liberal Party of Ontario.

Richard Patten, a senior manager with the YMCA in Ottawa, invited me to lunch one day to seek my advice on putting himself forward as the Liberal candidate for Ottawa Centre in that year's provincial election; he had heard of me through my Miska and Gale Liberal connections. He quickly impressed me as an honest and conscientious person sensitive to multicultural values and I gave him my personal approval, for what that was worth, offering him a Chinese name for use in campaigning in the Chinese community. The name I gave him, *Lick-Beat-Sing*, sounded similar enough to "Rick Patten" and, as well, its English translation was auspicious, "Energy-Guarantees-Victory". Shortly thereafter, members of the Chinese community were mobilized for handing out campaign flyers and erecting signs throughout the riding and I helped organize a major campaign event at the Yangtze Restaurant in Chinatown with the premier of Ontario himself, David Peterson, in attendance. Richard went on to win the election, ousting the incumbent MPP (Member of Provincial Parliament), my former tenant Evelyn Gigantes of the New Democratic Party. Richard served as Ontario Minister of Government Services and subsequently Ontario Minister of Correctional Services under Premier Peterson in what was the second-largest majority government in the province's history.

The following year, to my astonishment, I was invited to chair the provincial Liberal Party's major fundraising event in Eastern Ontario, the Trillium Dinner. I accepted, as I considered it an honour not just for me but also for the ethnic community. The Trillium Committee was formed and I was supported by a team of highly capable and experienced professionals and political organizers including Debra Davis, Don Grant, David Hill, Carol Hinds, Daniel Kennedy, Morris Kertzer, Norma Lamont, Isabel Metcalfe and Dalton McGuinty, Jr. – the latter would himself enter politics two years later and go on to become the province's premier. Our prime objective was to attract the highest attendance of party supporters in the history of the annual event.

Protocol required that the Eastern Ontario caucus of Liberal MPPs be briefed on our plans. That caucus meeting was chaired by the MPP for Ottawa South, Dalton McGuinty, Sr., the father of my committee colleague and someone I had first met some eight years earlier when he was a trustee for the Ottawa Board of Education and I was seeking the board's support in the protest against CTV's biased reporting on Asian students. The other caucus members present that day were Richard Patten (MPP for Ottawa Centre), of course, along with Bob Chiarelli (Ottawa West), Hans Daigeler (Nepean), Bernard Grandmaître (Ottawa East), Gilles Morin (Carleton East), Yvonne O'Neill (Ottawa Rideau) and Jean Poirer (Prescott Russell). Most of them did not know me so I decided to introduce myself with words that would quickly break the ice. "I am here to wash your feet," I announced, in reference to the biblical story of Jesus washing the feet of his disciples to convey humility and the fact that they all served one another. There was instant laughter. From then on, the Trillium Committee had their total support and I had initiated some relationships that would endure for years to come.

The Trillium Dinner did indeed sell out that spring and we indeed achieved the highest attendance ever at the event in the National Capital. The banquet hall of the Ottawa Congress Centre was full to bursting with more than a thousand supporters and included a particularly strong ethnic presence. Several hundred volunteers turned out to help the evening flow smoothly, including our nineteen-year-old daughter Kim. Loretta wore a colourful *cheongsam* gown and I sported my personal interpretation of a Chinese-Liberal necktie: red with a dragon pattern, red being a symbol of good fortune in Chinese culture and also the traditional colour of the Liberal Party. Loretta and I greeted Premier Peterson upon his arrival and we walked together in procession to the head table followed by the Eastern Ontario caucus MPPs, all of us led by Chinese lion dancers instead of the customary bagpiper. When the singing of the national anthem began, I could not keep the tears from my eyes.

In formally introducing Premier Peterson to the assembly, I spoke of the "changing colour" of Ontario since my first arrival as an immigrant two decades earlier – it had become Liberal red after forty-two years of Progressive Conservative Party blue – and how greatly I welcomed the new spirit of multiculturalism embraced by the new government, a spirit that enabled me to feel I now truly belonged. When I finally shared the words in my heart – "This is my home!" – there was thunderous applause.

Just when I thought the evening could not become any more gratifying – the record-breaking attendance, my intimate conversation with the premier over dinner and his donning of my proffered Chinese-Liberal tie after his own tie had been cut off in a traditional gesture of fun – it did. I was presented with a book bound in red silk and with a golden plate mounted on the cover engraved with the words 'Chairman Ling', and when I read the handwritten notes of appreciation from the MPPs and Trillium Committee members inside, I was rendered speechless.

In the July of that year, Premier Peterson invited my wife and me to a dinner for Princess Margaret, the younger sister of Queen Elizabeth II, at the official residence of Ontario's lieutenant governor, Lincoln Alexander, in Toronto. I was thrilled at the prospect of meeting not only the princess but also Mr. Alexander, a man of many 'firsts' including being the first visible minority to serve in a viceregal position in Canada.

There were several 'firsts' for me also that evening.

Loretta and I found ourselves the first of some two dozen couples in the receiving line to meet Princess Margaret, so I had no one ahead of me to observe and learn from – and it was my first time to be introduced to a member of royalty. When Her Royal Highness reached out her hand, I shook it heartily, greeting her with a warm, "Welcome to Canada!" She remained aloof and moved on. I later found out that it was not appropriate to have spoken without her addressing me first and that my handshake should have been much more fleeting and tepid. Next in line, Loretta, as always, knew better. She curtsied and maintained a graceful silence.

I was approached several times that year and after about running for political office myself. After some thought, however, I realized I was not prepared to give up my family's steady income for the unpredictability of political life and so I chose instead to continue doing what I could from a position of voluntary activity to help the efforts of others who were working to make Ontario an ever better place in which to live.

For the next couple of years, David Peterson and his majority government remained popular and I enjoyed seeing the premier during his occasional visits to Ottawa, once going skiing with him at Camp Fortune. The end was sudden and unexpected. Less than three years into his mandate and with the Liberal Party still enjoying the lead in public opinion polls, Mr. Peterson decided to call an early election. This turned out to be a huge mistake.

The Ontario economy was on a downturn in 1990, a fact that was not helped by the new free trade agreement between Canada and the United States which, some economists argued, caused Ontario assets and money to flow south of the border and created job insecurity at home. There was no 'defining issue' behind the campaign and so many voters believed that the premier was simply trying to win re-election before the economy dipped even further. It also did not help that the campaign was being run in the aftermath of the failed Meech Lake Accord, a package of proposed amendments to the Constitution of Canada which Mr. Peterson had vigorously promoted but many in Ontario felt gave too many concessions to Quebec at the expense of all other provinces including Ontario.

I offered the party advice on how to attract the ethnic vote and also helped out with the campaign in the Ottawa area. It was a somewhat different experience to my first foray into provincial politics, given the atmosphere. A photo in the *Ottawa Citizen* showing me welcoming Mr. Peterson and his young daughter Chloe to the Greek Community

Centre in Ottawa, however, remains a treasured souvenir in spite of the outcome. On election night, September 5, 1990, the Liberal's historic ninety-five seat majority government was decimated and the premier even lost his own seat, a loss that ended his political career. He announced his resignation as party leader that same night. In Ottawa Centre, Evelyn Gigantes won back her seat for the now-ruling New Democratic Party, though Richard Patten would turn the tables once again at the next election.

Happily, six of the eight ridings in the Ottawa area bucked the provincial trend and remained Liberal that sobering night, including the riding of Ottawa South. The people of that community were now represented by Dalton McGuinty, Jr., following the sudden death of his well-respected namesake father earlier in the year. I had known the younger Dalton for a while, not only as a colleague on the Trillium Committee but before that as a fellow law school graduate of my friend Lewis Chan of the Canadian Ethnocultural Council. I was happy to work first on helping him get selected as the party member whose name would appear on the ballot to fill his late father's seat in the provincial legislature, and then on the election campaign itself, donning my most comfortable pair of running shoes to accompany him door-to-door seeking votes in the community. He was the only rookie Liberal MPP elected that night, and six years later I would be supporting his bid to serve as leader of the Liberal Party of Ontario.

The leadership of the Ontario party was in a state of flux for a couple of years after David Peterson's resignation until Lyn McLeod was chosen in 1992, becoming the first woman to head a major party in the province. Three years later she stepped down after a provincial election in which even more Liberal seats were lost and the Progressive Conservative Party wrested power from the New Democrats. Dalton McGuinty threw his hat into the leadership ring and Loretta and I hosted a fundraising dinner for him at our home. At the leadership convention, he faced stiff competition but finally won on the fifth ballot and made a triumphant return to Ottawa South as not only the local MPP but also the leader of the provincial official opposition. Loretta and I were among the large group of supporters waiting at the airport to welcome him home.

Under his leadership in the 1999 provincial election, though the Progressive Conservatives retained power, the Liberal slate captured forty percent of the popular vote, the party's second-best performance in fifty years. Over the course of the next four years, Mr. McGuinty successfully presented his party as the 'government in waiting', promoting a platform that emphasized lowering class sizes in schools, hiring more nurses, increasing environmental protections, and holding the line on taxes. Meanwhile, a number of controversies erupted for the ruling Progressive Conservatives as well as a change in their leadership. Election Day 2003 saw the Liberals commandeering seventy percent of the seats in the legislature, forming a majority government under now-Premier Dalton McGuinty.

As a sixteen-year veteran of provincial politics, particularly as one coming from an immigrant's background, I felt a great sense of fulfilment. Throughout those years of ups and downs I had never lost faith in the Liberal Party.

The compelling and visionary Pierre Trudeau had been the one to awaken my interest in Canadian politics at the national level, making me believe that even though I had not been born in Canada, I indeed had something to contribute. Following his retirement in 1984, the leadership of the Liberal Party of Canada was won by retired finance minister John Turner, with another former finance minister, Jean Chrétien, coming in second place. Mr. Turner won the leadership but failed to win the country. That September, the Liberals were swept from power in Ottawa in a massive Progressive Conservative landslide. Mr. Turner would serve as leader of the opposition in the House of Commons for well nigh six years until he resigned in 1990.

When Jean Chrétien announced that he would again seek the leadership position, my hope for the future was renewed. I decided to actively support him. To do this required that I get myself selected by the Ottawa Centre Federal Liberal Association as one of its five allotted delegates who could vote at the nation-wide party leadership convention to be held in Calgary, Alberta. And not only did I want to be selected myself, I also wanted the other four Ottawa Centre delegates to also be Chrétien supporters, not ones who were rooting for any other leadership hopeful. I had to prepare myself for unforeseen challenges as party leadership elections had gained notoriety for their often bitter organizational rivalries.

Loretta and I arrived early at the delegate selection meeting in the auditorium of Ottawa Technical High School. The room was full and the air was electric. I made my way through the crowd, greeting people and shaking hands with friends and acquaintances from the Chinese, Italian, Lebanese, Vietnamese and other ethnic communities. There were quite a number of people seeking delegate status but I knew I could count on at least three people to cast their vote for me: my sister Donna (Dong-dong) and her partner Sam – Donna had come to Canada a few years after completing her college education in England and worked in interior design in Toronto, Montreal and Ottawa – and of course my Loretta.

Each delegate aspirant was allotted one minute for making a pitch to the audience. To make the best use of this brief time, I found myself dashing onstage and starting my speech almost before reaching the microphone. I spoke passionately about how Mr. Chrétien, who referred to himself as "a little guy from Shawinigan", had set a great example for me, "a little immigrant from Hong Kong", to persevere, to seize each opportunity, and to give back to Canada. The applause that accompanied my departure from the podium told me that my message had gone over well.

After all the speeches had been given, the voting began. Ballot counting went on until past midnight. To my great delight, the final results showed that I had received the highest number of votes, but best of all the other four delegates selected were also Chrétien supporters. The news on television the following day showed a little of my speech, including the finale during which I had raised my fist, repeating the name "Jean Chrétien!"

Some five thousand delegates from across the country converged on Calgary in June 1990, not only to elect a new leader of the Liberal Party of Canada but also to vote on a new national executive and a number of changes to the party's constitution. After I had signed in as an Ottawa-Centre delegate, Loretta and I picked up some campaign placards and put on the cowboy hats emblazoned with the name Chrétien that we had been given. We made our way to an auditorium full of empty chairs and asked an organizer in the room, "Where are our people?" Pointing towards front row seats close to the stage, he responded with a welcoming smile, "Those seats are reserved for you." We were confused, as there were no political signs or delegates anywhere in evidence. We soon discovered the reason. We were at the venue of a First Nations event, not the Liberal Party convention, and with our Chinese faces partially obscured by cowboy hats and sunglasses, we had been mistaken as members of the First Nations looking for "our people". It was a novel experience for once not to be perceived as immigrants! We quickly found our way to the right auditorium elsewhere in the convention centre.

The atmosphere was highly charged on the day each of the five leadership candidates made their pivotal speeches to the gathering: Jean Chrétien, Sheila Copps, Paul Martin, John Nunziata and Tom Wappel, each of them a veteran of the House of Commons. Several of the speeches were compelling, however I had learnt over the years that more than half of an election battle is won by having a solid campaign organization that is supported by strong financial and volunteer resources, and I knew the Chrétien campaign possessed all of these. The time for voting finally came and I went down to the floor of the arena to join one of the long line-ups heading to the voting booths. Looking up towards the area where I had been sitting, I spotted Loretta standing tall and waving her Chrétien campaign sign. Deep in my heart, I was grateful and impressed that my wife, a normally private person, had been so deeply affected by the "Chrétien spirit".

Mr. Chrétien won handily on the first ballot, capturing over fifty-six percent of the forty-six hundred-plus votes cast. He was sworn in as Leader of Her Majesty's Loyal Opposition on December 20, 1990.

In late 1992, Loretta and I were invited to a small cocktail reception hosted by Mr. Chrétien and his wife Aline at Stornoway, the official residence of the opposition leader and just a few hundred metres from our own home. It was an interesting experience to find myself sitting side-by-side in intimate conversation with someone I was used to watching on television or on a stage somewhere, Mr. Chrétien's legendary English vocabulary spoken with a strong French-Canadian accent conveying an air of freshness and high spirits. When it was time for us to head out with him to an Ottawa Senators hockey game, Madame Chrétien said goodbye at the front door and remarked with confidence, "Next year, it will be at 24 Sussex Drive." Her prediction that the couple would then be living in the official residence of the prime minister was indeed accurate.

The Progressive Conservative government under Brian Mulroney had become deeply unpopular, compounded by scandal and the introduction of a new sales tax, the Goods and Services Tax. Even after Mr. Mulroney was replaced by Kim Campbell, Canada's first female prime minister, and the ratings improved somewhat, antipathy towards the party continued. On October 25, 1993, the Liberals were elected to a strong majority government with one hundred and seventy-seven seats, while the Progressive Conservatives were all but wiped out, keeping only two seats in the worst defeat ever suffered by any major federal party.

And so it was that Aline Chrétien's prediction came true. And when Prime Minister and Madame Chrétien welcomed Loretta and me to our first garden party at 24 Sussex Drive, instead of using my name, he exclaimed, "You are the Doctor!" – no doubt a reference to the nickname I had been given by Liberal Party stalwart and future member of parliament Mauril Bélanger, a reflection perhaps of my habit of dispensing Eastern 'medicine' in times of challenge in the form of proverbs I had learned from my mother, my grandfather and Uncle.

Jean Chrétien served as Canada's prime minister for the next ten years. During that decade, he led the party to two more election victories, each time achieving a majority government. Under his watch, a great many positive initiatives were achieved including the deficit being eliminated, five consecutive budget surpluses being recorded, the national debt being reduced, and the largest tax cuts in Canadian history being instituted. He enhanced Canada's trade and cultural relationship with China and refused to support the U.S.-led invasion of Iraq in 2003. However, along with the sunshine, dark clouds were building on the horizon. Mr. Chrétien faced criticism on a number of fronts including not keeping an election promise to replace the hated Goods and Services Tax, and being accused of increasingly centralizing power in the Prime Minister's Office. In November 2003, he announced his resignation: A sound decision by a smart "street fighter" – his own label for himself – who had reached the summit.

The popularity of the governing Liberals, now headed by Paul Martin, also a former finance minister, began to fall sharply. The end was signalled by the eruption of the "Sponsorship Scandal" involving fraudulent use of federal government money that was intended to fund an advertising program in Quebec in an effort to combat separatism by raising awareness of the Government of Canada's contributions to the vitality of the province. The seat in Ottawa Centre was vacant following the appointment of Liberal MP Mac Harb to the Senate after fifteen years serving the riding and I became extremely sceptical that a new Liberal candidate would be able to hold the riding in the upcoming election, given the atmosphere. I decided to sit this one out, further persuaded of its hopelessness when the New Democrats presented their nationally respected former party leader Ed Broadbent as their candidate in the riding. I was right. He was indeed unbeatable.

Paul Martin's Liberal government managed to survive that election in 2004, becoming the first minority federal government in a quarter of a century, but the final blow was delivered the following year when the opposition parties banded together to pass a motion of no confidence in the government and another federal election was called. In January 2006, the newly constituted Conservative Party headed by Stephen Harper pushed the Liberals, led first by interim leader Bill Graham and then by Stéphane Dion, into the role of the official opposition. The third-place New Democrats held on to Ottawa Centre, however, with Paul Dewar, the son of a popular former mayor of Ottawa, taking over the reins from the now retired Ed Broadbent.

When yet another election was called just two years later, I knew it was time for me to get back in the game.

This time, the Liberal candidate in Ottawa Centre was Penny Collenette, a highly respected party stalwart whose impeccable track record in both the public and private sectors had earned her a place on a national news magazine's list of the fifty most influential people in Canada. A lawyer and human rights advocate, Penny possessed all the qualities of a strong candidate and I unhesitatingly went campaigning with her in Chinatown and the Little Italy areas of the riding where we knocked on doors, handed out campaign literature and made our pitch from top to bottom of high-rise apartment buildings. However it was not to be. It seemed to me that voters were faced with having to choose between two people who were worthy to represent them in Parliament – Paul Dewar had by now gained the confidence of many of his constituents – and so chose to opt for the familiar and stay with the status quo.

The country also stayed with the status quo, with the Liberals remaining in opposition.

Today, though no longer a card-carrying member, I remain eternally grateful to the Liberal Party for the way in which it embraced me as a full-fledged Canadian, and for the life lessons on winning and losing that it reinforced – not least for reminding me of the wisdom of the ancient Chinese proverb, "If there is light in the soul, there will be beauty in the person. If there is beauty in the person, there will be harmony in the house. If there is harmony in the house, there will be order in the nation. If there is order in the nation, there will be peace in the world."

CANADIAN MUSEUM OF NATURE – THE GUARDIAN ANGEL WITH FOUR WINGS

When the phone call came from the Prime Minister's Office, I could not have been more surprised. On the line was Penny Collenette, who at the time – it was February 1996, twelve years before Penny threw her hat in the ring in Ottawa Centre – was Prime Minister Jean Chrétien's director of appointments, charged with finding Canadians to serve in various honourary positions affiliated with the federal government.

Penny was known for having elevated this tradition of appointments from one in which they were made as a reward for political services rendered – "patronage appointments" – to one in which a person's skills were matched to the needs of the position to be filled, so when she told me that my name had been put forward for appointment to the board of trustees of the Canadian Museum of Nature, my instinctive response was one of bewilderment. I protested that I knew nothing about running a museum and that I was seriously lacking in knowledge of the natural sciences. Penny, however, suggested we meet to discuss what the position would require of me before making a decision. Curious, I agreed.

A few days later, I found myself navigating the corridors of the Langevin Block for our rendezvous – corridors whose every detail I had happily sweated over while planning their renovation two decades earlier. I easily found my way to the discreet spiral staircase that led up to the office Penny occupied close to the prime minister's private suite in the western wing. She greeted me warmly and Suzanne Hurtubise, deputy minister of the Department of Canadian Heritage, the department responsible for all national museums, soon joined us. Together they explained that the board of trustees of the Museum of Nature had been without a chairperson for quite a while and needed leadership that could help initiate the repair of the damaged relationship that had developed between museum staff and its senior management and also bring about a revitalization of the institution. They said that they believed that my non-museum background was a plus, that it could bring objectivity and freshness to the position – that what mattered was my record of success in guiding business associations and public organizations like the police services board. Strong leadership was needed from the museum's board and never more so than now, they said, given the challenges created by several years of severe budget cuts due to national deficit-reduction measures enacted by the federal government.

It sounded to me as though there were rather a lot of knotty issues to be overcome at the museum and I suspected that achieving success in this particular leadership role, especially when I knew nothing about museum management, could prove difficult. I told them I needed time to consider, which they gently countered by saying that the minister was waiting to brief me in her office. That got my attention. I had been an admirer of Sheila Copps ever since hearing her dynamic speech six years earlier at the Liberal convention where she had been the only female leadership candidate – she was now Canada's deputy prime minister as well as minister of Canadian Heritage – so I happily set off across the road to her office on Parliament Hill.

Ms. Copps was every bit as engaging, perceptive and knowledgeable one-on-one as she had been when addressing the crowd in Calgary. She had clearly been filled in on my résumé and seemed quite convinced, despite my own deep reservations, that the experience and multicultural background that I possessed could indeed bring a useful perspective to the management of the ailing museum. When she switched to speaking in French – a language I was not very comfortable using – our conversation was brought to an abrupt end by the urgent tones of a bell summoning all MPs to the House of Commons for an imminent vote. Hugely relieved, I quickly told her that I would pay a visit to the museum and then get back to Penny Collenette with my decision.

The Victoria Memorial Museum Building is an impressive stone structure somewhat reminiscent of a castle – and often referred to simply as 'the castle' – that was designed early in the twentieth century as an anchor to the Parliament Buildings visible at the opposite end of the mile-long avenue that stretches between the two. Indeed, 'the castle' even served as the temporary home of Canada's Parliament for four years following a fire that destroyed the Centre Block on Parliament Hill in 1916.

The first thing I experienced on entering through one of the three sets of imposing double front doors was a sense of letdown. I found myself in a rather gloomy, though spacious, lobby which then led to a multi-storied atrium that also failed to impress as it should have done, given its soaring height. Everything felt dated, tired. I bought an entrance pass and set off to explore, the sound of chattering children luring me up a broad marble staircase to the next level where I found youngsters enthusiastically engaged in natural science workshops. To my surprise I recognized one of the instructors. It was George McIlhinney, whom I had met at social gatherings for senior civil servants and diplomats in Ottawa.

George told me that he had been volunteering at the museum ever since retiring from a career with the federal government and found it a rewarding experience. He pointed to others also working with children in nearby rooms and I suddenly had clarity regarding a question I did not know was in my head but which I had unconsciously come there to resolve: Was there anything about this museum – almost foreign territory to me – that could ignite my personal commitment and passion? Watching George and his colleagues with the children, I had my answer. The Canadian Museum of Nature was more than a natural history museum; it was also about education, community participation, volunteerism and future generations. Those things, I cared deeply about.

I called Penny the following morning and agreed to let my name be submitted to the Privy Council for a three-year appointment to the museum's board of trustees.

The official citation signed by Governor General Roméo LeBlanc was dated March 19, 1996. Within mere days of the news getting out about my appointment, letters began arriving at my home, about forty in all. They were from museum scientists and from private citizens, mailed from communities across Canada and from as far away as New Zealand and Britain. They were letters of protest against the extensive layoff of museum professionals, scientists and technicians that had occurred over the past few years because of the budget cutbacks, and they pleaded with me to do something to reverse the situation. Some asked to meet with me in person to present their case. My challenges as the new chair of the board had begun even before my first official day on the job.

The number one task on my agenda was to meet with the top staff person, the museum's president and chief executive officer. He invited me to lunch at his office but I felt that the open communication I wanted to establish might be more easily achieved on neutral territory and so I suggested we meet in the dining room of the historic Rideau Club instead. I found him to be a self-assured man. He had held the president's position for more than a dozen years and spoke proudly of the museum, telling me of its many strengths. When I raised some of the problematic issues I knew existed within the institution, however, I felt that his answers were more perfunctory than I would have liked, making me wonder if perhaps he thought a rookie like me would want to be made to feel that all was under control, at least until I got my feet wet. Indeed, he assured me that he and his senior management team had striven to make things as "easy" as possible for the board of trustees in the absence of a chair. As we parted, he invited me for an official visit to 'the castle' so I could meet his senior team. I hoped that perhaps then I would learn more about the impact of the severely pruned operating budget, which had to be extremely difficult for management to cope with, and about the current state of staff morale, along with their vision for the future.

Louise Winter, secretary to the board of trustees and a long-time museum employee, greeted me at the front door the following morning and took me to the president's office. There, I was briefed first by the vice president and chief operating officer, followed by the vice president of collection and research, and finally the vice president of public programs, all of whom gave the impression that it was business as usual in spite of the budget cuts and layoffs. I then told Louise that I would like to tour all the museum's facilities and to meet as many staff members as I could, from directors and researchers to secretaries and carpenters.

Many of the museum's behind-the-scenes functions were accommodated off-site due to the space constraints of 'the castle' and over the course of the next couple of days Louise escorted me to plants and offices scattered across the city. As an architect I could see they were not always up to good functional standard for their purposes as research laboratories, production workshops and artefact storage facilities, but everywhere I went people were surprised and excited to be visited by the chair of the board. Many spoke openly with me and I sensed many damaged working spirits, caused in large part by the depletion of their ranks, and I was approached privately by employee union representatives who aired deep frustration.

It was clear to me that staff on the whole harboured the perception that their needs were being ignored. It would be my job to ensure their energy was revitalized, a challenge that should become somewhat easier with the recent relaxation of budget cuts. Something was already being done to address the physical plant deficiencies: the construction of a state-of-the-art building large enough to bring together under one roof all the scattered non-public functions was already in the works.

The first meeting I chaired was of the museum's executive committee, which was responsible for overseeing the activities of the board of trustees and its four standing committees (finance, building, human resources and community relations) and also for conducting the president's annual performance review. My fellow members on the executive committee were the chairs of the standing committees and we were joined at the table by the president. To my disappointment, the preset agenda produced a cut-and-dried session with no apparent pressing issues and no opportunity for in-depth discussion. I looked forward to something more substantial occurring at the finance committee meeting that was to follow immediately after. Before it began, however, Patricia Wright, its chair, pulled me aside for a quiet word.

A lawyer from Mississauga, Patti spoke frankly, telling me that she had been frustrated by a lack of meaningful financial information coming from management and she had a strong sense that there were underlying budget and staff problems that were not being shared fully with her committee or the board of trustees. She had been waiting for the chair position to be filled, she said, and offered me her support in turning things around. The perfunctory nature of the finance meeting that followed this conversation added weight to her comments.

I left both these meetings – my first as chair – not entirely dissatisfied, however, because I had learned two important things: first, there was a need for openness and trust to be developed between management and the board; and second, staff, from the bottom up, needed to experience sound leadership exerted by a strong board.

The first board of trustees meeting of my tenure was slated to be held in June, two months down the road.

Before June came, I had to appear before the House of Commons Standing Committee on Canadian Heritage. As a Crown corporation, an entity owned by the state but operating at arm's length from it, the museum was required to report to Parliament on an annual basis through this committee. As luck would have it, the chair of a sister museum, the Canadian Museum of Civilization, reported immediately ahead of me. Adrienne Clarkson was a former television host, dynamic, relaxed and fully bilingual. Her presentation that day easily commanded the attention of the heritage committee (she would be appointed Canada's Governor General – the Queen's representative in Canada – just three years later) and it was clear she would be a hard act to follow. I had been given a script by 'my' museum's president, but instinct told me to speak from my heart, so I started by saying that I was a rookie on the job. I spoke about budget and staff morale challenges, and equally about the museum's potential and my hopes for its future. I explained that what our museum was experiencing was a crisis as that word is defined in a Chinese dictionary: a combination of two characters, one representing "danger" and the other representing "opportunities".

The heritage committee's response was gratifyingly supportive. Best of all, for me, the laid-off museum scientists I had spotted among the spectators seemed relieved that the facts of the situation, as they knew them, were starting to be told.

In June, all eleven trustees gathered from across Canada for a two-day board meeting in Halifax, Nova Scotia. It was the first board meeting for six of us, all recently appointed by the Liberal government. The other five had been appointed previously by a Conservative government, however we quickly discovered that we were truly a nonpartisan group, sharing similar aspirations for the museum. The board was now at full strength and we wanted to have two days of deeply constructive sessions, starting with listening to what senior management had to tell us.

We new trustees were expecting an in-depth introduction to the museum's business agenda and anticipated future direction, while incumbent trustees, I later learned, were hoping for an improvement in substance over previous management reports. What we got, however, struck us as being little more than a visual presentation on regular museum activities, punctuated with remarks about how well the institution was doing. It was evident that we trustees were being treated more as observers than as advisors and decision makers whose responsibility it was to provide meaningful direction to management, a situation made all the more obvious when we were offhandedly informed that the museum's vice president and chief operating officer had departed a month earlier.

That evening, the executive committee met to discuss the situation. After lengthy and often emotional debate, we came to the conclusion that the most effective measure we could take to initiate the change that we felt was needed was to make a change at the very top of management, effective immediately. The following day, the whole board endorsed this recommendation at an in-camera session and it became my difficult duty to inform the president of our decision, no easy deed after his years of service. And there was still one more task to be done: the minister had to be brought into the picture before the news hit the media.

There was no answer at Sheila Copps' office – it was already past regular working hours – and so I tried the office of the director of appointments, the museum's presidency being an appointed position. Penny Collenette's assistant assured me that the information would be passed along pronto.

The board of trustees appointed acting vice-president and chief operating officer Colin Eades as interim president and CEO, though he made it clear that he had no interest in taking over the position on a permanent basis. Over the course of the next few months, he was to initiate a total restructuring of management and quickly introduced an 'Upwards Appraisal Process' in which experienced-in-the-trenches staff were moved into managing positions.

Colin Eades had his hands full during this period of change. On top of his two key 'interim' and 'acting' positions, he was also the director of capital projects and as such was busily occupied in overseeing the construction of the new facility that would house all the museum's non-public functions. That project was not without huge challenges of its own. It had been a source of contention ever since a site had been selected two years earlier – indeed the site itself was the bone of the contention.

There were those who argued its location in Aylmer, Quebec, about half an hour's drive from 'the castle', was totally inefficient, and others who accused the government of playing politics by selecting a site in Quebec rather than in Ontario. The biggest challenge, however, came from a third group of people who protested publicly and vociferously that the fifty-six-hectare site (one hundred and forty acres) included wetlands that should be protected, not developed.

Public Works Canada's environmental reports disagreed with their opinion of the site. So too did environmental assessments conducted by an independent engineering firm and by Axor Engineering, the company involved in the construction contract. We got in touch with Dr. Husain Sadar, director of the Centre for Environmental Assessment at Carleton University, and he suggested a way to break the stalemate: we could procure similar acreage of certified wetlands for permanent conservation. It was a wise suggestion, and it worked. We purchased a parcel of land to the south of Ottawa to be stewarded in perpetuity by our museum, protected from development and used only for natural sciences research. After that, the plans for the construction of the new facility continued without further disruption. The National Heritage

Building, as it would be named, was officially opened in Aylmer in the spring of 1997.

The search for a new president and CEO occupied a great deal of my attention. Traditionally, the federal government played a major role in the selection of the person to be appointed senior manager of a Crown corporation, often resulting in the name submitted by a board of trustees becoming lost in the shuffle. We did not want that to happen. I approached Penny Collenette and she agreed that my board could hire a headhunting firm to manage the search, on condition that the position be advertised only in the *Canada Gazette*, an official government publication.

I formed a candidate search and selection committee consisting of trustees of diverse professional experience and cultural backgrounds and we hired the executive search firm Ray & Berndtson. Within a few weeks, more than thirty professionals from across Canada had responded. We created a shortlist of eleven for interviewing. What we were particularly looking for were leadership attributes that included clarity in sharing ideas and a tendency to listen well. We conducted the interviews at Ray & Berndtson's boardroom in Toronto over the course of two days, followed by an exhaustive brainstorming session by our committee to reduce the shortlist to two names, two candidates whom I would then visit on their home turf for a final interview.

The first person to make that list was Joanne DiCosimo, executive director of the Manitoba Museum of Man and Nature and the only female candidate. She was a graduate of the Kennedy School of Government at Harvard and what had struck me most about her was how eloquently she spoke about believing in a bottom-up style of management. The second name to be added to the list belonged to another exceptional candidate who had a wealth of experience and impressed us as a superior planner and organizer with many clear ideas for initiating change.

We had come to the final phase of the selection process.

Colin Eades, our interim president, and I first visited the last name on the list, whose current museum beautifully reflected the skills and talents of the person in charge, the skills and talents that had earned him a place on our final list. In a private tête-à-tête over lunch, I took great care listening as he shared with me his suggestions on the changes he thought could help our museum, a topic about which he had many ideas to convey.

Then we traveled to Winnipeg, to Joanne DiCosimo's equally fine museum, a short walk from our hotel through the deep freeze of a prairie winter late afternoon. As we started off on a tour of her facility, Joanne asked Colin why he was not interested in taking on the president's position himself, making me realize that she was thorough in her mental processes. Later, at a quiet restaurant, she and I chatted one-on-one, covering a variety of topics including her experiences at Harvard and her ambition to take time off some summer to complete her Ph.D in England. We talked a lot about social and environmental issues and she asked many questions about the museum, about the board, and about myself. Rather than making specific suggestions on how our museum should be managed, she eloquently expressed a vision of the institution as an important resource to be managed for the pleasure and education of all Canadians. I was impressed by her community values and her skills as a listener and was soon satisfied that in her we had indeed found the right person for the job.

Back home, the board approved the search committee's recommendation and an offer went out to Joanne, who accepted and came to Ottawa for a make-or-break meeting at the Prime Minister's Office with the director of appointments – the final determinant. To our relief and delight, on July 2, 1997, our museum had its new president and CEO.

Right from day one of Joanne's appointment, the openness and trust between board and management that I had envisioned became a fait accompli. Indeed, two years later at a surprise party following my reappointment as chair for a second three-year term, I was delighted to be able to tell staff, "The museum's board and CEO are like a pair of chopsticks: one cannot function without the other."

Joanne DiCosimo quickly enacted her vision of the museum as a national resource, initiating and leading a process that resulted in first-time-ever collaboration among museums of natural history across Canada. She also reached out locally, developing the museum's capacity to raise funds from the private sector and introducing successful new programs to increase attendance, particularly among school children. A piece of plaster, however, was about to throw a wrench into everything.

The exterior stonework of 'the castle' had been extensively restored in the early 1990s but there had been little done to the inside. When the chunk of plaster fell off the wall in an area where people were gathered, it triggered an alert regarding the safety of the aging building completed way back in 1912. Engineers were hired to investigate. Their findings were alarming. Deteriorating wall plaster was the least of our problems, as it was quickly determined that 'the castle' did not comply with basic health and safety standards regarding mechanical and electrical services, structural design, and fire exit requirements. All were well below modern code. The magnitude of the repairs and renovations needed was enormous, an expensive undertaking far beyond what the museum's annual budget could cover. Joanne conferred with her management team and approached me with their vision of turning this major health and safety challenge into an opportunity for a total overhaul of the museum, its exhibits and its programs to better reflect its new philosophy. She suggested we take a bold step and approach the Department of Canadian Heritage for financing. The board agreed.

Joanne and I met with Alex Himelfarb, Deputy Minister of Canadian Heritage, at his office. This was the first hurdle we had to successfully navigate, as gaining his support for our proposal would go a long way towards winning the support of Minister Copps, while any resistance on his part would automatically have a negative impact on the minister's deliberations. I was glad that we were not having a totally 'cold' meeting, as he and I had met once before at a function hosted by a mutual friend. He appeared to be well informed of the situation at the museum and I filled him in on the details of the building's major deficiencies, ending with, "If we don't do anything, the building will be physically dead, the board of trustees will be morally dead, and the government may well be politically dead." This pronouncement was greeted with several long seconds of unnerving silence, followed by a smile.

Mr. Himelfarb took up our case with the minister, who in turn gained the support of the government. With a budget set at just over one hundred and thirty million dollars, the renovations could begin.

We hired the team of Padolsky, Kuwabara, Gagnon – PKG – Joint Venture Architects, and Colin Eades headed up the museum's capital project team with technical support from Public Works Canada. Needless to say, design challenges arose in abundance. Given the fact that Ottawa is located in a seismic zone and there are areas of quicksand-like Leda clay on the museum site, the exterior stone walls of 'the castle' would need to be reinforced for structural safety. It was determined that this could best be accomplished by interior modifications, however these modifications would encroach on precious floor space, space that would have to be recovered by excavating new square footage in the basement and adding an extension to the rear of the building, all with major impact on the renovation budget.

In 1912 the museum had boasted a massive stone tower on top of the expansive two-stories-high entrance lobby that projected out from the front of the main structure, but this tower had been demolished three years later when it was discovered that the unstable clay underneath could not support its weight. Bruce Kuwabara, the lead design architect for our project, came up with the idea of a lighter tower made of steel as a tribute to the original design. I liked the concept, but I had concerns.

The height of the new tower would extend well above the roofline of the main structure and would cast a long shadow on the neighbourhood to the north. People in the area would likely object to this and the Centretown Community Association – so familiar to me – would be up in arms on their behalf, leading to potential delays in the construction schedule. Besides, I wanted the museum to be a good neighbour. In addition, the tower as proposed served no practical purpose and it seemed to me our budget would best be spent on projects that addressed at least one of the many functional needs. The board agreed and the architects went back to the drawing board. What they came up with some weeks later was perfect.

The revamped design was for a tower not much higher than the main roofline and with no shadow effect: it would be in the form of a transparent "box" – a box made of glass. It would encase a dual set of scissor staircases – two interlocking stairways that wind around each other, one for going up and the other for going down – that would greatly improve visitors' access between floors and at the same time serve as a fire exit route, so essential for meeting current safety standards. The board endorsed this design and I heartily congratulated Bruce Kuwabara and his team for their creative thinking. This unique tower would be named the Queens' Lantern in honour of two monarchs: Elizabeth II, who personally unveiled the name plaque in 2010, and her great-great-grandmother to whom 'the castle' – the Victoria Memorial Museum Building – is dedicated.

It was during the complex renovation design phase that I was reappointed as chair of the board. Mid-way through that second term, I had my second encounter with a member of the Royal Family. It was in the spring of 2001 and I was one of several hundred guests invited to attend a reception for the Prince of Wales in the spectacular grand hall of the Canadian Museum of Civilization. When it came close to the time for the prince to arrive, people began to move towards the area where he would enter the hall, clearly hoping for a chance to meet with him face-to-face. I held back, not anxious to repeat the awkward "do not speak until spoken to" scenario I had experienced with the prince's aunt, Princess Margaret.

Deputy Prime Minister Sheila Copps – also the museum minister, of course – escorted Prince Charles into the grand hall and they began to move through the crowd, pausing for introductions and brief chats with people as they went. When she spotted me in the distance, Ms. Copps waved me over and presented me to His Royal Highness, saying I was the chair of the Canadian Museum of Nature. The prince shook my hand, enthusing, "Congratulations! What a lovely building!" Now that I had been spoken to, I felt free to respond. I clarified that I was not involved with the museum we were standing in but with its sister museum, one dedicated to natural history and the environment. "Jolly good!" he exclaimed, his face visibly brightening, clearly resonating with my areas of responsibility. "You must give him more money!" he added with spirit, looking directly at Sheila Copps.

In spite of this 'Royal Proclamation', however, fundraising from the private sector became essential to our renewal plan for our museum. We established a committee to raise capital for the many projects not covered by the restoration budget – new and renewed display galleries and exhibition spaces were high on that list. I was delighted that Dr. Adam Chowaniec, founding CEO of Tundra Semiconductor, and his wife, Dr. Claudia Chowaniec, agreed to serve as co-chairs of our national campaign and under their dynamic leadership we were successful in rallying community and corporate support from all across Canada.

My second three-year term as chair was extended for a year in order for me to continue playing a role in the final design stage of the renovations and in the initial stage of construction. I was grateful that my background in architecture helped me enormously in facilitating communication between architects, our project team, and the board of trustees.

When I stepped down in 2003, I was deeply moved to be awarded the title of Chair Emeritus and to have a boardroom in the National Heritage Building in Aylmer named after me. Most gratifying of all, however, was to see several hundred staff members turn out for my farewell breakfast in 'the castle', a group of them even performing a musical number composed for the occasion in a friendly nod to my own youthful days in a band.

I was aware of constriction in my throat as I responded to the amiable gathering, sharing my thoughts about my responsibilities as chair of the board of trustees for the last seven years during which I had viewed my role as that of a guardian angel, one with four wings. At any given moment, I said, I had been spreading at least one of those wings, whichever was needed at that moment. For the restructuring of the museum's management, I had spread the wing of intervention; for the task of finding the leader who could revitalize the museum, I had spread the wing of restoration; for building staff morale and initiating the developments that made new programs and new facilities possible, I had spread the wing of creation; and for preparing the way for an orderly transition in governance, I had spread the wing of succession. It was difficult to now say goodbye after working together – staff, management and board – as one unit, a cohesive team that had accomplished a great deal indeed.

Privately, however, I took a great deal of comfort in knowing that George McIlhinney, the friend who had first ignited in me a passion for the museum, would still be there, still sharing the wonders of nature with the excited and curious children, the citizens of tomorrow, who now poured into 'the castle' in ever-greater numbers.

LOOKING BACK ON IT ALL

As I look back on the challenges and the joys of each one of the activities that captured my interest and commanded a good deal of my time over the course of the past several decades, I feel lucky, I feel blessed and I feel grateful. In other words, I feel truly Canadian.

(TOP): As vice-president of the Chinese Canadian National Council, it was my pleasure to take the microphone while council president Dr. Joseph Wong *(centre)* admired the council's new logo as it was revealed by Canada's Minister of State for Multiculturalism, James Fleming, in 1981.

(BOTTOM): Over the course of three decades as a practicing architect on three continents, I designed a huge variety of projects – however my favourite has to be the Dows Lake Pavilion in Ottawa.

(TOP): Our 1987 trade mission to Hong Kong and Beijing led by Mayor Jim Durrell laid the foundation for Ottawa companies to begin doing business with and in China.

(BOTTOM LEFT): Skiing with Ontario Premier David Peterson *(left)* and MPP Richard Patten *(centre)* at Camp Fortune, just minutes from downtown Ottawa.

(BOTTOM RIGHT): Ready to cast my vote at the Liberal Party of Canada leadership convention in Calgary (1990).

(TOP): Police Chief Tom Flanagan is on my right and deputy chief Brian Ford on my left in this formal grouping of the Ottawa Police Force's senior officers taken just after I became chair of the Police Services Board in 1992.

(BOTTOM): Christopher Patten, "The Last Governor of Hong Kong", accepts a memento of Ottawa as he closes the first ever Festival Hong Kong in the capital city in 1992.

(TOP): Doors were opened for Ottawa firms participating in the city's 1994 trade mission to Beijing because of its chef de mission, Mayor Jacquelin Holzman, whose leadership lent official credence to the business negotiations.

(BOTTOM): I was pleased to introduce Peter Clark, chairman of the Regional Municipality of Ottawa Carleton *(seated left)*, to a 1995 gathering of the Canadian Chamber of Commerce in Hong Kong, a proactive body of business people with interests in Canada, Hong Kong and mainland China.

(TOP): Tung Chee-hwa, head of the Hong Kong Special Administrative Region, welcomes me to a business forum in Hong Kong in 1997, just weeks after sovereignty of the former British colony was returned to China.

(BOTTOM): Finding myself the recipient of a second Queen Elizabeth II jubilee medal a decade after receiving my first felt almost surreal. Her Majesty's Diamond Jubilee award was presented to me by Governor General David Johnston in 2012.

(TOP): The 'christening' of the Frank Ling Seminar Room in the Canadian Museum of Nature's facility in Aylmer, Quebec, with museum president Joanne DiCosimo *(first left)* there to give her blessing (2003).

(BOTTOM): I was delighted to bring together two of my great interests – the Canadian Museum of Nature and the Ottawa Dragon Boat Festival – by sponsoring the Nature's Dragons team composed of museum staff in the popular festival I helped found at Mooney's Bay.

(TOP): The long hours and challenges behind the renovations to the Canadian Museum of Nature were forgotten as Loretta and I witnessed the unveiling of the plaque designating the museum's unique new tower – the Queens' Lantern, named for Elizabeth II and her great-great-grandmother, Victoria – by Queen Elizabeth in 2010.

(BOTTOM): The museum has become a family affair, with its award-winning Donor Wall happily sponsored by my whole family.

(TOP): Loretta and I thoroughly enjoyed the gladsome pageantry of the Order of Canada investiture at Rideau Hall in 2005 – a highlight experience of my life and an extraordinary honour from my adopted homeland.

(BOTTOM): It was particularly sweet to receive the Order of Canada from Governor General Adrienne Clarkson, a fellow Hong Kong native whom I had also known as a colleague on the national museum scene in Ottawa.

Endgame

I consider myself a "Made in Hong Kong" product but with added value – value gained from diverse cultural life experiences: Chinese family commitment and consensus, British self-discipline and sense of duty, European adaptability, American vigour and optimism, and Canadian give-and-take, equanimity and perseverance. My worlds of East and West, seemingly so far apart at the beginning, have fused into a seamless whole, each beautifully informing and enriching the other.

In these pages, I have traced the rich journey that has brought me from Chinese beginnings under British colonial authority and Japanese suppression, through English educational experiences with a dash of European cultural influence, onwards through Southeast Asian lessons in political and personal stability, to settle finally in Canada, the "cold place far away" that the fortune teller had long ago foreseen would be good for me. He was right. It is in Canada – my home now for more than half of my seven-plus decades – that I have been free to create a life that has been everything l could ever have wished for.

Canada accepted this immigrant stranger, challenged me to be the best I could be at whatever I chose to do, and generously rewarded my efforts. Those rewards have been many, including being appointed to the ranks of the Order of Canada, an order whose motto, *Desiderantes meliorem patriam* ("They desire a better country"), reflects my highest intentions – for I have tried to live this life of mine from that place of noble purpose exemplified most powerfully in the lives of my mother and Uncle and Aunt.

Most fulfilling of all, I have been blessed with the gift of a stimulating, full and harmonious life with my beloved Loretta and with our two dear children and now our wonderful grandchildren. It is they, the ensuing generations, who motivated me to commit my life journey thus far to paper. Unlike me, they are products largely "Made in Canada" and their outlook is shaped by that fact of destiny and by their multi-ethnic community of friends, their frequent world travels and the borderless Internet. It is also, I dare to hope, influenced, as I have been, by their predecessors' values, at least those that have managed to filter down to one degree or another through Loretta and me.

Where will my journey take me next? Looking back over the course of my life has shown me clearly that each time one door closes, another opens without fail and I find myself in a place beyond my earlier imaginings. Not knowing for sure what comes next is part of the glorious adventure. Ever since being caught outside during that terrifying air raid when I was six years old, I have chosen to hang on to the trust implanted in me in that moment by my mother – that no matter what is happening around me, even the most difficult of circumstances, all is indeed well. It cannot be any other way when I can always pray standing.

Loretta and I along with our daughter Kim, our son Theo and our grandchildren pay our respects at my mother's grave in the Chinese Christian Cemetery in Hong Kong, with its commanding view of the beautiful waters of Victoria Harbour (2012).

I was deeply moved to see the sign that today adorns the exact spot in Hong Kong where, in 1944, caught outside in an air raid, I held onto my mother's hand and asked the question, "Mother, can you pray standing?" Her response gave me the immovable foundation on which to build my life.

My brother Yuen-shun (as a teenager he adopted the Western name Ronnie), sister Dong-dong (Donna) and I enjoy getting together as often as we can. A photo of the three of us, taken at a family reunion in Vancouver in 2012, adorns the souvenir poster sent to all who came to the gathering, with our family name highlighted in Chinese characters – *haú* ("mouth") above *t'in* ("heaven" or "sky") – symbolizing our unbreakable family ties.

Roots and Wings

Baby and the Chinese Origins

I was born on October 1, now the National Day of the People's Republic of China, and in 1937, the year of my birth, that day happened to be the twenty-seventh day of the eighth lunar month of the Chinese calendar, the day the birthday of Confucius is celebrated.

My family name in Cantonese is Ng, which Westerners find difficult to pronounce, the easiest way being to close the mouth and utter the sound "Oonn" from the throat. In Mandarin, the lingua franca of China, Ng becomes Wu, which was the name of a state in ancient China in the area of what today is the province of Jiangsu. In the dialect of that ancient time and place, the name Wu meant "big" or "great". The State of Wu was one of the vassal states during the Western Zhou and the Spring and Autumn periods (11ᵗʰ century BC - 473 BC). Historical records show that when Wu was conquered by the State of Yue in 473 BC, refugees fled south to the Zhongshan region and adopted the name of their defeated state as their family name – indeed, the Wus/Ngs went on to become the largest clan in the Zhongshan region. All Wus/Ngs are members of China's majority ethnic group, descendants of the Han Dynasty. When my grandfather was alive, he sometimes spoke of a Wu/Ng Family Directory, however no such document has yet come into my hands.

My grandfather chose the given names Chung-Fong for me – it is Chinese tradition for the paternal grandfather to name the grandchildren. Chung was one of the given names of Confucius and I'm sure my grandfather harboured the hope that sharing the name might help me develop the Confucian virtues of family and community duty that guided his own life. Fong in Chinese means "Precious", and also has the same sound as the word for "Carrying on the shoulder" and for "Elder brother". I believe my grandfather was giving me the message that I must always support my elder brother, the first grandson of our family, whom he had named Yuen-shun ("Head of state" plus Shun, the name of a revered Chinese philosopher).

My father's eldest sister and her husband – Aunt and Uncle – nicknamed me Baby, no doubt because it sounded more affectionate than Chung-Fong and I was indeed the baby of our family for a long time – eleven years – until the arrival of my sister. The Cantonese accent soon modified the pronunciation of "Baby" and so throughout my life I have been called Bēbē by my older relatives and closest friends.

Starting with my generation of teenagers in Hong Kong, it became fashionable to unofficially adopt a Western name. I was a huge fan of American movies and music and particularly loved Frankie Laine's rendition of the haunting ballad that resonated throughout the Gary Cooper movie *High Noon*, so I picked the name Frankie, which later morphed to Frank when Old Blue Eyes – Frank Sinatra – replaced Mr. Laine as my all-time favourite singer. And so Frank Chung-Fong Ng, or simply Frank Ng, became the name I was known by in Hong Kong, in England and in South-east Asia.

During my two years working at the London office of Booty Edwards and Partners, my very un-Western surname created some confusion.

With clients, I would offer clarification by spelling out, "N as in No one, followed by g as in good," and would then receive letters addressed to Mr. Good. Similar problems arose when I moved to Canada and I realized I had to do something about the situation, as it would be impossible to make a name for myself professionally when few could spell or pronounce it. When I noticed letters arriving at my desk addressing me as Mr. King or as Mr. Ling, I realized these were Western interpretations of the sound of my name. I thought the former too royal and Anglo for me and chose to adopt the latter as my legal name, and so it was that Ng Chung-Fong officially became Frank Chung-Fong Ling.

ROOTS

My family's ancestral home was located in Shan Chang, a village in what was then the county of Zhongshan in Guangdong Province in the south of China. The original house, a small single-storey structure of traditional Chinese style with a central living space surrounded by bedrooms, has been demolished since my last visit there with my father in 1987. Indeed, the whole village has been replaced by a jungle of high-rise apartment buildings, a result of the rapid growth of the area that has come to be known as the Chinese Riviera, one of the country's premier tourist destinations.

During our visit, my father and I were standing at a spot marking what had once been a gateway into the old village. My father told me that over a century earlier my grandfather's father had tried to leave the village, having had enough of life in a poor farming family, but on reaching that old gateway his passage had been blocked by his father – my great-great-grandfather – who was angrily wielding a shovel. He later succeeded in leaving with the support of his mother and made his way north to the city of Guangzhou (Canton) to start a new life. That's where my grandfather was eventually born and raised, though the attachment to the ancestral village remained strong and it was considered by all to be the true family home.

My grandfather was given the name Ng Ding-Sung ("Born of a sacrificial vessel, an emblem of imperial power"). He grew up to be a Chinese scholar of modest financial means and so, unlike more well-to-do men in those days, he had only one wife, my grandmother Kwok Yuk-Chan ("Precious jade"). The Kwok family came from the village of Ts'ui Mei not far from Zhongshan. Together they raised five children, my father being the third child and only son.

Aunt, their eldest child, was born in Yokohama, Japan when my grandfather was posted there briefly as an employee of the Singer Sewing Company. She was named Ng Pui-Sheung ("Admiring the goddess of the moon"). After she completed high school in Guangzhou, my grandfather, thinking of career opportunities in Western society for his children, decided to send her to study nursing in British Hong Kong, where she was accepted into the groundbreaking Nethersole Hospital and went on to graduate from there as a nurse and a midwife. It was at the hospital that she met Uncle, Dr. Wong Tse-Chuen ("Handed down son", meaning the son who inherits the family name and legacy), a young graduate of the University of Hong Kong Medical School.

Uncle was born in Hong Kong, graduated as a top high school student from Queen's College, and was supported through medical school by his widowed mother, a devout Christian who used her modest income as a domestic helper and cleaner to assist him. With my grandfather's consent, Uncle and Aunt were married in Hong Kong and she too became a Christian. Then, sometime in the early 1920s and with the backing of her devoted husband, she moved my grandparents and her four siblings, including my father, from Guangzhou to Hong Kong. Her youngest sister would later return to China when she married an official of the Nationalist Government, but everyone else remained in

Hong Kong, two of my aunts even following in the footsteps of their elder sister by also marrying graduates of the University of Hong Kong Medical School.

My father, Ng Chong-Hang ("Walking with strength"), became a Christian due to the example of Aunt – the most influential teacher in his life – and it was at Youth Fellowship gatherings at Hong Kong's Hop Yat Church that he met my mother. They fell in love and were married in 1932.

My mother, Chung Kam-Sun ("Charmingly beautiful and contemporary"), was born in Hong Kong in 1911, the eldest of six children and only daughter of her father's concubine – she never spoke of his other wife or children. Her father, Mr. Chung, had been a wealthy shipping merchant from Xinhui in south China, once owning the house next door to Uncle's house at 116 Pokfulam Road. He went bankrupt as a result of intense labour action in 1922 in which over thirty thousand seamen from Hong Kong and Guangzhou went on strike for higher wages. Since he had lost almost everything, my mother had to help support her five siblings and so immediately upon graduating from Ying Wa Girls' School, she became a teacher there.

My father once shared with me his memories of the time immediately after his wedding to my mother when the newly-weds, in keeping with traditional Chinese custom imposed by my grandfather, had to pay respect to our ancestors by visiting the ancestral home. What today is a journey of a few hours was in those days an arduous three-day expedition, sailing first to Macau from Hong Kong and then riding in rickshaws the rest of the way, all the while toting heavy luggage. The whole family had gathered in the village to await their arrival and for the next three days my mother had to sit formally on display in the living area of the house adorned in her ceremonial Chinese wedding regalia – a custom known as the viewing of the bride – while my father was free to spend each evening out on the town with friends. As I listened to him recall the experience, I couldn't help but feel relief that my mother no longer had to endure the old Chinese ways to please my grandfather or anyone else.

My mother passed away at the young age of fifty-six in 1968. My father emigrated to Toronto some eight years later but found the climate difficult and so within two years he went back to live with Aunt in Hong Kong, where he passed away in 2004 at the age of ninety-five. His ashes were laid to rest peacefully beside my mother in the Chinese Christian Cemetery near Pokfulam and within close proximity of the graves of my grandfather (1869-1959) and grandmother (1871-1972).

Uncle Wah-chiu, my mother's favourite brother, emigrated to Canada with his wife in the early 1990s and passed away in Toronto in 2000 at the age of eighty-four. Auntie Wan-fun, as sociable as ever, remained actively engaged in life in Toronto until she too passed in October 2012.

Uncle passed at the age of seventy-two in 1964, with Aunt living on until 1983, when she passed away at the age of eighty-five. I was grateful to be able to be at her side during her last few days – something I had not been able to do for Uncle – and then to organize her funeral and pay a final tribute to her in person. In keeping with their selfless lives, both Uncle and Aunt had requested that their ashes not be interred in a gravesite that needed tending but instead be scattered into the waters of Hong Kong's Western Harbour in view of their home at Pokfulam.

WINGS

From October 1, 1937 – Day One for me – my life has been inordinately blessed by the unwavering presence in it of unconditional love, generosity of spirit and inspired optimism that exuded so freely from my family in Hong Kong. Here on the other side of the Pacific Ocean, the Wu/Ng/Ling family can only flourish and thrive, sustained as it is by its roots in such richly nourished and deeply fortifying beginnings.

CPSIA information can be obtained at www.ICGtesting.com
Printed in the USA
LVOW10s0044080316

478108LV00033B/1627/P